LIBERATE

STORIES & LESSONS ON
ANIMAL LIBERATION
ABOVE THE LAW

This compilation first published in the United States in 2019 by Warcry.

ISBN 978-1732709652

All contents © 2019 by Peter Daniel Young

For information, submission guidelines, bulk requests, or general inquiries, please contact:

peter@peteryoung.me

Also published by Warcry:

Flaming Arrows: Collected Writings of Animal Liberation Front Activist Rod Coronado (Rod Coronado)

From Dusk 'til Dawn: An Insider's View of the Growth of the Animal Liberation Movement (Keith Mann)

Underground. The Animal Liberation Front in the 1990s.

Cover image: Animal Liberation Front raid of University of Iowa, 2004
Cover design: Robyn Lowe

"Your laws will have no meaning past the setting of the sun."

Earth Crisis

Dedicated to those left behind.

Testimonials

"Peter Young explicitly told members of the audience to commit crimes." *Michael Whelan, Executive Director, Fur Commission USA*

"A frequent flying hipster." *Forbes*

"Entitled." *Travel Pulse*

"An outspoken defender of the animal rights movement." *New York Times*

"His decidedly non-terroristic appearance causes…. consternation and confusion." *Techdirt*

"Be aware of any suspicious activity around (your) farms in the coming days, as activists tend to be energized after his appearance." *Fur Commission security alert to fur farms before a University of Wisconsin lecture*

"An arrogant vigilante." *USA Today*

"I was unprepared to witness first hand the unapologetic arrogance exhibited by Young." *Mindy Patterson, Founder, Cavalry Group*

"Attained legendary status among like-minded extremists." *Mason City Globe Gazette*

"It seemed like he was suggesting that the audience free the animals from the basement… Hearing that was pretty shocking." *Oberlin College student, after lecture*

"He believes all of his illegal activities are justified as long as he hides behind the word 'compassion.'" *Beloit, WI farmer*

"Covers barnyard arson the way Peter Parker covers Spider-Man." *Toronto Star*

"(Peter Young) did tremendous damage to many people in the fur business, and shows no remorse." *Dennis and Jill Preissner, third generation mink farmers*

"A motivational speaker for the Animal Liberation Front." *Teresa Platt, Fur Commission USA*

"(A) self-appointed spokesman for the Animal Liberation Front." *FBI agent Mark Kitsmiller*

"Young… travel(s) the country urging activists to commit crimes in the name of animal rights… (His) appearances are often followed by eco-terrorist activity." *Washington University police memo*

"The suspect refused to provide even basic personal information." *San Jose Police Department Officer Cooley*

"Brazen." *Linda Zimbal, Wisconsin farmer*

"An elevated, if controversial, figure within the culture of activism." *Seattle Weekly*

"Unrepentant." *The Associated Press*

"There is little doubt that Young will return to his old ways. Do not believe for a moment that he has been rehabilitated." *Target of Opportunity*

"He toes the line on advocating people going out and committing crimes." *Cedar Rapids, Iowa FBI agent*

"Encouraged college students to break laws in order to achieve the change they want and provided guidance on how to do so." *CBS Cleveland*

"Told UC Berkeley students… to stop protesting and start freeing animals from Bay Area research labs." *Inside Bay Area*

"He incited people to break the law, and if caught he'd do it again." *Federal judge Stephen Crocker*

"Notorious ALF activist gone vegan evangelist." *San Francisco Magazine*

"I'm not a vegan and I actually very much disagree with his cause, but… I thought that was pretty brilliant." *Ryan Holiday, media strategist*

"I'm happy to hear my advice got someone sent to federal prison." *Bill Nye, on advice imparted in a 1990 conversation.*

"Is convinced the FBI is following him everywhere." *Oakland Tribune*

"Had to keep his whole life a secret when he was a fugitive sought by the FBI." *Wall Street Journal*

"You will not be allowed back here. Don't even try." *Canadian border patrol*

"He won't be allowed to return to the state — ever." *Dawn Elshere, South Dakota state's attorney*

Contents

LIBERATE

STORIES & LESSONS ON
ANIMAL LIBERATION
ABOVE THE LAW

All transcripts were heavily edited for length and redundancy. All speeches had content added for clarity, and to more accurately reflect the intended message. In others, excerpts from related talks were spliced in. Every lecture transcript was treated to significant revisions.

"Fear is the feedback you receive when you're about to maximize your potential as a human being."

No Plan Is Too Big

At 18, a friend and I visited what I will call for the sake of obscurity a "large animal research laboratory in the Seattle area." A wing of the building was under construction, which created a crucial design flaw: a side door used by workers that never fully closed—exactly how the best stories begin.

We quickly found ourselves deep inside this lab at 1 a.m., explored the building, then left to discuss how best to exploit this access with the rest of our group.

It was the perfect storm: Replicable access to a building with animals, a core group willing to do what it took to get them out, and a reckless disregard for the law. The three pillars of animal liberation.

Over the next week, the question of "what next?" hung in the air. We met with a former employee of this lab who was able to confirm the presence of animals in the wing we had access to. We bought a lock pick gun (a device for amateurs I later learned is no substitute for actually learning to pick locks), and we did dry-runs to test parking and exit points.

Just a few blindspots remained (with answers I would later learn over the next many years): How do you find animals once inside a building? (*A: Wander, follow your nose, look for clues like empty cages and bags of bedding in hallways, hone in on any wings of the building that are visible from the outside but suspiciously inaccessible inside. Animals are almost always on the top floor or the basement.*) Were the vivarium doors alarmed? (*A: Rarely.*) Were there motion sensors once inside? (*A: Animals might trip them, so rarely if ever.*) How does one transport animals from a building to a vehicle? (*A: There's very little that can't be transported in either plastic tubs or duffel bags.*) If we found large animals, how do we sedate them? (*A: I'm not a vet, but Ketamine administered properly is said to be effective on many large animals.*) And how does one bypass alarms? (*A: Doors are more psychological barriers than real ones. Go through, over, or around. To quote an expert: "The best way in is never the door."*)

In 1996, those wishing to answer such questions had few resources to draw from. The internet was in its infancy. The "authoritative" resources were three ALF "primers" - crude photocopied manuals that, even at my novice stage, I strongly suspected were not authored by anyone who had carried out sophisticated ALF activity.

The remaining resources were a short list of periodicals and one-off zines (e.g. *Memories of Freedom*) from which small amounts of tactical advice could be drawn, but all of which left more questions than answers.

The few (anonymous) people who knew what they were talking about, weren't talking.

Pervading all of our questions was one core belief that, even if we had found the answers we sought, guaranteed our failure:

This is out of our league.

For an otherwise-motivated activist, this limiting belief condemns more animals to death than a thousand meals at McDonald's.

And despite the "perfect storm" of people, place, and resources; our plan was neutralized by two things: Lack of tactical guidance and a failure of confidence—our failure to conquer the "inner game" of activism.

The plan to raid this lab was never carried out.

That how-to manual we sought remains unwritten. If and when it ever is, I've curated the book you're holding to be its compliment: broader animal liberation strategy, tactical guidance in story-form, the "inner game" of taking action, and virtually every principle (if not tactic) I wish I'd known at 18, standing in that lab at 1am.

Fast forward many years. After a succession of events that led me from criminal charges to fugitive status to prison, I found myself in the loose role of "ALF spokesperson."

I never respected a "spokesperson." My respect is reserved for those in the trenches, not the ones doing the reporting. So as this role increased, my discomfort with it grew at pace.

To offset this, whenever asked to fill the "spokesperson" role, there was one secret filter to my words. Everything I ever wrote or spoke on the subject of animal liberation was crafted for one specific avatar, an audience of one: *me at 18 years old*. What would have motivated a younger me to move quickest from idea to execution? What were the psychological hurdles? What were the tactical? Every word spoken or written was to this end.

Of the several books I wish I'd had at 18, the one you're holding is the only one that has been written.

Let History Be Told By Those Who Lived It

Beyond that, this book has a more obscured agenda. As I stepped away from the cheerleader role, some scurried to fill it. And I watched some of the worst fears about misrepresentation of the underground animal liberation movement come to pass. Because the anonymous nature of the ALF's work brings with it their inability to speak for themselves, the subject of ALF history, methodology, and motive is ripe for exploitation by non-participants with a personal or political agenda,

So I watched self-appointed "historians" capitalize on this, spinning the ALF as "anarchist" (in my experience, anarchists always talked most and contributed least), trying to build a name for themselves on the backs of other's work, and hinting involvement in activity I can state for a fact they were not involved in (and in fact, due to their egotism and untrustworthiness, were actively kept *out* of.)

For these reasons, the secondary agenda of this collection is to create an indelible historical record that cannot be rewritten by revisionists or frauds.

When available, let the stories of the ALF be told by those who lived them; let the tactics be taught by those who practiced them; and let the history be told by those who made it. I am but the smallest part of this, but the uncredentialed archivist is none at all.

The Accidental Anthology

After over 100 lectures, it became easy to lament the transience of messages delivered from a podium. All that remained for the effort was a stack of boarding passes, cheap applause, occasional audience feedback, and a cobbled-together folder on my computer of video recordings and audio files from the rare organizer (with more initiative than me) who thought ahead to preserve the moment.

At some point I learned you can pay people $1 a minute to transcribe record-ings. After handing off my files to them, they returned a megafile of over 15 hours of edited transcriptions. A book began to take form.

I edited these transcripts down by over 80%, then added a collection of loose ends comprised of published writings, unpublished writings, and podcast interviews. Then rounded it out with scraps from the editing room floor for a (largely unnecessary) final chapter. And I had a book.

In Part One, I immediately betray the book's central mission of "actionable content" with an assemblage of personal interviews & writings, absent of any tactical guidance and merely contextualizing what's to come.

In Part Two, the action. The principles of moving from idea to execution. When many talk but few strike, what is the exact architecture of beliefs that creates the warrior mindset? I've spent years looking at this question and deliver specific insights.

In Part Three, two short entries on the subject of Research & Investigation. Because you can't shut down what you can't find.

In Part Four, I move from high-level mindset to hyper-specific: Working out-side the law to rescue animals, and the history of those who have. From the laser-focused tactical ("*How They Got In*") to the esoteric and editorial ("*The Enemy Within*"), this is the section specific to those who have broken the law - or want to.

In Part Five, guerrilla media-generation. When an action (of any kind) happens, the work doesn't end there. You insure an impact that extends far beyond by accessing the media through a secret back door. This is the poor-man's public relations formula: what to do when you have no money, no contacts, perhaps not even a story. I open up my media playbook to generate massive publicity without PR firms or media connections.

In Part Six, what happens after you get caught: prison. Few subjects relevant to the animal liberator are both so under-reported and so willfully misrepre-sented when they are.

In Part Seven, how to respond to attempts by the government to stop our work. Passivity will always find an excuse. The true threat we face isn't "government repression," it's how we respond to it.

Then, Outtakes. With so much left on the editing room floor across dozens of lecture transcripts and interviews, I offer a small sampling of excerpts across many years. When I felt an item had value that wasn't covered elsewhere - either a useful point, historical curiosity, or engaging anecdote - it was included (in 9-point font) here.

The book ends with a deliberately-positioned message to any animal liberation activist advancing in years, and how the greatest threat to your long term efficacy isn't the FBI, it's irrelevance through blind conformity to your "radical activist" identity.

Absent from this collection is material best left unpublished (e.g. my attempt at an industry-specific ALF primer in 2000, completed but never released), content voyeuristically interesting but perhaps inappropriate (e.g. transcripts of confrontations with hecklers, such as the forest tribe of roadkill-wearing Oberlin anarchists who showed up to confront my lack of an "intersectional" approach to who-knows-what), and material that is lost forever (e.g. recordings of classes I gave on lock picking and creative techniques for sneaking into things).

Regrets Are For The Guilty

Whenever I read a book where much time has passed between its composition and publication, I hold my breath. Because most often, the author's foreword contains some variation of the sentiment, "I was young and naive when I wrote this," souring what follows. I'm not going to do that here.

I'm not without these misgivings, but they do not undermine this book's premise. Let me be clear that 80% of any "revisions of belief" I have experienced falls into one category:

"This, but better."

This, but bigger. This, but more strategic. This, but in a more specific context. This, but optimized for impact.

In the end, the only messages I would avert wholesale today are those that are specific to the "movement." I made the error of delivering messages to an echo chamber of this kind often. Ideologies, scenes, and tribes are transient. And among each, their cultures can change over years such as to be unrecognizable. An outcome, however, is forever. Any message to a "movement" or scene will rapidly find obsolescence as its fate. When the focus of a message is a mission, that message is timeless.

As a final disclaimer, the reader will encounter frequent redundancies for which I must be forgiven. As is unavoidable when drawing from dozens of sources offered to varying audiences, some war stories and talking points will be repeated. Some of them many times.

I write this on the 20th anniversary of the month a friend and I were pulled over near the Zimbal Minkery in Oostburg, Wisconsin; leading to arrest and prison. Not an event I wish to define me, nor an anniversary I even remembered (I was reminded of it in a call from a reporter two weeks ago). Yet were it not for this incident, I would not have had the platform to share these stories and lessons, and some chapters in this book (e.g. "*Prison*") could not exist at all.

When The Smoke Clears, What Remains

What happens after the action is over? For the animals rescued, they are either unavailable for a status update (having returned to the wild), or have lived out their lives in a more domestic hiding — every bit the fugitives their rescuers sometimes become.

For the activists, the outcomes are not so binary, the endings not always so happy. Where are they now? On one end, they have entered the mainstream animal protection movement. In the middle, those whose identities as "liberators" went from life-mission to costume, fading into internet bickering, chasing cheap applause online, and micro-scene obsolescence. On the other end, those who reversed even the most core principle that all sentient life must be defended (see Rod Coronado's bow-hunting videos). And outside the spectrum entirely, the many who simply vanished.

The greatest threat to the 20-years-later radical is not prison. It is their potential nullified through 9-to-5 jobs because they were so married to an "activist" identity that they failed to develop a Plan B. It is being so marred in nostalgia that their "radical" identity becomes a prison, as they whither away into echo chamber irrelevance. And perhaps the most insidious neutralizing agent of all, the cult-like hypnosis of burying oneself alive in a scene of political homogeneity, with effects compounding over decades, oblivious to the opinion-incest feedback-loop that has turned them into out of touch ideological zombies, entirely unable to relate to anyone outside their ever-shrinking circle.

Calm Before The Storm

As I write this, we are at an unprecedented level of inactivity for the underground movement. Those niches that champion direct action most are those most responsible for its demise — descending ever-deeper into a toxic culture of identity-politics, intra-scene cannibalism, critique-based virtue signaling, and abandoning focus on outcome as they fetishize process at the expense of product.

What's worse, large segments of the grassroots culture have shifted from confrontation to cowardice, from battle cries to real crying. If attention-seeking martyrdom is bad, attention-seeking victimhood is orders of magnitude worse. At least animals benefit from the former.

Reflecting on 20 years of observation on the ALF, I would offer the next generation three major revisions from which the greatest victories will rise:

Working alone: The greatest obstacle to ALF actions will alway be the lack of solid people to work with. A more effective and prolific ALF will abandon the "three to five person cell" model and emphasize working alone.

Militant unemployment: The single most destructive (and under-discussed) impediment to action is employment. Of all the ways to make money, it is the highest effort and lowest yield. And it leaves its victims with little time or energy with which to fight. Your job is the #1 cause of burnout, activist retirement, and inaction.

Wildlife liberation: After lack of people to work with, the second greatest hindrance to rescues is lack of homes. Releasing native mink is the most popular workaround, but mink represent but the tip of the iceberg for wildlife farming in the US. The research-savvy liberator could spend a lifetime targeting the vast underground of wildlife farms and never be exhausted of options. From skunks to coyotes to quail to turtles, there is no state without hundreds of easily-targeted, vulnerable captive wildlife operations.

17

Warcry

This is a book about back to basics. A few people, one night, a target, and a plan (or no plan at all - that usually works too). Animal liberation doesn't have to be fashionable. It doesn't need to answer to the prevailing winds of any movement. The only vindication it needs is the result it achieves.

This is a model (and its consequences) for anyone with a trusted friend, a tank of gas, and no regard for unjust laws. And the first two are negotiable.

Consume this book as a voyeur, and you will be rewarded with a few good stories.

Consume it as a warrior, and you will be rewarded with a partial blueprint for making the next chapter of animal liberation history.

Peter Young
La Jolla, California

Sentencing Statement To The Court

Speech transcript
US Federal Courthouse
Madison, Wisconsin
"I will remain unbowed before this court."

After pleading guilty to freeing mink from six fur farms, I was brought into court from my jail cell in Dane County Jail (Madison, WI) to be sentenced. Before handing down the sentence, the judge asked if I wished to address the court. In the audience were over a dozen fur farmers, dozens of friends and supporters, and "more FBI agents than I've ever seen in a courtroom" (to quote my lawyer).

This statement was for everyone in the room that day. Moments later I received the maximum sentence.

This is the customary time when the defendant expresses regret for the crimes they committed, so let me do that, because I am not without my regrets.

I am here today to be sentenced for my participation in releasing mink from six fur farms. I regret it was only six. I'm also here today to be sentenced for my participation in the freeing of 8,000 mink from those farms. I regret it was only 8,000. It is my understanding of those six farms, only two of them have since shut down. I regret it was only two.

More than anything, I regret my restraint, because whatever damage we did to those businesses, if those farms were left standing, and if one animal was left behind, then it wasn't enough.

I don't wish to validate this proceeding by begging for mercy or appealing to the conscience of the court, because I know if this system had a conscience I would not be here, and in my place would be all the butchers, vivisectors, and fur farmers of the world.

Just as I will remain unbowed before this court—who would see me imprisoned for an act of conscience—I will also deny the fur farmers in the room the pleasure of seeing me bow down before them. To those people here whose sheds I may have visited in 1997, let me tell you directly for the first time, it was a pleasure to raid your farms, and to free those animals you held captive. It is to those animals I answer to, not you or this court. I will forever mark those nights on your property as the most rewarding experience of my life.

And to those farmers or other savages who may read my words in the future and smile at my fate, just remember: we have put more of you in bankruptcy than you have put liberators in prison. Don't forget that.

Let me thank everyone in the courtroom who came to support me today. It is my last wish before prison that each of you drive to a nearby fur farm tonight, tear down its fence and open every cage.

That's all.

Part I

Personal

Sidestepping this book's central mission of "action-able content," I offer context for what's to come in this assemblage of personal interviews & writings.

Fugitives Have More Fun: Confessions Of An Eco-Terrorist

Lecture transcript
Farmhouse Conference
Hollywood, California
"The best lives will always belong to those who break the most rules."

This was a "coming out" talk.

After years under a gag order by lawyers, admonished to never discuss my whereabouts while a fugitive because of potential legal consequences, I went ahead and did it anyway. I opted to tell the whole story, for the first time, to a room of non-activists in Hollywood who had no idea what they were there to see.

The inside joke pervading this talk was that the audience that day was quietly peppered with people I had known while a fugitive, though they could never publicly admit it. They already knew this story, or parts of it, because they had lived it with me.

When an event organizer asked, "Tell your life story in 30 minutes," this is the story I told.

My name is Peter Young, and I'm a convicted eco-terrorist.

This story is going to be important for me, because legally I have not been able to talk about most of what I'm going to tell you until now. Much of this I've never told anybody else, including some of my closest friends.

I spent eight years as a fugitive, hunted by the FBI. I was facing a potential life sentence for freeing mink from fur farms where they raise them to make fur coats, 82 years for what they call a "crime."

There are people here in the audience right now whom I've known for years, whom I spent many years lying to about every facet of my life. They had no idea who I was. They had no idea of my background. I couldn't reveal myself because there was a lot on the line. I'm going to share just a little bit of that story.

I was asked to tell my entire life story in 30 minutes. Here it is.

When I was 13, my dad was a radio disc jockey in Seattle. He was dating a newscaster on the local CBS affiliate. They were friends with a lot of local media people, one of whom was Bill Nye the Science Guy. Do you know who Bill Nye is?

Group: Yeah!

One day, my dad, the newscaster, Bill Nye and myself were all hanging out. They were all griping about their very cush jobs. And Bill Nye turns to me at age 13 and says, "Peter, I'm going to tell you something." He's says, "Listen to what I'm about to tell you, and don't forget it for as long as you live." He said,

"*Don't ever, ever, ever get a job.*" He said, "*It's not worth it.*"

Fast forward five years. I turn 18. I graduate from Mercer Island High School outside Seattle, and I decide I'm never going to work another job for the rest of my life.

I had to figure out how I was going to accomplish this.

I reasoned, "I can probably shoplift or dumpster dive most of my food. I can probably rely on some petty scams to get just enough money for the bus or what have you, and I can move into an abandoned house and essentially live for free without spending almost any money or working any job ever again."

So this was my blueprint. I decided I was going to be militantly unemployed, but I was going do it with *style*. I was going to live in abandoned houses in the richest neighborhoods. I was going to eat the most expensive stolen food. I was going to infiltrate parties at the nicest hotels. This is how it began.

I was 18 years old and had just graduated. My first mission was to find an abandoned house. The plan was to walk around residential neighborhoods in Mercer Island, Washington. If anyone knows Seattle well, you'll recognize Mercer Island as a very wealthy enclave. It's an actual island, but in a lake. So I committed to walk down every residential street until I found an abandoned house.

We can all agree this sounds like an incredibly improbable recipe for free rent. Why would they leave an abandoned house empty in one of the richest zip codes in the whole country? Well, that's one of the cool things about being 18: you don't have that voice in your head telling you something can't be done. You just go out and do it, because you don't know otherwise.

So I walked up and down every street with a crowbar. In a matter of hours, I found an abandoned yet well-maintained house that was owned by the Department of Transportation. I did some library research. I learned the legal status of this house was such that plans to sell or demolish the house had been shelved for at least two years. Perfect.

I kicked the back door in. I installed my own lock. And I proceeded to live in this abandoned house for two years.

This house had a view of downtown Seattle that people pay millions of dollars for. And in fact, it was a million dollar house classified as surplus property by the DoT. All I had to do was dodge the police that came around once a week to shine their flashlight in the window, and the house was mine.

So I moved into this house. Mission accomplished.

I would spend my days skateboarding. I would spend my days reading. I would spend my days doing activism. I would spend my days crashing other people's parties at fancy hotels and just doing whatever I wanted. I was living my punk rock fantasy, and the world was my playground.

If any of you are coming out of the punk rock scene, you know the mantra, "Young 'til I die." That was how I chose to live my life. I wanted to be young until I died. I wanted to do everything and see everything. I did not want to spend one precious moment of my life working a job, so I opted out of 9 to 5.

After reclaiming my town and after being successful at it, I decided to apply this model to traveling. I wanted to see the country and do anything and everything, and do it all without spending any money.

I got a ride with a friend to Eugene, Oregon. I walked to the edge of Eugene and put out my thumb on the freeway. Got a ride to a town called Florence, Oregon. On the coast, I found an abandoned boat where I spent two nights. I would go to sleep looking out over the ocean and the Oregon coast, watching the sun set. The next night, I got a ride down to Gold Beach, Oregon, where a family who owned a Mexican restaurant picked me up and took me into their home. They fed me. We had a campfire. The next night, I got a ride down to Arcata, California, where I hid out in the Humboldt State University Library overnight in the stairwell and walked around the library all night in my socks. The next day, I got a ride to Santa Rosa, where a guy picked me up, gave me $100, and checked me into a hotel for free.

I was living the dream. This was everything I'd wanted. It was more adventure than I ever could have hoped for.

I would hitchhike for several months at a time. And I would always return to this abandoned palace on Mercer Island where I lived, and things were going very, very well for me.

Concurrent with this, the biggest part of my life was animal rights activism. At age 17 I learned what was happening to animals in factory farms. I learned about how they pack six chickens in a cage that's barely half the size of a sheet of newspaper. I was horrified by it, and I wanted to stop it. So I participated in animal rights activism that would run the spectrum from leafleting outside of McDonald's to civil disobedience. Like the time I went to a slaughterhouse owners convention, in Portland, Oregon, and hid out under the table before their convention. When they started, I ran out, and took over the stage. I told them I wasn't going to leave until they stopped killing animals. I got arrested.

And if you go pull up the *Willamette Weekly* archives from 1996, there's a photo of me getting handcuffed while dressed up as a cow.

This is what I was dedicating my life to. Freedom for myself, and freedom for others. It was important to me to use the time I had reclaimed from an employer, the time that I had taken back, and use it for something bigger.

But I was getting increasingly frustrated with my activism because going through legal channels was not getting the job done. Animals were still being killed by the billions, and some friends and I got together and decided we needed to escalate our tactics.

One trusted friend and myself got together, and we decided we were going to raid fur farms. We had learned that the mink raised for fur coats on these fur farms are genetically wild, and are native to North America. This makes mink one of the few animals raised in intensive confinement that you can release directly into the wild. So it alleviated the burden of having to find homes for thousands of animals.

We concluded our most efficient actions as activists would be carrying out ALF actions. We also concluded that within this framework, raiding mink farms would offer the best bang for our buck. We learned that a few people can go into a fur farm and open 1,000 cages and save several thousand animals in less than an hour. So we decided, "This is what we're doing."

So we obtained a list of fur farms from the internet and made a plan. We were already known to police locally as suspects in ALF activity around Seattle. So the plan was to travel eastward and hit as many fur farms as we could before pelting season, which is a time in roughly late-November or early-December when every animal in every fur farm in the country is killed for their fur.

We obtained a pair of bolt cutters. We got $60 together from a crude receipt scam we pulled at Barnes & Noble. We got some black clothes that we probably shoplifted from a thrift store. We borrowed a car. And we set out to hit as many fur farms as we could before the animals were killed.

After raiding the first farm of this campaign, it was immediately evident we were having more success working outside the law than we ever did waving signs outside of a research lab. That farm was forced to shut down.

We began to go down the line, from farm to farm. We went to Iowa. We released 5,000 mink and 100 foxes a couple days later. Over the next week, we raided three more fur farms and released somewhere between 8,000 and 12,000 animals.

It was supremely rewarding in that finally there was no gap between my thoughts and my actions. I was living entirely consistent with my beliefs. You can say whatever you want about being a criminal, but if you do it well, it will serve you. And not just personally, but also this world.

This was something I was learning at a very young age. At this time, I'd been living in that abandoned house for about 2 years, so this puts me at about 20 years old in this story.

Several days later, after we'd hit the sixth fur farm in our campaign, something went wrong. We were driving past the largest fur farm in the country in Sheboygan, Wisconsin, and the owner recognized the description of our vehicle that had been put out on a fur farmer email list.

She saw us driving past her farm. She got in her car and gave chase. She called the police. The police surrounded our vehicle. They asked us for our consent to search the vehicle. We told them, "Hell no you cannot search our vehicle," which you should always do if the police ever ask to search anything. They decided they had probable cause to impound our car and apply for a search warrant, which is what they did.

Because we were so broke and so driven, we did not carry out the normal security protocol of throwing away tools, and clothing, and other forensically-incriminating material after each action. This is what you should do. Instead, we had simply kept most of the tools that we had and used them in every single action. That linked us, and what was in our car, to every single crime we had committed and every single fur farm we had hit.

The police let us go. They said, "Report back to the police station in 24 hours to get an update on the search warrant we're going to apply for." That was a date we neglected to keep. When the police tell you, "Please come back to meet up with us in 24 hours," and you know they've just confiscated enough incriminating evidence to put you away for a decade, that's not a request you want to comply with. We knew, at that point, it was just a matter of time before we were charged with these fur farm raids.

I knew that my life had to change, and I knew what was coming was an indictment. I didn't know what they were going to charge us with, but I knew they were going to charge us with something big. It might be as low level as burglary and it might be as big as terrorism charges, but we knew the charges were coming.

We became fugitives. My co-defendant was probably a little more nervous than I was. He immediately got on a plane, flew to Europe, and went into hiding. I decided to stay in this country and lay low. I knew that the judicial system was not going to act in fairness. The judicial system was not going to say, "Hey, here's a guy who did not act out of a profit motive, but acted out of his conscience," and factor that into my sentence. I expected to go to prison for a very long time. In response to this inevitability, I became a fugitive.

There are only two rules for being a good fugitive. The first one is get an ID under a different name. The second one is don't call your parents. If you can do both of those things, you can be very successful as a fugitive.

I hid out in Washington DC, and obtained a stack of books on how to get a new ID under a different name using forged documents. I read every book there was on this subject.

Then I went to the DMV and walked out with an ID under a totally different name. I was reborn.

Keep in mind, I had not been charged with anything at this point. I just knew it was coming, so I decided to lay low in Gainesville, Florida and live as a fugitive without actually having been indicted yet. I would wake up every morning, I would go to the Gainesville library, and I would check the internet, waiting for news to break that I had been indicted on federal charges.

Eleven months goes by and that never happened. And I thought, "Maybe by some fluke they lost the evidence." I thought if they were going to charge me, they would have done so in 11 months. So I decided to resurface.

I went back to Seattle. I contacted friends I hadn't seen in a year. I contacted my parents for the first time in a year. I decided I was going to move in with a friend of mine in an apartment. Essentially, I just resurfaced. The friend I was going to move in with told me, "Your room is not going to be empty for two days so make yourself busy, come back then, and we'll have a place for you."

It was a homecoming. I was coming back to Seattle after spending a year as a fugitive. To fill those two days, I hopped a freight train up to Bellingham, Washington, 90 minutes north of Seattle.

I'll never forget, on my second day there, coming out of a record store and walking right into a friend of mine from Seattle. I looked up and said, "What are you doing here in Bellingham?" And he shoves this piece of paper in my face and he says, "Peter." He said, "Your life's going to have to change."

I looked at the document, and it was a press release from the Department of Justice stating that they had indicted my co-defendant and I on domestic terrorism charges. We were facing 82 years in federal prison.

This was much worse than I had anticipated. I had anticipated maybe burglary charges. So my life had to change. This friend gave me a fistful of cash and said, "Run for your life," and that's exactly what I did.

I took a Greyhound to Tucson, Arizona. I rented a cheap apartment with this money. Everything had to change. I knew I couldn't hitchhike anymore. I knew I couldn't hop freight trains anymore. I knew I couldn't dumpster dive. I couldn't do anything that might subject me to a police interaction. I decided to commemorate the last several years I had spent enjoying a level of freedom most will never know by writing stories about my experiences living in this abandoned house and living this suburban criminal lifestyle. So I sat down to write.

This time in Tucson was very lonely. I had no friends. I spent six months writing what I planned to release as a massive 100-page photocopied memoir, what they call a "zine," that would be a collection of stories about my life. It was also going be a how-to manual on everything I'd learned about how to live without spending money.

I made 10 copies of it, scammed from the chain copy store. It was 110 pages. It was very cumbersome. Even if you're scamming copies, 110 pages is a lot of copies. I made 10 copies of the zine at Kinkos.

When this project was completed, and my lease in Tucson was up, I had to make a decision: Do I want to live the rest of my life in solitude, living a boring, monotonous life, working 9 to 5 just to avoid the government? Is that really freedom? Or does freedom come with living consistently with your core principles and core identity?

I had to make a decision at this point. Do I want to get a job and not be in prison, but be in a different kind of prison, a 9-to-5 prison? Or do I want to live consistent with my beliefs and convictions, come what may?

I decided I was going to return to the lifestyle I had been living all along, because it's what made me content. And if I was arrested and went to prison, at least I would go down knowing that I was living consistently with myself.

So I put out my thumb, and I hitchhiked to Little Rock, Arkansas. Again, I'm a wanted man at this point.

I had all ten copies of my zine in my backpack. I gave one copy away to a girl who worked the bulk food section at Whole Foods in Little Rock. Then I hitchhiked another ride, and I gave a copy of my zine to the guy who picked me up hitchhiking. I made only those 10 copies and gave exactly 10 copies of the zine away over the next two months. Then I just forgot about this project. It was something I'd written, I was proud of it, but it was just a zine. There's a million punk rock zines. They all fade to obscurity quickly. Very few of them ever have a circulation of more than 50, and mine was just another one for the pile.

Fast forward six months. I was still traveling, they hadn't caught me yet, and my email inbox started to blow up. I began getting half a dozen, a dozen, or 20 or more emails every day from people all around the country who had read my zine. I only made 10 copies so I couldn't figure out what was going on. It was this endless barrage of people saying, "This zine changed my life. I quit my job after reading this zine. This is incredible." I couldn't figure out what was happening.

What I pieced together was this: I gave one copy of my zine to a particular person in Little Rock, Arkansas who gave it to a band who stayed at his house. The band loved it, made a million copies of it, took it on tour and spread it like fairy dust all over the country. It went analog-viral. Kids were scamming copies and reproducing it at an insane rate. I estimated there were tens of thousands of copies of my zine that had essentially been bootlegged and spread all over the country in a very short amount of time.

Quickly, my life got very weird. I was the most solitary, isolated person you can imagine, doing what I did, traveling as a lone fugitive. I did not think there was another person in the world living my lifestyle. And suddenly, I was getting emails from all over the country from people saying, "Come stay at my house. We'll take you out dumpster diving. I want to hitchhike with you."

Then it got weirder. A publisher got wind of the buzz, and offered me a publishing deal. I moved to San Diego, lived in a broom closet on the UCSD campus, and wrote new material for a book version. Once released, the book quickly sold tens of thousands of copies out of the gate. Almost overnight. I was forced into major visibility, at least within a small subculture. It was a visibility that I didn't want.

Not only did I not want this visibility, it was dangerous to me as a fugitive. As I was becoming increasingly visible in these circles, I was getting increasingly nervous about what this would mean for my freedom and my fugitive status.

Things got weirder still. My life became a constant game of dodge ball, where I couldn't let people take pictures of me, and I couldn't let my picture on the internet. I had to lie about who I was to everyone I met. I would be at shows hanging out with people, and I'd see someone from my past walk in the room, and have to duck out. This was happening consistently, and it was this cat-and-mouse game of having to avoid my past while still being very visible in my present.

It became much more difficult to manage as a fugitive being out in the mix like this. I would give speaking events, and have to worry about who was taking my picture, if it might end up on the internet, and who might see it and recognize me. Meanwhile, I have my poster up in post offices all around the country. They actually used to put up fugitive wanted posters in post offices. I had my own. This was increasingly difficult to manage.

So I moved to Santa Cruz, California. I got an apartment three blocks from the beach with my girlfriend at the time, and I pulled back from that spotlight.

No one at this time in my life knew who I was. Not a single person knew my real name. Everybody I've talked to who knew me during that period said they knew something was suspicious about me, but they couldn't put their finger on it. It was a lot of little things, like that I never talked about my parents.

One time my girlfriend, who I'd been with for a year and a half, comes in the living room and sits on my lap. She looks me in the eye for a long time, and finally says,

"How do I know you are who you say you are?"

You can imagine everything that's running through my head at that moment.

I found out from her later she had spotted a blank birth certificate I had hidden in our apartment, just in case I needed to get another ID under a different name again. Which I had to do on a couple of occasions. She started to connect the dots and realized that maybe I was hiding some part of my past.

I had many "close call" stories like this. There was a band who invited me to tour with them, who decided they were going to book some last-minute shows in Canada. I very abruptly, with no warning, ejected myself from the tour, because I couldn't cross the border and interact with customs. They were very confused by this. Things like this were always coming up. But overall, my life was really, really good.

Fast forward to March 21st, 2005. I was living in Santa Cruz. I went to Starbucks in San Jose, California to meet with a friend. The events of what happened at that Starbucks are still blurry to me. I don't quite know what happened, but it ended with me in handcuffs in the back of a police car. Two police came up to me and thought I was acting suspiciously. They accused me of stealing several CDs from the Starbucks, which absolutely wasn't true. I stonewalled them. I refused to answer any of their questions. They got very angry with me. They threw me in the back of their car.

They took me down to the jail, fingerprinted me, and my true identity was revealed in a matter of seconds. Police came to the cell, and said, "Peter Young? Is that your name?" It was a name I hadn't heard in 8 years.

I refused to talk to them. They slammed the cell door, and I heard one of them say, "We got ourselves a terrorist!" They all started high-fiving each other.

I'd been a fugitive at this point for eight years, and my life was changing once again. I was facing 82 years in federal prison.

They took me out of solitary confinement in Santa Clara County Jail and up to Alameda County Jail, which is near Oakland, California. They threw me in this holding cell that was the size of your bathroom. It had 50 guys in there, packed like sardines. This is my first experience being among other prisoners. The cell door closes behind me, and I'm faced with 50 tough looking guys staring at me in total silence, and I'm looking like I just stepped out of a Banana Republic.

I get shipped out to Wisconsin where my charges originated. The newspapers are reading, "*Man Pleads Not Guilty to Terrorism Charges.*" The word "terrorism" is getting attached to my case. Everything is looking very bleak.

After five months in jail, my lawyer successfully had the most serious charges dismissed. I plead guilty to the remaining charges and received a sentence of two years in federal prison.

Relative to the expected outcome, I considered this a happy ending to a challenging time. Not just the jail time, but the entire eight years I spent as a fugitive. Fugitive life was fun, but being relieved of it was welcomed.

I received a lot of support in prison. I received more letters than I could ever answer. I received more books than I could ever read. The support wasn't about me. It was about what I had done, what it represented, and how it resonated with people. I was someone charged as a domestic terrorist for saving animals that were raised for fur coats. Even my meat-eating grandmother could get behind that.

Two years later I was released, and my life got crazy once again. I was thrust into an entirely new life. I stepped out of prison, and almost immediately went to a get-out-of-prison party that was held for me at a house here in L.A. owned by one of the child stars in the 90s sitcom "Home Improvement."

Again, I was stepping into another life, but one I could feel a lot better about. Before prison, I had spent a lot of years being an unintentional spokesperson for a hedonistic punk rock lifestyle. That was great, and my writing helped a lot of people achieve freedom. But I felt much better being back in the animal rights movement serving something higher. Helping animals that have no voice. That was something that was more satisfying in terms of having a role in this world. I was back in my own skin again.

My life changed. I could talk to my parents again. Universities began inviting me to speak, offering four figures for a speech. Sometimes these schools were the same schools that I had exploited the resources of as a fugitive. These are the same schools that I'd slept in the library of overnight, or the same schools that I had scammed the dining halls at, were now paying me to come speak about animal rights issues. The irony was awesome.

That's my adult life in a nutshell. It's been a strange ride. Not a lot has changed in the fundamental ways. I'm still vegan, still travel wherever I want, whenever I want.

I don't think Bill Nye is in the audience today, but if he's watching this video later, I just want you to know, Bill Nye: I have spent less than 18 months of my adult life employed. Thank you, brother. That was great advice.

If there's any message to this, it is that life serves the risk-taker. The best lives will always belong to those who break the most rules.

Lessons From A Fugitive On The Run

Live interview transcript
Unmistakable Creative Podcast
"So I went back to the house, broke in, and lived there for two years."

I was the unlikely guest on a podcast that leans towards CEOs, celebrated authors, and venture capitalists. From shoplifting advice to free rent to how being a fugitive impacts relationships, this is the conversation that happens when the only goal is "provocative content."

Today I catch up with Peter Young who has a fascinating and somewhat hilarious story which I hope you enjoy.

Peter, I came across you by way of our mutual friend, Ryan Holiday, who has been another one of those people who has referred an insane amount of really fascinating guests to our show over the years. So on that note can you tell us a bit about yourself, your journey, your background, your story and how that has brought you to what you're up to in the world today, and then what you're known for.

My name is Peter Young. If you Google my name, you're going to see the word "eco-terrorist" in just about every mention. I'm an animal rights activist and have been for many years. It's something that's very important to me.

In 1997 a friend and I went on a multi-state campaign to free mink from fur farms. We were ultimately indicted and faced up to 82 years in federal prison for cutting fences and releasing animals at these farms.

I went on the run, I became a fugitive for 8 years. I was arrested in 2005, served 2 years in prison, and got out in 2007. There's a lot more we could go into but that's the synopsis.

Well, it's an ongoing joke that you have to commit a crime to get on the show. One of the things that's always interesting to me is the journey before the journey, kind of childhood growing up. What causes you to grow up to be the kind of person that feels so compelled to do something about an idea that you go and you cut fences at farms? There's gotta be something internally, I think, that causes you to be that provocative and that audacious of a person?

Anyone who goes to prison, people wonder: What's the story here? What's your family life like? What did your parents do to you? Other than a divorce when I was 10, there is little turbulence in my childhood to mention.

I came from a flatly middle-class background. I grew up in Silicon Valley. Los Gatos, California. Later moved to Mercer Island, Washington, outside of Seattle. It was a rather un-tumultuous upbringing. The clearest impetus to criminality I can identify is getting involved in the punk rock music scene at age 15.

The punk rock scene imparted a sense of urgency that it's the obligation of all of us to not just complain, but take action. I trace that stirring of a higher calling to those days. Eventually this stirring lead me to prison.

There's two things here that interest me, and these just came up as I was thinking about the way you've described this. And you talked about the '90s and activism, you talked about punk rock, and the theme that keeps coming up over and over for me is this sense of mission and community. And I'm really interested in what lessons you brought from those days that could be applied to the real world?

Fundamentally it was getting away from critique-based politics, and critique-based lives, and shifting towards action-based lives. The internet has poured gasoline on the fire when it comes to people who fetishize opinions. Fundamentally what I took from the punk rock scene was an emphasis on action over words.

In activism, today the internet is a place for talkers to look like doers. People should be measured based on what they do and not what they say, and the internet has flipped that around.

That's actually a really interesting way of looking at it and I've never thought about that. I mean this is like a minefield that we could dig into for an hour. You can get on Twitter and you can just start saying things, even though you're doing absolutely nothing. We somehow equate what they're saying and what they're doing. That's a real disconnect.

You can become a world-renowned figure in a field without having contributed much. We can just talk about the activist world, but there are people whose credibility and credentials are built entirely on the internet with almost no real-world application. The lines have become blurred. People confuse the two. It's become epidemic.

There's a role for spokespersons. But people need to be honest about what they are. If you are somebody who writes a blog, say that you're somebody who writes a blog. Don't say you're a crusader for the revolution. Just be honest. That's all we can ask of anybody.

Without a doubt. Let's talk about what leads to the point of you thinking that, okay, to be honest and to stay true to who I am, my level of activism has to go to such a point that I'm going to start breaking laws and freeing mink from farms. What drives you to that point? Take me through that journey.

It was a cold and pragmatic equation. I had spent a couple of years protesting outside of various targets. At the end of a couple of years, I recall one particular conversation where several friends and I sat around and said, okay, we're not here to get our names in the paper. We're not here to yell at strangers on the street. We're here to save animals. Are we accomplishing this? No. So we started to do that math and say, okay, how can we make that happen.

Interestingly enough something got my attention that you just said about yelling at strangers on the streets. I actually wanna talk about the psychology of protesting in front of these stores and things like that, and kind of what lessons you have brought from that in terms of human interaction. I'd imagine with the amount of exposure you've had to human beings, there's gotta be some incredible lessons that you've brought from it about human psychology and human behavior, which I'm really interested in.

Eventually I took a direction that most activists, unfortunately, don't. I began to study psychology. Activists are in the business of changing minds, and if I didn't start reading books like *Influence* (Cialdini) and other crucial texts to understand what motivates people, I would probably still be on the street shouting. I don't necessarily discount that as a tactic. It depends on your target and desired outcome.

We used to go to the opening day of the opera house in Seattle every year. We did that because it's the only place in Seattle you see fur coats. People wear their fur coats out to the opening day of opera. Our explicit goal was to shame people. This is a tactic that might be effective when every other tactic has failed. People who are still wearing fur coats in the 21st century, they've heard it all. They will not change through continued education, and the only thing you can do is shame them. That's a limited example where this might be effective.

I became motivated to become a vegan and an activist through a form of shaming. I was listening to bands who were calling me a murderer and calling me a sadist for eating animals and for not taking action. That worked on me. It doesn't work on most people. What motivates people ultimately depends on their psychological makeup.

Let's shift gears and talk about what it's like to be a fugitive. We've had a lot of people who've spent time in prison on this show. We never had somebody who was a fugitive on the run for as long as you were. So let's get into what that whole experience was like.

This is the fun part. For legal reasons, I actually have not been able to talk about my fugitive days until relatively recently. Pretty much anything you ask, I've never been allowed to talk about until now.

The only two rules to being a fugitive are to have an ID under a different name and to not call your parents. If you can accomplish those two things, you can be a successful fugitive.

I caught the tail end of when taking on a new identity using crude forgery was fairly simple. When we were pulled over near a fur farm in Wisconsin and abruptly let go, we knew charges were coming. They had confiscated our car with tons of evidence, so we knew it was just a matter of time. So I went on the run.

The first thing I did is purchase a few books from a publisher that has since gone out of business called Loompanics. They published an A to Z catalog on how to do every illegal thing you could think of. Several of those books were about how to get IDs under fake names. This was in 1997 and these books were written in, like, 1981. I had no business following outdated books as blueprints for felonious activity, but they were all I had so I did it anyway.

I literally walked from Kinko's with my fake birth certificate and a photocopied power bill to the DMV. You could still see the white out tape outline in the photocopy. I just walked right to the DMV and walked out with an ID under a new name.

To any fugitives or aspiring fugitives out there: If you're going to get a new ID, don't pick a name that's an inside joke. You potentially have to live with that name for the rest of your life. I think the first name I took was the first name of one of the Beastie Boys and I tacked it onto the name of one of my favorite punk rock songs or something. Bad idea. When I walked out of the DMW it hit me, "Oh my God, I might have to be 'Adam Firestorm' for the rest of my life," or whatever my last name was.

Once you have the ID, the only things that can trip you up at that point is not having a Social Security number. I was not able to work a normal job because I had read a lot of books on this, and the Social Security Number is how people get caught. Fortunately, I had spent most of my adult life committed to not working, so this was irrelevant.

I didn't call my friends. I didn't call my family. I had this ID. And I lived that way for eight years.

The thing that intrigued me that you said the most is that you can't have any contact with your parents, as one of sort of the big rules of being a fugitive. What's the psychological impact of that kind of disconnect from the people you love in your life on you and on them?

This is something I've only talked about with a couple of ex-girlfriends because it seems to come up.

Well, I've been known to ask weird questions from to time to time.

No, this is great. I don't think I've fully recognized the impact of my fugitive years until recently.

To put it in one sentence, it makes it very difficult to get close to people. That's as much from the absence of contacting friends and family for eight years as it is not being able to let anybody get too close while I was a fugitive.

A way this manifests is that I am constantly accused of being evasive about things. I can't shake this habit. An ex-girlfriend told me she noticed that every time I tell a story, I leave out names. I refer to everyone in my stories as "my friend." She said it makes me seem like I'm hiding something.

The reason I got into this pattern of being vague is that it's a small world. If I was telling a story while a fugitive, there's always a small chance if I mention a name, the person I'm talking to might know that person. They might say, "Oh, you know, so and so?" Then they'll call that person. That person will be like, "I know that story but I don't know that name." Then quickly the whole thing will unravel and I'm in prison.

To this day, I have not fully shaken this. I'm unable to really let my guard down and not appear to be hiding something, always.

What about with your parents, how did it affect things with them? I mean, to not hear from your son for eight years, I think my parents would be horrified.

My parents come from Northern California and grew up in the '60s. They understand. They get it. I'm sure it wasn't fun for them. Honestly this has never come up. It is the elephant in the room. My fugitive days are never spoken of.

They understand it had to be done. They understood it was unjust that I was looking at a life sentence at age 21 for freeing animals. I expect they saw it as a calculated decision. Even if I ended up only spending two years in prison, there was no way I could have known that up front.

So you mentioned that for you personally, you end up being really evasive. You have these disconnects. It's really hard to get close to people. One of the things that I've heard about being a fugitive is that there is this like just endless weight on you that you can't shake throughout the entire period. In fact, it's almost liberating by the time you're done with it, because you've been living with this false identity for so long.

I can't say that was my experience. When I went on the run I very quickly developed another life and other friends and another sense of purpose. I was a writer, I was publishing books. I had this other life I built very quickly. I went on the run when I was 20 years old. So there was more of my adult life spent as a fugitive than not.

Prior to that, I lived in an abandoned house in the second-richest zip code in the state of Washington, Mercer Island. It was a multi-million dollar house with a view of downtown Seattle. The house was owned by the city, so it didn't look abandoned. My life by many measures was already a fugitive life. It was a very easy transition from that life to a real fugitive life because I was so off the grid and outside the system as it was.

The really interesting thing for me is that you have this huge passion as an animal rights activist, and you have to make this pretty drastic identity shift. I'm guessing you did nothing related animal rights at that point?

I couldn't do anything that was on the front lines, like picture-in-the-paper kind of thing. I had to avoid that, but I continued to contribute in the ways I could.

You brought up the social security number. What about the rest of it? We talked about relationships, but what about day to day functioning as a fugitive, like getting credit cards and bank accounts? Is it just I'm changing my name and you're a whole new person? It's funny because as I'm thinking about this, I'm like, huh, can I change my name and basically forget my student loan debt ever existed?

It's harder now. The DMV's have gone on lockdown after 9/11. With bank accounts, you nailed my number one pain point as a fugitive. Everything else I found was fairly easy to get around. I had a couple of long term ex-girlfriends when I was on the run. Neither had any idea who I was. If you were to ask them right now about any red flags I displayed, the first thing they would say is, "He just refused to get a bank account. I couldn't understand why he was always using my bank account." Anyone I lived with, I figured out a reason, an explanation, a justification for needing to use their bank account. So that just came through the support of friends who didn't know what they were supporting.

What's interesting to me is now it takes us back into the psychology of all of this. It sounds to me like one of the most valuable things that has come from all of this is an incredible ability to persuade people.

I got deeply into learning about communication in those years, and that was inspired entirely by my needs as a fugitive. This is a whole book that I need to write. So much of what I was doing depended on me socially engineering people on the criminal end. And building rapport with people on the other.

I needed support and I had to learn how to build rapport to get that support. I couldn't be honest with people. When I was arrested and the FBI raided my house, there were 15 books next to my bed on communication skills because I was very seriously pursuing this subject as matter of survival.

Let's do a deeper dive into this. I know you said there's an entire book here. What are the lessons in communication from a fugitive on the run that could be applied to our own lives and our everyday situations, as crazy as it sounds, even if we're not fugitives on the run?

The biggest thing is to always have your story prepared. To this day, and I'm not embellishing this in the slightest, if I go to Whole Foods and somebody cornered me and said, "What are you doing here?" I will have a whole story chambered that has nothing to do with the truth. I don't mean I would just deliver a story like "I'm here to buy groceries." I mean a totally fictional, alternate story because the truth of my life during those years was so often incriminating.

After I develop this made up story, as I'm walking around the store, the story is playing in my head as to how I can make it better. Everywhere I was when I was a fugitive, I had to have a story. There was a lot of aspects to that life I've only alluded to that we can get into, but there were a lot of financial hardships involved. I had no stable income so I had to get very creative. I figured out a way to get everything for free.

Okay, we're gonna talk about that.

As I'm saying this, I'm thinking, "how much do I want to admit to? What do I not want to admit to?" "Getting everything for free" could run the spectrum from dumpster diving to shoplifting, to developing scams at chain stores that would get me by. But I always had a story, and I still always have a story.

You said there are parts you've alluded to but we haven't dove deep into, let's get into them. How you get all this stuff for free, everything else. This is the part that I feel like has a lot of depth.

Let me clarify. Activism also might be the even bigger factor in this need to "always have a story" because when you're an activist, it often involves being places you're not supposed to be. Let's say we wanted to compile research about a university research lab. We would go in college student clothes and see what we could find by going places we weren't supposed to go. We'd see if we could get access to the animals and so forth.

My activism has taken me to a lot of places that I was not supposed to be. In those situations, you have to have a story. This is where these two subject intersect, the activism and the fugitive status.

You mentioned being able to get everything you needed for free, I would imagine that's a fairly useful skill to have even in the world today.

If you name something, I could tell you exactly what scam I had to get it for free. I mean literally everything from free Greyhound bus passes, to phone cards in the pre-cell-phone days, to food. I had a trick for everything.

Let's talk about food, it's interesting. I mean, the reason this also intrigues me so

*much is because I keep wondering how this would all work in the day and age
of social media, and if it would be possible. And I know to some degree, a lot
of crazy things are possible only because one of our former advisers and mentors
literally walked out of this door with $10 and a laptop 3 years ago, and visited all
50 states, and worked one on one with 500 people and started multiple businesses.*

*So that became very clear to me in terms of what's possible, but I wanna hear
this from a perspective that you have of how you got things for free. Let's start
with food. I think it's really funny that you have like a hack or something for
everything.*

I practiced a technique that was called the left-hand technique. You can
do this to this day, no technology will ever make this obsolete. It exploits a
massive blind spot in every supermarket. I want to be clear on two things.
One, I don't do this today. Two, I only did this at chain stores. Whether or
not that's a rationalization your listeners buy into, that was my rule.

The left-hand technique is where you take something cheap that you can
afford like a couple of carrots or a small candy bar. Then you get the item you
want, or multiple items, and you hold them in one hand. You get in the line
and you hold the items in the hand that's closest to the door, the direction
you're going be exiting. Left hand or right hand. You get in line and you put
the item you want to buy, the cheap item, on the carousel, and you hold the
items you want for free casually at your side. Out of sight of the cashier.

The genius in this is that if there's a loss prevention agent or other kind of
security watching you, as soon as you get in the line, you're no longer suspect.
You're in line, so you're obviously paying for those items. There's no way to
shoplift right in front of a cashier, right? Unless you hold the items casually
at your side. Now, this sounds implausible, but I did this thousands of times
and never got caught. It exploits a visual blind spot as well as a paradigm
blind spot of store security.

Let's go to the next one that I'm interested. And what about shelter?

When you're 18, you don't know things "can't be done." This is the best part
about being 18 that I try to maintain to this day. When I was 18, my dad
said, "You have to get a job or go to school." And I did not want to do either
of those things. I lived on Mercer Island, Washington. Anyone can Google
that, it's a haven for the rich. It's not an island in the ocean, it's an island in

a lake, three minutes from downtown Seattle. Everybody has lived there, Bill Gates, Paul Allen, you name it.

So I decided I was going find an abandoned house in the second-richest zip code in the state of Washington. No one had told me it "couldn't be done." I got a crowbar and walked up and down every street with my girlfriend at the time. Within three hours, we found a house that looked empty. We looked in the windows and it appeared severely flood damaged. I did some research, I found out the house was owned by the Department of Transportation. It was not scheduled to be rezoned to residential for at least two years.

So I went back to the house, broke in, and lived there for two years. The house, when it was eventually auctioned off, sold for like $1.5 million or something. It had a view of downtown Seattle, it was a house -in one of the richest zip codes in the state, and it was all mine for two years. That was my biggest housing hack.

There's something you said there that really actually intrigues me, it's that part of that story that I think is probably the most relevant thing to somebody listening. You said when you're 18, you have this sense of not knowing that something can't be done. How do you renew that sense of not knowing something can't be done when you're an adult, when you've gone through life and have seen things that can't be done?

You look for people who have done those things that "can't be done." You'll always find what you seek. This gets into NLP and limiting beliefs. You have to identify those limiting beliefs and train your focus on evidence that disproves those beliefs.

Talk to us about the transition from being a fugitive to life in prison. Like you said, we've had people who spent time in prison here. We've had drug dealers and we've had bank robbers who've been in maximum security facilities. I don't know what your prison situation was like, so I'm really interested.

I was on the beach in Santa Cruz at 10 a.m. and I was in solitary at 3 p.m. That's how abrupt the transition was. Culturally I can't imagine a more abrupt transition for anyone. The circles I moved in in Santa Cruz, they couldn't have been further from the people I encountered in Santa Clara County Jail.

They put me immediately in solitary. For one, I was labeled a terrorist. Also I refused to take their TB test because it had an egg byproduct in it. As a vegan, I wasn't going take it. I was in solitary with an Aryan Brotherhood guy, among others. There were only three other people in that cell block who weren't in for murder. When I say solitary, there was one person allowed at the cell at the time. So guys would come to my door and talk.

What I found interesting is that the first day of county jail was really bad. The first day being in the federal system was really bad. My first day in prison was really bad. But once I cleared those hurdles, prison was not bad.

There was one instance when I got to MCC Chicago, which is a federal holding facility in the downtown Chicago. They push you through to the door and shut the door behind you. I'm standing there holding a bedroll, and all the prisoners were lined up on the second tier. Guys are whistling, saying, "We've got fresh meat here." It was the scene we've all seen in movies. Exactly what you think jail would be like. What you don't realize is, they're not serious. They're making fun of what they see on TV. They're acting out a parody. That's not how prison is.

What I found is that if you want to survive in prison, the same social principles apply as on the outside, the same rules of communication apply as the outside world. If people don't like you outside of prison, people aren't going to like you in prison. It's no different. The actual rulebook is different, the culture is different, but the way you build rapport with people and the way you get people to like you outside and inside prison are exactly the same.

So it's not this like terrifying, "Everybody here is gonna try to kill me and rape me" environment that we've probably been brought up to believe?

Here's the thing, I can only speak from my experience, which is a small sliver of the entire range of prison experiences. I was not in a minimum security prison, I was actually in a medium. The average sentence at the prison I was at was 16 years. So I was around some serious heavy hitters. But it was not a state prison. The culture of federal prison is much different than state prison. You have 50 state prison cultures, and then you have the federal prison culture. Each of those is distinct.

While medium security federal prison had me around a lot of real tough people, it was not the Darwinian struggle that I had been told prison would be. The people in prison who do the best were the people who were the nicest, while not being supplicant. As counterintuitive as that sounds, that's really how it was.

How did that whole time alter your perspective on life and your world-view and all of that? I mean, how did that time change you as a person?

It makes what we worry about out here seem petty. For the rest of my life, I will look at almost no one as having a real problem. It makes me less sensitive because I'm always thinking, "Look, I was in solitary eating only oatmeal for six months. Like, be quiet." It changes your perspective and raises the bar as to what it takes to be affected by an experience. The downside of that is it has a numbing effect.

I wanna talk about one other thing here, and this will kind of start to bring us full circle. We had a friend here who actually also spent time in prison named Meg Worden. She was kind of the gateway to our guests who have all been to prison. With her, it was like, wow, these people have fascinating stories, I wanna talk to more of them. One of the things that she actually said that I never forgot was that coming out of prison was actually much harder than going in because of this sort of reintegration process into a normal society. Given your background as a fugitive on the run, I'm really interested in how you navigated that whole transition of coming back out.

I think those problems she spoke of start to happen when you do more than two years. In fact, I've heard two years is a threshold.

I was so privileged in prison. I had a massive amount of support when I got out. I had six people meet me at the gate with money. I had everything. I was at a hotel in La Jolla, California within two and a half hours of getting out of prison. I had a very privileged experience.

I did find myself under somewhat of a cloud when I got out of prison. I suspect this was that I had a sense of purpose during my fugitive days, and I couldn't reclaim that. I couldn't go back to that life. I couldn't even acknowledge it. I was told by lawyers to not ever talk about anything I did while I was on the run. You have to walk away. You have to forget.

When I was arrested, I had books I'd written that were about to be published. I had a massive life I had to just walk away from. Everything had to be abandoned. Projects I'd spent years on. I had to walk away from all of it.

I was emotionally challenged by this, and I could not talk to anyone about it. I couldn't say, "Oh, I used to write these books and do all these things." I couldn't admit to anything. So I felt very isolated from everybody even though I was around a lot of people.

It's funny because I think about what you're describing as the vacuum that any creative professional experience is after they manage to put a big project out the door. I've heard this author say the day their book publishes is one of the most depressing days ever because it's done. The thing that you've been working on for nine months is done and over with. I felt the same thing when we finished an event last year, there was a sense of emptiness. How do you recover from that kind of a loss and get back to some semblance of normal and functioning?

It's exactly like being a fugitive twice over. I was a fugitive on the run. I had to abandon my life before being a fugitive. Then when I got out of prison, I had to abandon my life as a fugitive. It's just a bunch of spaces that are empty and you have to fill them. I had to find a new sense of purpose, which was not hard because I adopted a spokesperson role in the animal rights movement.

That began to feel empty very quickly because then I've become what I despise. I'm just a guy at a podium, cheerleading actions I'm not carrying out myself. I eventually realized I can't be that guy anymore. I might do it once a year, but I can't be that guy full time.

In the last couple of years, a lot of statute of limitations issues have cleared up. Things that prevented me from connecting with my past life. I'm just now starting to revisit those things. It's been over 10 years, but all those things I had to walk away from, such as unfinished books, I can finally revisit those and bring all the disparate parts of my life together.

There's a Heraclitus quote, "You can't swim in the same river twice." It is hard to go back to things and pick things up 10 years later, but that's what I'm trying to do.

Captured:
The First Prison Interview

Interview
No Compromise Magazine
Dane County Jail, Madison Wisconsin
"My faith in direct action has not changed, only my wish for the ALF to go bigger and go for the throat."

When the ink dried on my federal plea agreement, my lawyer cleared me to speak publicly for the first time.

This interview was the first that had been heard from me since becoming a fugitive almost 9 years prior.

You were wanted by the FBI for seven years. What led to your arrest?

My only "mistake" was moving several copies of the same CD across the room at a Starbucks while an off-duty cop observed from outside. By no stretch of the imagination was it "shoplifting," but when a search turned up items deemed suspicious (such as a book titled "*Evasion*" and what they thought was a handcuff key taped to the rear of my belt), they decided to arrest me anyway. Fifteen minutes after the cops ran my fingerprints, the warrants from 1998 came up, and this new chapter of my life began.

With so much discrepancy among media reports of your case, give us the nutshell version - from the actions to the recent plea agreement.

It was just before pelting season 1997, and within a month all mink on American fur farms would be dead. Given the heat in the Northwest from reports of recent successful and failed mink liberations, as well as our visibility as Seattle activists, we looked towards the Great Plains. When the smoke cleared two weeks later, six fur farms had been visited with 8,000 to 12,000 mink and 100 foxes released.

There were several close calls, such as when Tom Fasset walked up on us as we opened one of what was to be 2,000 cages. (I always wondered if they caught that one mink, and I found my answer in the FBI evidence turned over last month: She got away.)

There's no question that we exceeded the bounds of safety – moving from one farm to the next, even hitting two farms in one night. And while it proved in the end to be our undoing, I can say I appreciate the sense of urgency that drove us this far. As bad as jail can be, I'd have always felt worse doing nothing.

Eleven months later, we were indicted on four counts of Extortion (20-year max sentence, each) and two counts of Animal Enterprise Terrorism (one year max sentence, each).

Seven years later I was arrested. Factoring in my famously harsh judge, if found guilty, I was told to expect eight to twelve years. The case against me was mostly circumstantial, resting on a list of fur farm addresses, bolt cutters, and my co-defendant Justin Samuel's testimony. I was moved from California to Wisconsin, where it became clear that they were more interested in who my friends were for the last seven years than in an old case, even offering me a deal of one year if I would tell them.

Their case fell apart when my lawyer filed a motion citing a 2003 Supreme Court ruling that "extortion" could not apply to political cases. Those charges were dismissed, and my maximum sentence unceremoniously dropped from 82 years to two. The feds lost interest, and in the end I settled on a deal of two years for the mink releases and one count of obtaining a driver's license with forged documents.

Why did you target the fur industry, and what effect did your actions have?

We hit the fur industry because, in terms of immediate effects, I know of no action with greater yield than a mink release. The most common criticism of live liberations – that the liberated animals are just replaced -- does not apply. A mink farm's closed breeding system means that when its animals are gone, they're gone. Two of the farms we visited are now closed.

Above all, we raided fur farms because we had no excuse not to raid fur farms. It's just too easy. Two people can liberate 1,000 mink every 15 minutes. I believe if most people knew the simplicity of these actions, they would spend a little less time on the internet and a little more time tearing down fences.

It's important to evaluate not only our victories but also our failures. Can you offer an analysis of the mistakes which led to your indictment?

The plan was to hit as many farms as we could in as short of time possible. After the second release in Sioux City, it became clear the Midwest fur farming community was on alert. They began waiting for us, and we were followed several times in the coming days. The first mistake was not admitting we were too visible to continue. I have nothing to offer in my defense except that we were angry and very determined.

Mistake #2 was working with an emotionally unstable, dogmatic pacifist. I found out the hard way that being an informant for the FBI falls safely within a code of "Gandhian nonviolence."

Our two-week campaign ended when a farmer followed us as we passed the Zimbal Minkery in Oostburg, Wisconsin. She called the police from her cell phone, and in minutes we were surrounded. After refusing consent to a search, our vehicle was confiscated. Above all, I regret not cutting through the fence of the Sheboygan impound lot that night and removing the evidence from our car. That would have solved a lot of my problems.

Take us through a few milestones of your activist history.

Becoming vegan in 1994 was most significant, no question.

My shift to activism was inspired by the mid-90s straight-edge scene. Bands like Abnegation brought me from the "self-hating vegan" phase to one of action, and understanding this was not another "single issue," but something much more urgent than I had admitted. We listened to the Earth Crisis demo every night before masking up and hitting those farms in 1997. I've been vegan and straight edge for 11 years.

The moment I knew that this is war came when we discovered a chicken slaughterhouse operating in a nondescript building just outside downtown Seattle. Animal liberation was suddenly no longer an abstract struggle but one to be fought in my own neighborhood. We crouched in the bushes, looking through a cracked window, watching the massacre. It was this image-- flailing birds hung by their feet and carried to their bloody end-- that branded into my mind a promise that I would dedicate the rest of my life to seeing it end.

Lastly, a crucial milestone came later that year while reading the paper and learning that anonymous activists had broken into a Seattle-area pig slaughterhouse and removed the bolt gun used as a killing device. Soon after, a second article appeared reporting another local slaughterhouse had its office ransacked and three chickens rescued from the killing floor. It was these reports of simple actions with life-saving effects that imparted upon me a profound message: While we may not win in our lifetime, there can be many small victories along the way.

Sadly, your co-defendant Justin Samuel turned informant. What are you feelings on him today?

He is a disgrace and I wish him the worst.

As the victim of a snitch, weigh in on the subject of how they should be dealt with. Compassion, banishment, or something in between?

Any person that utters one word of excuse for an informant should ask himself how many apologies he would make if the snitch's victim were a close friend, loved one, or even him or herself. The first step is confronting the privilege of distance.

I hope any snitch who works to bury a liberation activist in prison, yet still remains convinced he has a rightful place in our movement, will continue to work for animals. Absolutely. What pains me is that there would be one person willing to work by the snitch's side. In Justin Samuel's attempt at reintegration, there were a few. I don't expect to regain trust in those elements of our movement that allowed Justin to move through it unchallenged, those who looked away for the sake of harmony and those who allowed Justin to be present in large groups of activists (such as David Agranoff's wedding) without showing him the door with force. My concern is as much for myself as for the message it sends, for the snitch culture it breeds and its future victims.

During the mid-90s, there was an upswing in activism and direct action. What are your memories of this volatile time?

A lot of hooded sweatshirts and camo. I remember liberal use of the term "vegan revolution." I remember communiqués that read like hardcore lyrics, with lines like "This is a warning to those who transgress the natural order." It was a climate of militancy that perhaps lacked good strategy. In the mid-90s, direct action did surge in the actual number of actions, but it was very scattershot, most often occurring at the retail/restaurant level. A message was sent, but at the end of the day, I'm not sure how many lives were saved. While we recently may only see a few significant actions a year, I'm impressed with a big action and good strategy more than I am with a brick and spray-paint.

Over the years, have you followed direct action? What specific actions did you find most significant?

The 1999 raid on the University of Minnesota, number one. The activists' ability to liberate animals, do $3 million damage with their hands and leave the FBI with no idea how they had gotten in was remarkable. Nothing like it had happened in ten years. If we assume those responsible were not active in the 80s, we can take a lesson from a group that started from scratch, taught themselves the skill, and went big.

And the Ellsworth, Iowa fur farm that was emptied twice in one week, shutting it down. This was an especially celebrated action to me, as someone who knows the pain of hearing of those I set free being recaptured, but not having the courage myself to return to settle the score.

Offer your analysis of direct action today. What's missing from the ALF's strategy?

First, trust no one who claims himself an expert on the ALF Mine is not an authoritative analysis, just a personal one.

Lessen emphasis on the "two-five person" cell structure, and reconsider the power of the individual. One person on a bike with a backpack can potentially do as much damage as several, without the burden of consensus and the threat of snitches. The biggest limitation of direct action will always be the lack of solid people to work with. One person will not be able to do large scale liberations, but silent actions for which a lookout may not be necessary, such as break-ins for the confiscation of data, would happen more often if people considered the one-person cell.

Additionally, the 80s model of using actions to expose atrocities with video footage should be revisited. There's value in reclaiming the A.L.F's now-tattered Robin Hood image. I can think of two examples of chicken liberations in which footage was taken and played on the evening news, giving the public its first glimpse inside an egg farm. Merge education and liberation.

Taking out targets whose work is not easily absorbed by others is good strategy. The business of a demolished KFC can be picked up by the one across the street, but there are only so many labs that are genetically engineering chickens without legs.

What I believe would see the greatest surge of direct action is providing people with more names and addresses. This is what made *The Final Nail* so successful in the 90s, and it's what has made the anti-HLS campaign so successful today. It is something that would make animal abuse something with an exact physical location, erasing most people's excuse for turning away. Knowledge bears responsibility. I would like to see a *Final Nail* for labs. This, I think, would really set things off.

And I won't win any friends with this one, but I believe that limiting our use of numbing agents such as alcohol, drugs, computers/e-mail, and television would go a long way towards eliminating distractions and keeping us motivated to act.

My faith in direct action has not changed, only my wish for the ALF to go bigger and go for the throat.

How do you feel about your plea bargain?

I'll say this: Last night I read the FBI case file, added the number of animals never recaptured, and divided it by my sentence. It works out to about 12 hours per mink.

Have you received adequate jail support? How could it improve?

"Adequate" would fall a little short. Within days of my arrest there was a website, support fund, phone-line assault on the jail to win me vegan meals, money, and a lot of mail. It's been incredible. To any activist with federal warrants, I would recommend an arrest in the Bay Area. The locals will take care of you. When I was extradited to Wisconsin, one generous person even uprooted her life and moved to Madison to do jail support full time.

As overwhelming as it's all been, the best gesture of support came ten days after my arrest when 58 foxes were released from an Illinois fur farm, with the action claimed in solidarity with me. My vision of improved jail support? A better liberated-animal-to-letter ratio.

What are your plans after your release?

To be right back out there, doing my part. You'll never be able to count me among the ones who stopped fighting.

Part II

Principles Of Taking Action

Any speaker with integrity has only one role: Using the platform to most quickly move people from their seats to action.

These are my attempts to deliver on that obligation.

Seven Laws Of Militance

Lecture transcript
International Animal Rights Conference
Luxembourg
"The only true remedy for fear is action."

This is my attempt to distill down the core differences between talkers and doers. More than any lecture, this is the one I wish I had heard when I was a new activist.

Here it is: The seven laws that separate the people who hesitate from the people who liberate.

Let me share a story with you that was shared with me many years ago. Again, this happened many, many years ago. So all the police officers in the room can turn off your recording devices, this will not be useful to you in any prosecutions.

Someone was aware of an animal research laboratory in their town. They were aware of documentation about animal abuse that was held in a specific place, inside a specific building, at this specific university facility.

They had no one to work with. They didn't know anybody else. They knew they wanted to do something to expose the cruelty in this laboratory. They had no skills. They had nothing working to their advantage.

One day they were reading a newspaper and came upon a statistic.

"On average, one out of 38 times that you leave your house, you accidentally leave the door unlocked."

This person thought, "That's interesting. How can I apply that to my project to get inside this laboratory?" This person reasoned that it's probably more likely that you would leave a door unlocked at your place of work than your home.

This person went to this particular building, this particular door where this documentation was held, late one night. They jiggled the doorknob. It was locked.

This person went back the next day and did the same thing. And the next day. They reasoned that, statistically speaking, if they went 38 days in a row, they would find the door unlocked once.

On the 27th day that door was unlocked. And what they found inside... well, the rest is history.

What happened there? What is that accomplishment? What is it that this person did? Is that a skill set? It's not a skill. Everyone can jiggle a doorknob.

It's a mindset. That person exploited a loophole and used it to achieve a victory for animals. This is a mindset you can cultivate in yourself.

What makes a great activist is not a set of skills, it's the way they think.

I began this journey into decoding what makes great activists several years ago when I started a book project. I was compiling stories of successful activists who had done great things and achieved some great victories and taken some big risks for animals. These stories were most often shared with me anonymously, because their stories primarily covered ALF actions.

I began to look at the common denominators to understand the following: what makes these high-achieving, bold activists different from the rest of us? What made these victories happen? How do these people think?

There is a formula I've decoded. I distilled down this mindset into seven principles, seven ways of thinking that separate highly effective activists from people who merely talk.

These are those seven principles, which I call "the seven laws of taking action."

Law #1: "Highly effective activists know that nothing is ever as complicated as you think it is."

Another story: This one also involves a laboratory and a person who wanted to get inside. Again they had no idea how to do that. They had read a lock-picking book once, several years before.

They made a lock-pick at home. Literally, from a small piece of metal they picked up off the street. You need a second tool called a "tension tool" to pick locks. They didn't have that, so they used a steak knife. They had no idea how to pick locks, other than this book they had read several years ago. They didn't even own that book anymore. So they found a hidden door at the university, just for testing purposes. It was a broom closet.

They spent five days, several hours a night trying to pick this lock. They had no book, no training. Just persistence. After five or six days, they got it down to where they could pick that lock in under five minutes. This was the same type of lock used on every door on the entire campus. While I won't go into specifics, ultimately this led to a great victory for animals and animals were saved.

As a speaker, you need to have a target audience. You can't please everybody, and you can't cater a talk to everyone. So when I give a talk, I try to think, "Who am I speaking to?"

The answer I decided on, years ago, was this: "I'm going to make my talk for me when I was 18 years old." Like, "What did I want to hear from the podium when I was a new activist?"

When I was 18, all I wanted to hear when I went to a talk was specific how-to information on how to break into buildings and save animals. That's what I wanted to hear.

There's one thing that I learned after many years of being an activist, which is that specific how-to information isn't important. Because when you have a strong enough "why," the "how" will always take care of itself.

When you have a strong enough purpose, the details about how to accomplish that will always resolve themselves. This is central to this principle of nothing ever being as complicated as you think it is.

When I was in prison, I was surrounded by people who we call criminals. I was in with one guy who used to drill into the roofs of banks and break into safety deposit boxes. I was in with another guy who would rent semi-trucks and back up to Walmart distribution centers, where his crew would walk-in like they owned the place, in the middle of the day, and load the semi-trailer with expensive electronic equipment which they would then sell on the black market. I knew people who did a lot of bold and creative things.

One of the things I learned from being around people who did all these crimes for money is that it was actually quite appalling how many more people are willing to take greater risks and do more for money than most of us ever will for animals.

What can we take from that? The only thing I can take from that is that they desire money more than we desire animal liberation. We don't want it badly enough.

When I was 19, there was a chicken slaughterhouse in Seattle. I used to look in the window of this place at night. I would go there at night obsessively and look in the window. I would see chickens that had escaped from that day's killing session just running loose within the slaughterhouse. I would go there night after night and see these chickens.

And one day, me and my friends got together, and decided, "We have to do something." We had no skills. We never went to burglary school. We simply had a purpose that was strong. We went there one night. We had bolt cutters. I believe that was the extent of our tools. We just showed up at this slaughterhouse at 1:00 a.m. We went around the back and scaled the wall. So now we're on the roof, thinking, "All right, what do we do now?"

We're walking across the roof. We see a staircase that descended into the loading dock. We thought, "Now we're getting somewhere." At the bottom of the staircase there's a door. We took the bolt cutters and cut the chain that held the door closed. We were making progress. Now we're inside. We get to the killing floor of this slaughterhouse and find three chickens. We put them in a box and took them to safety.

Getting inside a slaughterhouse is perceived as a challenge. I think if you put the average person outside the slaughterhouse and said, "How would you get in?" They would say, "I have no idea," and then turn around and walk away. Yet there is something about putting yourself in the situation with an open mind and just allowing opportunities to present themselves. That's what we did that night.

Law #2: "Nothing happens until you get out of your house and start trespassing."

In the interest of making this relevant to the entire spectrum of activism, I should say, "Nothing happens until you turn off your computer and go outside."

This is something I call "the proximity effect." Allow me to explain.

I used to sit and obsess endlessly over where laboratories were. This was before the internet. Today, you can look up the address for many, but not all, animal research laboratories. Years ago, this was impossible.

We had no idea how to locate these labs. I set on this quest to find local labs for a year with little progress. One day, my friends and I just said, "We know of a place that breeds rats for labs. Let's just go there and see what happens." We went there and just walked around. We had no plan. We look in the window of a truck and see a binder on the seat of this truck that says "delivery list." We smashed out the window and took the binder. And we effectively had a master list of every laboratory in the state of Washington. This was huge. This information was not public.

This only happened because we put ourselves in a situation with no plan, and just allowed opportunities to present themselves. I'm not a religious person. I'm not a superstitious person. But there is an almost cosmic force I can't explain that I've seen play out time and time and time again. Which is, if you put yourself physically in a situation where you want something to happen, opportunities present themselves. It's as though the universe has a contract with you that if you put yourself there, it will meet you halfway and present an opportunity.

It would be impossible to overstate how many times I've been in a situation where I visit a place and suddenly see opportunities. "I can step on that power meter, then swing over to that ladder that goes up to a window that's open." You just see things.

So if you want footage of animals in a laboratory, you're almost certain to sit at your house and think, "How can I get this footage? I probably have to get a job there." Or, "there's no way I can get this footage." The answers will rarely come to you in your head. The answers will rarely come to you in a physical safety zone.

I can almost promise you, if you go to that laboratory, an opportunity will present itself.

In my early days, I would watch Animal Liberation Front videos. I always wished the videos would start just two minutes earlier. They're in the building, they're walking around, they're loading up animals. But I always wanted to know, "How did you get in the building?" I would watch these videos and wonder.

One thing I've learned since is that how they got in doesn't so much matter. If you put yourself there, chances are you will find a way in. Do with that what you will, but I have almost never been somewhere that I couldn't get into.

That's when ideas become actions, when you bridge that gap between your living room and where you want something to happen.

Law #3: "Demystify legal consequences."

This breaks down into three categories.

The first one is fear of police and interacting with police. This will happen to almost every activist at some point.

The second one is a fear of jail. Whether or not you're doing activism that is overtly against the law, in the back of our minds, we all think prison may happen to us.

The third is assessing the true likelihood of getting caught.

When I was a fugitive for a number of years, I had a game I would play to numb myself to police interactions. I had obtained an ID under a fake name. It was a real ID. So I could be stopped by police, they could run the ID, and it was fine. I knew one day I would be arrested and I knew one day the consequences would be severe. So I played a game where I would bait the police into stopping me - while I was a wanted fugitive.

I did that because I wanted to numb myself to interactions with police. I did that so when it actually resulted in an arrest, I wanted to be so comfortable being in the presence of police and talking to police that I felt no fear.

When I got arrested, I had a bail hearing where they decided if they were going to let me out. The lawyer for the FBI got in front of a judge and said, "Mr. Young has been in police custody 32 times during the time that he was a wanted fugitive." I had actually been stopped by police 32 times during the eight years I was wanted by the FBI.

Another reason I would bait the police into stopping me was because I knew one day it would come out that I had been in their custody 32 times, and it would make them look really stupid and also be really funny to talk about, like I am now. So that was part of it.

Have you heard the statistic that the number one fear amongst human beings is a fear of public speaking? It ranks higher than death.

I don't believe that because I can tell you that most people, if they have to get up in front of an audience and speak, they will do just fine. I think the number one fear of people is interacting with police. Because almost nobody can keep their mouth shut when they talk to police. Almost no one does fine. History has proven this.

Interacting with police is massively intimidating to most people. The most effective activists overcome the fear of interacting with police because it will be necessary in their work as an activist.

The next one is the fear of prison. This is something I think is necessary to overcome. We must have a sober assessment of what prison really is and also what it is not. If I had to put my prison experience in just one sentence, it would be, "The parts that I thought were going to be bad were not bad. And the parts that were bad were things that I never thought would be bad." I'll leave it at that.

Don't rely on the media to feed you your idea of prison. Find someone who's been to prison and ask them questions. Remember no single prison experience is going to apply across the board. There's a million prisons in a million states, countries, and jurisdictions. Get a well-rounded account of what prison is. Understand that, most of the time, it's not a fate worse than death.

Last element in demystifying legal consequences is having a sober account of risk. We like to think that a likelihood of prison is much greater than it really is. Humans have a terrible ability to assess probability.

Right now, people in the US are very scared about this law called the Animal Enterprise Terrorism Act. And it's a real law that has real consequences for real people. That should not be downplayed.

Yet among the poster children for fear of this law was a case where four people who were indicted for legal protest activity. They weren't ALF activists. They were engaging in legal protest activity. This sent shockwaves of fear through the entire animal rights movement.

A sober assessment looks like this: There are four people who got indicted yet there are 9,996 other people who protested that same year and did not get indicted. By that math, you have a 0.04% chance of getting indicted under the AETA.

We tend to focus on the negative, anomalous events and assume we're next. We don't have a well-rounded statistical perspective of true risk. We completely fail at assessing probability.

Law #4: This has two sides. The first is a sense of urgency. The second is something we'll call "speed of execution."

A sense of urgency is an elevated level of empathy.

Here is another story shared with me about an incident that happened many years ago. It was an unreported action that happened where some activists learned that there were salamanders held inside of a specific room in a specific university building.

They had a narrow window in which they could access this building and the room with the salamanders. They were told that the room was left unlocked, because no one knew it was there. It was a room within a room, so they weren't concerned about anyone getting inside. They went in in plain clothes, no ski masks, no gloves, no planning. Because there was so much activity in the university, they expected they could just walk into this room, surrounded by students, pick up the salamanders, and walk out. And that's exactly what they did.

They rescued, I believe, several dozen salamanders. It was never claimed. It never got publicity. There was never a communique sent out. It was only accomplished because of a sense of urgency, which is the elevated level of empathy where you actually see the world through the eyes of the victims, of the animals.

"Live your life as though you were the persecuted."

Speed of execution is the other side of that coin, the unemotional side. Effective activists know that the speed with which they actually carry out their actions determines how effective they will be.

Conservatively, 95% of the missions I planned which I postponed never happened. Most of those times, I postponed them because of an obstacle that was in my head, or because I was trying to achieve some perfection in a plan instead of completion.

In the startup business world, they have a term, "minimum viable product." They know that their success in the marketplace depends on how fast they can get their product out to the public. They will rush the software, or whatever the product may be, to market. They know it isn't perfect, they know it's flawed, but they get it out to the market because they know if you wait for perfection, that day never comes.

This is not to be confused with haste or introducing unnecessary risks. Handle the fundamentals, manage risks, but after that, focus on doing something instead of doing something perfectly.

There's an amazing book I encourage everyone to read, it's called *The War of Art*. Not *The Art of War*. This is a different book. The author talks about something called "The Resistance." The Resistance is that little voice in your head that talks to you every time you have a big plan with big goals and big consequences. Whether this is for animals, or whatever it may be. And The Resistance is that voice that tells you not to do it. The author Steven Pressfield says, "That's how you know you're onto something good, when there's a voice in your head telling you not to do it."

I've seen this in myself. Every time I have a great idea, immediately my mind goes towards, "Why can't this work?" Most of us have some variation of this.

On this idea of speed of execution, how many people here have noticed the more you talk about something, the further away you get from actually doing something about it? There's actually a term for this I found in a psychological journal. It's called "narcotizing dysfunction." When we speak about something, on a psychological level your mind equates talking with having done it. That's why people in punk rock bands tend to not be activists. They're on stage talking about how cool and militant they are, and they don't actually do anything. The people who talk the loudest are the ones doing the least.

And this is a very dangerous thing, I started noticed this in myself. I have a book I've been working on and I would always say, "I'm working on this book. I'm working on this book." Consequently, I never made much progress in the book. Well, I stopped... with the exception of right now, I stopped talking about this book because I knew the more I talked about it, the further away I was going to get from completing it.

There was a term we had when we were doing ALF activity many years ago. There were certain people we called "recon artists." It was a play on words, merging "reconnaissance" and "con artist." Recon artists were the people who would go out at night and look at potential ALF targets. They would do this all the time. And they would talk about it, "Oh, I went and checked out the slaughterhouse and this fur farm." They were fiercely focused on looking at potential targets, on staking them out, and doing recon. They would spend months and years staking out their targets. The more time they spent researching, hiding in bushes, watching buildings, and taking notes on security, the further they got from actually doing anything with that information. That's narcotizing dysfunction.

This is why speed of execution is crucial.

Law #5: "Identify your limiting beliefs and obliterate them."

Effective activists understand there are beliefs in your head that hold you back. They understand their "beliefs" may not actually be factually correct, objectively true, or supported by any evidence at all.

My house was raided by the FBI some years ago. They were investigating a raid that happened at a laboratory in Iowa in 2004. 400 animals were taken out of this lab.

After the FBI finished ransacking our house, a roommate and I were driving around, processing the situation. My roommate had been an activist for a long time. I was reading the warrant to him while he drove. He says, "It's crazy that in 2004 people were able to get inside this lab and get 400 animals out and do half a million dollars in damages." He said, "It's crazy they could do that in the year 2004." And I said, "Well, why is that?" He said, "Well, because everybody knows it's impossible to break into labs these days." He said, "It's just impossible. After the 80s, when there were tons of labs getting broken into, all the labs locked themselves down and it was impossible from that point to break into a lab."

And I said, "Let's explore this. How do you know? What is your evidence for this belief?"

He said, "Oh, come on, man. Everybody knows you can't break into labs anymore."

I said, "Well, maybe, maybe not. So let's explore the evidence. What evidence do you have to support this?"

He continued to say, "Come on man. Everybody knows it's impossible." So I said, "Have you ever even been to a laboratory?" He says, "No. But they're all secure now. Everyone knows that."

And so we lapped around this point about 10 times. I got him to admit that he had no evidence to support this belief. None.

This is a fantastic example of what they call a "limiting belief." We all have these beliefs. Beliefs about things that "can't be done." We might think we have evidence to support the belief but, in reality, the evidence is not objectively true. The evidence is usually rooted in emotional convenience.

A lab wouldn't have to lock their doors if they had us all believing there's no way anyone could get inside. Do you see how that works? Limiting beliefs hold us back more than any kind of government surveillance, more than any government repression. Our biggest enemy is our beliefs.

What's interesting about beliefs is that they can be changed. You can find evidence to support any belief. For example, consider that story I just told you. My friend had his "evidence" to support the belief that you couldn't get inside a lab after the 1980s. The people that broke into the lab in Iowa had a different set of beliefs. Both were equally sure of their beliefs. One found one set of evidence to support their belief, the other found another set of evidence. You can find evidence to support any belief.

Let's say there is a man or woman across the room you want to talk to. You think she might be interesting and worth knowing. If you think of yourself as an unattractive person, you're not likely to talk to that person. Yet someone who considers themselves interesting and attractive will be comfortable going over and talking to that person.

For both people, I could find 10 or 20 or 100 people who would say they're unattractive. I could also find 100 other people who would say they were attractive. It's merely a matter of where you focus your attention. You can find evidence to support any belief.

There's very little that's objectively true. It's like my friend saying a lab raid is impossible. The people that carried out that lab raid in Iowa had a different set of beliefs.

Who do you think got more done the night of that lab raid in 2004? The person that believed the labs couldn't be broken into? Or the people who sought out evidence that labs could be broken into?

Effective activists choose beliefs that translate to action.

Law #6: "The high-achieving activist does not care what you think of them."

We all know people who, before they do anything or say anything, they'll look to their left at the person next to them, look to their right, and only then will they will decide what to say or do. Figuratively speaking.

They survey their social landscape and decide what's going be fashionable for them to do, and they act based on the greatest social incentive.

There's a quote I read, "I don't know the recipe for success, but the recipe for failure is to try to please everyone." High-achieving activists don't get into debates on the internet. They don't care about debates. They're too focused on taking action. High-achieving activists don't survey the crowd and decide to do what's fashionable. They don't even know what's fashionable. They're too focused on their outcome.

There is an even more elevated level to this. People who have actually *delegitimized* opinions, where opinions themselves have no merit. Actions are the only things that count. The high-achieving activist knows the only true measures of an activist are your actions. It's not how well-favored you are by other activists or the public. It's what you do and how effective you are for animals.

The only cool thing about prison culture is this: In prison, all that matters is what you do. What you say has no merit. You're either somebody's best friend, or you're stabbing them in the throat. There's no in-between. It is culturally forbidden to trash-talk or criticize somebody. You're either their best friend or you punch them in the face. That's it. What I appreciate about this is that it strips away all the nonsense and gets down to action. You're either doing something or you're shutting up. There's no in-between.

Focusing on opinions will always come at the expense of your mission. The high-achieving activist answers to the animals and nothing else.

Law #7: "Demystify fear."

It is using fear as fuel. Early on in my activism I noticed something important. We all think of doing risky things and get nervous. When we imagine a risky situation, we physiologically experience fear as though are in that experience where we are at risk. This is natural.

Yet there is something incredible I observed when, for example, I was going to farms at night. I experienced fear before we got in the car to drive to the farm. I experienced fear in the car driving to the farm. I experienced fear when we parked. I experienced fear as we pulled down our ski masks and passed out tools. And as soon as we got out of the car and began advancing on the farm, as soon as there was no turning back, the fear vanished. Completely gone.

Why does that happen? It happens because when you're in the moment where you're taking action, when you are in the moment where you're irreversibly committed to your mission, fear is absent.

Fear only happens in anticipation of something. It never happens in the moment.

If you thought about the role of fear in your life, you would see this holds true. Almost none of the things you have feared in your life, 99.999% of the things you feared never happened.

In this way, fear is actually the worst measure of how dangerous something is. Fear will deceive you. The fear mechanism is inaccurate, and it lies.

If you look at fear from an evolutionary biology perspective, it is biologically natural to experience fear. If you see a predatory animal on the horizon, fear is what motivates you to evade the predator.

Here are two things about fear: Fear is meant to be very brief. And fear is meant to be a servant of intuition.

Today, we live in an artificial world. We're so detached from our natural origins that it's extremely rare for us to experience real, true fear. Do you ever notice how today people actually invent things to be afraid of? We'll actually go and watch scary movies because on some level it is a biologically natural thing that we lack. We do things like bungee jumping. Weird things. Because we literally never experience genuine fear.

I heard a story about somebody who lives in Los Angeles. There were wildfires that were literally three hours from their home. They received a phone call from their mother, who said, "Oh my God, are you okay? I just want to make sure you're okay." And the person said, "Mom, you know those fires are three hours away. Why are you calling me?" And she said, "Yes I know. But I just want to make sure." We literally invent things to be afraid of.

As activists, it is tragic and toxic how often we do this. We are inventing things to be afraid of. One, on some level we crave it. Two, it justifies our inaction. Three, it makes us feel important.

I had a friend who was in jail in a remote location. There was one vegan kid in that town who could go visit this friend. People contacted this vegan guy, and asked, "Hey, this guy needs jail support. Can you go to the jail and visit him and drop some money off so he can eat?" This kid said, "No, I can't do that." He said, "I don't want to be put on the FBI's list."

This person was so irrationally fearful, so terrified of being put on a "list" that he wouldn't go three blocks to visit this activist in jail. That's an example of inventing fear.

The point about fear is that in the modern age, the fear mechanism is triggering at the wrong times. While fear originally, biologically speaking, was a great preserver, in the modern age fear has become a prison.

There is a fascinating study done on robbery victims who had been held up at gunpoint. One of the things that came out of the study was that, in the moment they had a gun in their face, not one person said they experienced fear. They were very focused. They were very present. They were thinking,

"How can I get out of this situation?" But fear was absent.

I've been in many situations that I believed would be intimidating in the moment. Afterwards, I found it curious that my heart rate hadn't even increased. My heart rate increased each time I thought about that situation, before and after. But in the moment, the survival instinct was so acute, there was no fear.

The only true remedy for fear is action.

If you have something you're fearful of, anywhere on the spectrum of activism, the remedy for that fear is to do it. Take action. Because when you're in the moment, fear is absent.

Fear is the feedback you receive when you're about to maximize your potential as an activist. Fear is the feedback you receive when you're about to maximize your potential as a human being.

Don't fear fear. Understand that fear is sending you a signal that you're about to do something awesome.

The Seven Laws of Action, again:

1. Nothing is ever as hard as you think it is.
2. Get outside, where things really happen i.e. The Proximity Effect.
3. Demystify legal consequences.
4. Adopt sense of urgency / speed of execution.
5. Identify and destroy your limiting beliefs.
6. Answer to the animals, not the opinions of humans.
7. Demystify fear.

You should do these things because the only true measure of an activist is your actions. In fact, the only true measure of your life are your actions. Nothing else.

Lessons From The Underground

Lecture transcript
NYU
New York City
"It is our obligation as activists to be their claws and fangs."

Transcript of a talk I gave many dozens of times in my first two years after prison. This represents an early attempt to impart subtle lessons while walking that fine line necessitated by both probation, and state and federal incitement laws.

Since the governent is calling animal rights activists terrorists now, I'm justified in calling what you see here terrorism.

Projector slide of primate in vivisection lab.

If anything is terrorism, and if activism is terrorism, this is definitely terrorism.

Projector slide of cat in vivisection lab.

This would be another animal I believe is experiencing terror. And this is another animal I think was sufficiently terrorized.

Projector slide of pig in factory farm.

We can safely call this terrorism.

Now let's talk about counter-terrorism. Those first two animals you saw, the cat and the primate? Both of those animals were rescued in overnight raids from laboratories. The laboratories they came from were trashed with handheld tools, and those animals were given new homes.

Sometimes there are happy endings.

Courting A Point Of No Return

Anyone who is responsible for actions like these, who has ever broken a law for animals and gone to what we consider "extremes," I believe can point to a specific moment in time they identify as being a "point of no return." I don't just mean a catalyst, or the beginning of a process. I mean, one moment they can identify as being that point where they knew they were going to do whatever it took to get those animals out of these places no matter the consequences.

I had one of those moments that I will share with you.

I lived in Seattle at the time. This is going back a number of years. And I was involved in various vegan outreach efforts, and also adhered to a classic protest formula. But everything changed one day when a fellow activist and friend showed up at my door.

It was about 2 a.m. He looked very stricken. He had chicken feathers all over his jacket. I invited him inside. He told the story of missing the last bus back to the suburb where we lived, so he had to walk home.

In the process of walking home he stumbled upon a nondescript building that he discovered was a chicken slaughterhouse in full operation. This was literally on the fringes of downtown Seattle.

Until that point, to me, what happened to animals was very abstract. It was something that happened far away, out of state, or in the distant countryside. It wasn't something in my immediate physical realm.

That all changed when he told me there was a chicken slaughterhouse within three miles of my house. So I told him, "You need to take me there."

The next morning we went down to the slaughterhouse. It was about 5 a.m. We snuck down the alley behind the slaughterhouse. We stood on a crate, and within a matter of two or three minutes, I saw several hundred chickens getting grabbed by their feet, hung up on this conveyor device, and having their throats slit right in front of me.

This was an entirely new reality for me, the fact that animals were dying in my own neighborhood. I became obsessed with this chicken slaughterhouse. I began to go down to this place, my friend and I, a couple times a week.

What we learned is they would park semi-trailers full of chickens across the street before they opened for the day. And they would leave them there overnight. So we would go down to this parking lot and spend time with these birds. We'd talk to them. If we had Clif Bars in our pockets or something, we'd feed these birds.

And there would come a point every night, usually around 4:45 a.m., where we'd hear some tremors in the distance. We'd hear footsteps. We'd hear car doors closing, and we knew that was our cue to leave because the slaughterhouse was about to open.

Every single night on these excursions we would disappear down that same alley. We'd stand on that same crate. We'd look through that same window. And we'd see those same birds that we just spent time with 20 or 30 minutes before, getting grabbed by their feet, hung up on this conveyor line, and killed right in front of us.

I would go home every night from these excursions feeling as complicit in the deaths of those birds as if I were the one in the slaughterhouse doing the killing. As if I were the owner of that slaughterhouse.

That's what I identify as the point of no return for me. What I saw, that first day at that slaughterhouse.

It was the burden that comes from knowing, for the first time, I had the ability to affect what was happening to animals, because it was happening in my neighborhood. It was no longer an abstraction. This was a radical paradigm shift for me.

Bearing Witness, Militantly

With this new mindset, the fact that there were animals everywhere in my neighborhood, my friends and I got together and set out with the explicit goal that we were going visit every single animal abuse facility in Western Washington. Every lab. *Every factory farm. Every slaughterhouses. Everything.*

I can tell you now that was an overly-ambitious goal. We did not understand the scale of animal abuse industries. But it was our mission to set out and see what they were doing to animals with our own eyes.

At the time, this was not explicitly reconnaissance for illegal activity. It was just something we felt we had an obligation to do. We had an obligation to know what they were doing to animals in our neighborhood. So we began to go where these animals were, and we began to research where they were imprisoned.

This predated the internet. We had to get guerrilla in our tactics. We would drive around and look for businesses that had some kind of tell in the name, like the prefix "bio," or something that indicated it was a pharmaceutical company. Then we would pull over, go around the back, and dig through their trash. We'd investigate. Is there animal bedding back there? Is there a bag of food for animals? Is there paperwork that we can look at to get an idea about what they're doing? We'd get up on the roof, we'd put our nose to the vents. Could we smell animals?

We'd go to slaughterhouses. The addresses of these places are very easy to find. When they dropped the animals off we'd follow those semi-trucks back to the factory farms to learn where these animals were coming from. Again, this is something we felt we were obligated to do as activists, to uncover what was happening in our towns.

When we began to do this research we were absolutely shocked at what we found. This is going be as true for Seattle, as it is for New York City, as it is for any major city in the country, and a lot of not-so-major cities. Every time you began to look below the surface you're going find animal exploitation in your town that blows your mind. And that's what we found.

Hiding In Plain Sight

One of the very first places we went was an address we found in a business directory at the library. The information we had indicated this was a product-testing laboratory. The classic facility that will do anything you pay them to do with any animal, with whatever product you're trying to get on the market, for a price.

So we went to this place and it was in a strip mall. I remember there was like a vacuum cleaner wholesaler on one side, and I think there was like a car insurance place on the other And there it was, in between, in a faceless storefront, with blacked out windows, and a little plaque on the window with the name of the lab.

We thought we had the wrong place. It was too small, too nondescript. We went around back, got up on the roof, and put our nose through the vents. We could smell rabbits and we could smell rats. This was a place we would walk by every day. It was right across the street from the library in a town called Bellevue, right outside Seattle.

There was another place. The information we had told us they were doing research on dogs, and that they had 150 dogs in this building. We showed up to the place, and it was literally a house. And we were quite sure we had the wrong address once again. Sure enough, we went around the back, and saw it was connected to a hospital. We put our ear to a vent that was right about ankle level, and could hear dogs barking from the basement of this house.

I would ask anybody to tell me what the appropriate response is when you're standing outside of a building and you know there are 150 dogs inside. These are dogs that are in no way different than the dog you have in your home that you love and you care for. What is the appropriate response knowing those animals are just feet away? Is it to stand outside that building with a sign reading, "Please stop killing animals," hoping one day these researchers will heed your call?

Or, is the only appropriate response to do whatever is effective to get those animals out no matter what it takes?

This was the climate of the movement when I got involved in activism. It was a very volatile time. There was a real energy in the air.

The Animal Liberation Front

At this point, the underground animal liberation movement had existed for many years. The ALF was not new. But the pace at which things were happening was unprecedented. There was this emerging consciousness that patience wasn't virtuous. It was not virtuous to stand outside a building waving a sign.

The consciousness that was emerging said that this patience was criminal. And it seemed like every single day we would hear of some new illegal action that had happened the night before for animals.

This was everything on the spectrum of small-scale actions of questionable value. For example, people going to McDonald's, breaking out windows, and spray painting, "Meat is murder."

All the way up to more strategic actions. There was one action in Seattle I'd like to showcase because I think it captures well what just a few people can do with just a few hours of their time.

Some activists went to a pig slaughterhouse outside Seattle. Rather than burn the place down, or spray paint it, or do minimal property damage, these activists did something else. They broke into the slaughterhouse overnight and simply rounded up every tool in the entire building that was used to kill animals. Every knife, everything. Everything that was used to kill animals was simply rounded up, removed from the building, and discarded off site. And I remember the communiqué that was released after this action stated,

"This action was carried out to guarantee at least one blood-free day in the slaughterhouse."

I think that captures so well what just a couple of people – maybe even one person - can do with just a few minutes of their time to have direct impact on the lives of animals.

My friends and I were very inspired by this momentum. We decided to throw ourselves into the front lines of this movement. To go out and take what we knew they would never give, which was freedom for these animals.

From Symbolism To Vandalism

This was a period as an activist where I'd been learning many lessons. I had spent a couple of years following a classic protest formula. Then something big hit me one day after taking a hard look at what I'd been doing with my activism.

My realization was that there is one thing that is worse than doing nothing at all. And that's doing something that gives you the *illusion* of being effective.

We had been guilty of exactly that. Guilty every time we carried out protests and would go home and feel good about ourselves. Because when I began to reflect on actual results, and how many animals we actually saved… I had nothing to say. I couldn't justify it.

To be clear, there were many things I did that I feel fantastic about. Vegan outreach is one example. One of the best things you can do for animals is to educate the public about a vegan diet. That may, in fact, be the best tactic against the meat industry right now.

Yet there are many things I did that I couldn't justify, such as standing outside of a research laboratory with a sign. What did that accomplish?

As activists, we were asking ourselves every single question you could possibly ask, except for the one that mattered most: Is this effective?

We asked ourselves questions such as: How can we get more people to our demos? How can we more effectively phrase our protest slogans? But we never asked ourselves the only question that mattered, which was: Is this saving animals?

The Target

It was around this time I began to learn about the fur industry in western Washington. Seattle is a hotbed for the fur industry. Within about a one-hour drive from downtown Seattle, you can find about six mink farms.

When we began to learn about the fur industry we did what we always did when we learned about a new industry. We simply found out where potential targets were and went there.

I'll never forget the first time I went to a fur farm. We had an address that we got from a publication called *The Final Nail*. It was a fur farm directory published by activists. We had this address, and we drove out to this farm in Granite Falls. It almost seemed too easy. We pulled up, and there were 20,000 caged mink at this fur farm.

There were about 30 or 40 sheds and thousands of animals in a very small place. It was incredibly accessible. You could simply hop the fence and have free run of the entire place. It seemed too easy. And, as it turned out, it was.

We hopped the fence. We were there about five minutes, walking up and down the sheds. And a pickup truck came screeching up. Two farmers jumped out. One of them had a shovel. We hopped the fence. They gave chase and pursued us into the woods. We got away.

The next night we went to another fur farm nearby. It was a repeat of the exact same scenario. We showed up, we were there for a few minutes. And a truck came screeching up. We took off into the woods.

We couldn't figure out how they knew we were there. It was 2:00 A.M. or 3:00 A.M. Upon doing research, and looking more closely at the makeup of these farms, we realized what it was.

A very few fur farms, mostly in the Northwest, will have what are called photoelectric sensors. These are invisible beams that surround the farm. If you break the beam, it sets off an alarm at the farmer's house.

We realized very quickly that you could simply step over the fence, drop to the ground, roll under the beam, step up on the other side, and have free run of the farm. Totally undetected.

There Is Always A Way In

I mention this to highlight an important point: Every single time we would find a target and decided we wanted access, we would find a way. Every single time we set ourselves to get inside a place, we always got in. Animal abuse facilities – and I'm not just speaking about farms – are not as secure as you think. You can always get in. You can often just walk into a slaughterhouse. You may have to go on the roof, or get creative. Yet we would always get in. There's always a point of access.

There was one laboratory in Seattle and it was connected to a hospital. And this place kept all their animals in the basement. It was very easy to determine. Most labs keep their animals either in the basement or on the roof.

This place had their doors alarmed, double alarmed, locked, and triple locked every which way you could imagine. The one thing that they didn't think about was in a little-used wing of the building, there was an elevator. You hit the down button in that elevator, and it would drop you right down into those labs.

Our infiltration tactics were very amateur at this point, but we always found a way in. And so we'd see things, horrible things. Things similar to what you saw in the slides I began with. And we'd go home and just try to forget. Yet there comes a point where you can't forget. There comes a point where you've simply seen too much.

Flashpoint

We reached that point in the fall of 1997. I remember sitting down in the lobby of the Student Union building at the University of Washington with a friend. We had a fur farm list. We had an atlas of the Midwest. And we mapped out what was going to be our attempt to get as many of those animals out of those fur farms as we could before they were all killed during pelting season in November.

A friend of mine many years ago told me that for him, working outside the law for animals was something he likened to the reflexive response of putting your hand on a hot stove. It wasn't something you thought about, you just recoiled. You just did it. The situation was so bad that you didn't think about it, you just did it. It was a natural response to an extreme circumstance.

So we got in our car and drove east.

Mink Liberation

In the fall of 1997, there were six mink releases across the Midwest in a two-week period.

The Turbak Mink Ranch was a farm in Watertown, South Dakota. The farmer killed approximately 12,000 mink every fall for the last 30 or 40 years. He woke up the morning of October 16th of 1997 and found about a third of his animals were gone.

A few days later at the Circle K Fur Farm in Sioux City, Iowa there were 5,000 mink and 100 foxes released. Every mink on the farm and about half the foxes - gone.

Within the next 10 days, there were four more mink releases across the Midwest.

According to police reports, every single one of these raids followed the same model. There was no claim of responsibility made. There was no communiqué issued. There was no graffiti left at the scene. There was no property damage other than a cut fence. The farmers would simply wake up in the morning and find most or all of their animals gone.

When this two-week period was over, somewhere between 8,000 to 12,000 mink and 100 foxes had been released into the wild.

It would later come out that two of those farms had to close down permanently.

Anyone who has ever carried out both extremes of activism will tell you these are the kinds of results that writing letters or waving signs will never accomplish.

Total Siege

Around this time there was a New York Times article about the ALF's fur farm campaign. It said that farmers were so on edge during this time, they would actually sit overnight in their pickup trucks with shotguns waiting for animal liberators to arrive.

Another was a *Chicago Tribune* article specifically about that two-week campaign. It was a front-page article in which they had a quote from a mink farmer who said, "It has been a very, very rough two weeks."

I would say so. You wouldn't want to be a farmer during that period of time in the Midwest. Raids were happening at a pace of about one every three days. Two other cells were out targeting farms in the West at the same time as us. Two other large mink releases, that we had nothing to do with, occurred in Idaho and Illinois during this short period.

It was a total siege.

Counter-Siege

In the center of this storm, another person and I were seen passing the largest fur farm in the country. The Zimbal Minkery, in Oostburg, Wisconsin.

Little did we know the FBI had put out a bulletin across a five-state area alerting law-enforcement as well as mink farmers to be on the lookout for our vehicle.

And so on October 28th, when we passed the Zimbal Mink Farm, Linda Zimbal got into her car and gave chase. In minutes, we pulled into a parking lot, and it was like one of those scenes in the movies where all the cop cars come screeching up and surround the vehicle. We were ordered out of the car. We were asked consent to search the vehicle, which we refused. So they said, "Okay, we're just going to confiscate your car and apply for a search warrant."

And would you believe that after they pulled over their main suspects in this campaign that had cost the fur industry by some estimates over $1,000,000, they politely asked us to please report back to the police station 24 hours later.

That was a date we neglected to keep.

Into The Night...

There was absolutely nothing more heard about our case for the next year. But a year later another person and I were charged with four counts of extortion under the RICO Act, and two counts of a little-known charge called Animal Enterprise Terrorism.

When they eventually obtained a warrant and searched our vehicle, they found items they believed indicated our involvement in these mink releases. They found ski masks, fur farm address lists, detailed notes on farms, bolt cutters, and so forth. With all this evidence, it didn't take a tremendous leap of logic to determine we might have *something* to do with these mink releases.

We were charged in a six-count indictment. Cumulatively we faced a possible maximum of 82 years in prison.

They had their indictment, they had their search warrant, they had their arrest warrant, they had all their evidence. The one thing they did not have... was us.

The Hunted

For the next seven years, I was considered a federal fugitive. Does anyone want me to talk about where I was during those seven years?

Audience: Yes!

You and FBI both. So we're not going to talk about that.

But I do want to take a minute to remind you about something serious. I want to remind you that there are several activists out there right now who are being hunted by our government for actions ranging from sabotage against a laboratory to burning down a horse slaughterhouse that never reopened. I would encourage you to ask yourselves this question: What would you do if one of these people showed up at your front door and asked for sanctuary? One of the people who is being hunted by our government right now for trying to, allegedly, make the world a better place? Would you stand on the side of the butchers and the vivisectors of the world? Or would you stand on the side of those who are trying to make the world a better place? Keep those people in mind. They're not often spoken of, but they are out there.

Just as animals are so often the hunted, sometimes in fighting for a better world, we too become the hunted. And for the next seven years, I was the hunted.

Caged

In 2005 I was arrested in San Jose, California. In a Starbucks.

You can make your jokes because I've heard them all before. I got arrested at a Starbucks, yes. When I was in prison I got a stack of letters **this tall** from people who said, "Dude, you deserve two years just for *being* in a Starbucks."

When I was arrested I faced a long legal battle. If found guilty, based on the sentencing guidelines, I was told by lawyers to expect between 8 to 12 years in federal prison.

I had a long fight. I was in seven or eight different jails. And when all the smoke eventually cleared I was sentenced to two years in federal prison.

The last memory I have in county jail before I was sent to an actual prison was after my sentencing in court. They sent me back to my cell. They told me to pack my things up. They told me I was going to be shipped out any minute. And I began to round up all the paperwork in my cell. I began to sift through the legal documents. A lot of it I hadn't wanted to look at before that moment because of the potential sentence I had hanging over my head of 12 or more years. I remember pulling out all the police reports from the different jurisdictions that investigated these mink releases. And I remember sitting down for the first time and actually doing the math on how many mink were released, and how many they say were recaptured, and then subtracting.

When I did the math, it turns out I was going to serve about 12 hours per mink that was never recaptured. That's 12 hours per mink that we can say had a reasonable chance of living its full life in the wild.

I remember thinking, "I am honored to be able to give so little to get so much."

Your Best Investment As An Activist

Think of those pictures I showed you at the beginning of this talk. Why aren't we all more motivated to take action to stop atrocities like this? I can speak personally and tell you I've never been terribly motivated by what I've read on a piece of paper. I've never been motivated by what I've been told about an injustice. More than anything, what I've been motivated by is what I've seen with my own eyes.

I think that's always going to be that point of no return: when you see what you're fighting for with your own eyes.

When a problem exists only on paper, generally your solution is also going to exist on paper. You're going to write letters on paper. You're going to make signs out of paper. You're going to write essays on paper.

But when you see what you're fighting for with your own eyes and that problem crosses over into the 3D realm, your solutions tend to carry over into that realm as well.

That is why I always tell people the best investment you can make as an activist is to see what you're fighting for with your own eyes. Don't just know about it, go see it.

I know there are slaughterhouses right here in New York City. I know there are labs right here at NYU. There are a lot of opportunities. Some might take more finesse than others, but there are a lot of opportunities to see what you're fighting for with your own eyes.

When I did this in Seattle, it gave me the motivation as an activist to last a lifetime. I can never forget the things I've seen. Even if I tried, there is no way I can unsee them.

Those things that I've seen on egg farms, as an example. And if any of you here still eat eggs, I'll share this for your benefit. As someone who's seen many egg farms close up, I'll tell you exactly what we're talking about when you eat an egg. They pack five or six chickens into a cage about the size of half a sheet of newspaper. They can't even lift a wing. They spend their whole lives that way, largely in darkness and filth, crammed in with other chickens.

Again, these are places you can just walk into. There's no need for repelling down through a skylight. I would just walk into places that keep pigs in metal crates their entire lives. They can't even turn around. So if you eat eggs or eat animals, you would do well to ask yourself how you can justify that knowing what I just told you.

That is the responsibility of knowledge, to confront the obligation that comes with that knowledge. And I don't just mean this for consumer choices, I mean this in terms of your activism as well. If you know there is a laboratory here at NYU, what is the obligation that comes with that information? You have to ask yourself.

This information is all there for the taking. We live in what they call the "information age." We don't have the excuse of ignorance anymore. You can go to websites like *FinalNail.com* that list most of the slaughterhouses in the country. Most of the vivisection breeders in the country. Most of the fur farms in the country.

You can inform yourself about what's happening in your own neighborhood. I have here a piece of paper that is going to be passed out that has some great resources on it.

More Targets Than Time

The Fur Commission USA is a fur industry trade group. I remember them saying about our case, after we were indicted, that we had acted "opportunistically" when we chose to raid fur farms. They were trying to say that somehow we had seized upon some small weak link in the animal abuse infrastructure and pounced on it. As though ALF activity is so difficult and only easy targets like fur farms can be targeted. That could not be further from the truth. There was nothing opportunistic about it.

When we decided to go after fur farms, we had so many options we didn't know where to start. There was one lab, and I won't even go into specifics. I remember this place had a lot of animals, it was a horrific place. You could tell just from looking in the dumpster what they were doing to animals in that place. And I remember they had a whole wing of the building that was under construction. You could see very clearly through the windows. You could not only see the cages of certain animals, but also that all their alarms were dismantled while they were doing construction. That was one of the places that we had as an option. It was totally possible for us to break through the window of that facility undetected at night, and get those animals out.

Slaughterhouses were another easy target. We had tons of ideas. Choosing one was simply a matter of what offered the best effort-to-yield ratio. That was the only equation. It wasn't that we didn't have numerous other options. It was simply an equation of: how can we most efficiently save the most number of animals in the least amount of time and with the least amount of risk?

When I say effort-to-yield ratio, I can put this in solid numbers. I remember one time, we timed ourselves at a fur farm. There were two of us. In 15 minutes we were able to release 1,000 animals. Those are the kinds of results you can not achieve with any other tactic.

Out Of Sight, Out Of Mind

These industries thrive on one thing, and that's out of sight, out of mind. And when you remove that veil of secrecy, you go a great distance towards taking away their power.

I have just barely stepped foot on NYU, so I can't say for a fact what I'm about to share is true on this campus. But I go to a lot of universities, and there's one thing I've taken note of over the years. Do this at NYU: walk around, and just simply look at buildings that have a name that might indicate they experiment on animals. Whether it's the psychology building, and psychology departments almost always experiment on animals, biology, anything with word "bio" in it, neuroscience, health sciences, and so on. These are going to be telltale signs that there are animals in these buildings. When you see a building like that, on this university or any other large university, look up at the top of that building. Most of the time, between the top row of windows and the actual roof of the building, you're going to see a windowless gap. It might be one floor. It might be several. That's where they hide the animals.

Think about what this means. There's actually secrecy built into the design of these buildings. They're not worried about animal rights activists. These buildings predate the animal rights movement. They're not worried about animal rights activists seeing what goes on inside. They're worried about *anybody* seeing what goes on inside. It shows you clearly that these people knew from day one that what they do is sick and wrong.

Everyone needs to carry that burden of having seen too much. Please investigate what's happening in your town. In my experience, you can simply walk into an egg farm about half the time. Slaughterhouses are also not as secure as people think.

Laboratories may be a little more secure, but I'll share a story: During my time doing activism at the University of Washington, we had a tables set up one day. A guy came up to the table and said he worked in the labs. And though he supported animal research, he saw some very bad things in those labs that he did not support. He said that the university was so on edge about people seeing what went on in these places that even he, as an employee, on a regular basis, would get confronted in the halls and asked to identify himself because they were so paranoid of potential outsiders. He revealed to us there was only one person that ever got to walk through that building and was totally immune to suspicion. Just one. He said the FedEx delivery guy got to go wherever he wanted. And I always remembered that. The FedEx guy gets to go wherever he wants.

Recently I was in a thrift store and saw a FedEx uniform. Those aren't that hard to find…

Haunted

Do most of us know who the Weather Underground was? They were an infamous anti-imperialist group that carried out a series of political bombings in the 1970s. They made a film about the Weather Underground, and there was a quote from that film that I think captures so well what makes a good activist. The Weather Underground members were fugitives, they got arrested, they served prison time, they got out. After all of this, the interviewer asked them, "Why would you go so far?" And I'll never forget what this person said. They said there wasn't a single moment between the years of 1960-whatever to 1974, there wasn't a single moment that they were not *haunted* by the images of what was happening to the people in Vietnam.

This captures so well what makes a good activist. It's not just that you have loaded yourself up with a lot of data. It's something that happens on a very emotional level. Sometimes, the only thing that can put those images out of your head is to simply go out between when the sun sets and when the sun rises, and do what has to be done.

When I go somewhere new, and I know I'm going to be there for more than a month, I obligate myself to get on the internet and find out what's happening in that town. I will simply go to the nearest university and force myself, as hard as it is, to stand outside these building and look up, and know that in this building, there are imprisoned animals.

Speaking of haunted, there was one time I'll never forget. We had an address for a fur farm in Montana. The information we had did not indicate the kind of species on this farm. So we showed up at this farm, we parked on the street, we walked down a very long dirt road, and we came up over the apex of this hill. Something was very off about this fur farm. The average mink cage is about **this** big. We were looking down on some cages that were maybe the size of this podium. It was a full moon, and I remember looking down at the back-lit image of some very, very large animals. To me, from a distance, I thought they might even be primates, I wasn't sure. My friend and I sat there, looking down at this place. We stared at it for a good three, four, five, seven minutes. Just looking down, trying to figure out what we were looking at. Then it hit me in a split second. We were looking at more lynx in one place than might have existed in all of the wild in the entire state of Montana. Legally, lynx are a threatened species, but you can still raise them for coats. I spoke about being haunted. That will do it.

Terrorist

I just found out two hours ago that the police showed up at my old house in Los Angeles and were asking about me. Incidents like this happen all the time. More broadly, we've seen an increase in hysteria around animal rights activists. I realized right away when I was arrested that mine was not the average case. I realized there was one word that was going to have a tremendous impact, not just on the outcome of my case, but on the conditions of my incarceration. That word was "terrorism."

It has been applied to something as small as breaking out the window at McDonald's, or to rescuing an animal from an abusive situation. I don't need to tell many people here that it's the fur farmers of the world who are the true terrorists. It's the vivisectors who are the true terrorists. Activists are counter-terrorists. Nonetheless, it's worth talking about the weight of that one little word, "terrorism," and how it affects a politically-charged case.

The first thing I noticed having a "terrorism" case is that they became absolutely obsessed with knowing who my friends were. I realized that they weren't going after me, they weren't going after Peter Young, they were going after an entire movement. They were looking at me as their entry point to dismantle this movement of "terrorists."

The way this specifically manifested is within days of my arrest, they executed search warrants all around the Bay Area in California. They raided two or three homes, they searched a storage unit, they impounded a car, they subpoenaed phone records. These were people they weren't trying to link to any specific crime, these were people who were just believed to have some association with me during the time I was considered a fugitive. When all the smoke cleared, they had visited somewhere between 50 and 100 people around the country, knocking on doors, asking, "How do you know Peter Young?"

I remember my first lawyer, who had no experience with a politically-charged case, pulled me out of the cell and brought me into the attorney booth in Santa Clara County Jail. He's scratching his head and he's saying, "you know, I can't figure this out, these people are more interested in who your friends are than what you're actually accused of doing." He said, "they're trying to create a master list of who your friends are."

I feared this was going to have some serious ramifications. Some people that had no reason to think they were ever going to be an FBI target all of a sudden were a target, simply because they were believed to have some association with me. Literal guilt by association.

When I was arrested, I had a backpack on me. The FBI took this backpack and scrutinized it down to the pieces of lint inside. One thing they came up with was a little scrap of paper at the bottom of my bag. It was something a friend of mine, unbeknownst to me at the time, had slipped in my backpack. It had quote on it from the book *Catcher In The Rye*. She signed that quote, "Holden Caulfield."

Keep in mind, Holden Caulfield is the protagonist in the best selling fiction book of all time. Suddenly the FBI became verrrry interested in who this mystery "Holden Caulfield" person might be. They began to run Holden Caulfield through their databases. They did a criminal history check on Holden Caulfield. And they found him. Turns out, there's a man named Holden Caulfield who lives in Tempe, Arizona. So some very poor, unfortunately named old man got a knock at his door, confronted by FBI agents asking, "How do you know Peter Young?"

No One Talks, Everyone Walks

When you get arrested, they're probably going to let you sweat it out for a few months. But at some point they're going to come to you and they're going to offer you plea bargains. They're going to offer you plea bargains that involve naming names. Some of those plea bargains might not even involve implicating anyone in any crimes.

When I got arrested, they let me sweat it out for about three months. Then they began to approach my lawyer. When we hired this lawyer, we said look, we're letting you know right now, cooperation is not an option. And he said, yes, I understand that, and I would not encourage you to ever do anything like that. But he also said he was obligated by some lawyer-code to pass on any information to me that the prosecutors gave to him, including plea bargains that involved naming names.

The first plea bargain they offered was when I was looking at between 8 and 12 years. They came to me and said, "We're going to cut you loose in three years. All we want from you is, when you get out in three years, simply go back to the animal rights movement and feed us information. We want you to be our mole in the animal rights movement." They asked me to tell them who I knew, who those people knew, and so on.

So we threw that one back in their face. They came back again and said, "Okay, now we're going to give you two years. All we want from you is, simply give us a complete list of every single person that you associated with during that time you were a fugitive." Now, it's very telling when you look at this plea bargain offer. They did not actually want me to implicate anyone in any crimes. All they wanted was names. I could have easily given them a complete list of names of every person whose couch I stayed on, or the people I hung out with. There was really no reason to think anyone would have gotten in trouble. I could have walked out of prison and everyone in the FBI would have been happy. But naming names, no matter how benign, is a terrible thing to do. You never give information to the police, no matter how seemingly harmless. You just don't talk to police. And that's not legal advice, that's just decent-human advice.

Then they came back a third time, when I had my felonies dismissed, and said, "Now we're going to give you one year if you give us that list of names." It's very telling to look at the fact they didn't want me to implicate anyone in any crimes. They wanted more names for their list.

Next thing you notice having a "terrorism" case is that they make an immediate attempt to exaggerate the scope of the conspiracy to encompass not just you and your friends, but the whole animal rights movement. Specifically in my case, they tried to implicate national animal rights groups in funding and training us. To be even more specific, they said PETA did this. They dropped that theory pretty quick, yet initially they were trying to say that it wasn't possible someone could get together with one other person and go carry out such a crime spree. This kind of autonomous action is totally outside their paradigm. They think it has to be a broader conspiracy.

It's funny when you look at just how basic, low-tech, and under-funded our entire campaign was. When we left town, we had literally $60. I still remember that number. We had no idea how we were going to even make it past Idaho, let alone eat. Often to eat we would have to dumpster dive at grocery stores. I remember in Wisconsin there was a supermarket chain that would take their bananas when they got too ripe and instead of throwing them out, they would wrap red tape around them and sell them for 10 cents a pound instead of 70 cents a pound. Because we were desperate, we learned very quickly we could take the red tape off the old bananas and wrap them around the new bananas. So we got new bananas for 10 cents a pound. Point being, this was something that we had to do just to survive. So if PETA really was funding us, shame on them for only giving us 40 cents a day.

Their Only Weapon

Having the word "terrorist" associated with me affected me in jail. When I was arrested, I was put in a cellblock at Santa Clara County Jail, a jail holding 1,000 people. They put me in a cell block with what was considered to be 14 of the worst of the worst prisoners in the entire jail. There were only three other people in that cell block who were not in for murder. I was considered to be this caliber of criminal. I couldn't leave my cell without being shackled at the hands and the feet. When they pulled me out of my cell, the entire floor had to lock down. I was seen as this level of threat.

You've heard of Con Air? Like in the movies? That actually exists. It's a 100-person capacity retired commercial airliner. Everyone on it is shackled at the hands and the feet. They fly federal prisoners and drop them off at prisons around the country. On most Con Air flights there will be one or two people that are deemed so high-risk they have to have what's called a "black box" that goes over their handcuffs as an extra safety precaution. Of course, I'm the guy who gets the black box.

I remember sitting there on this plane, and there was a Hells Angel's bodyguard sitting on my right, and there was a guy who was in for kidnapping on my left, and both of them are sitting there looking at the black box nervously like, "What the heck did this guy do?" So I told them, I released some animals from some people's backyards. And they're like, "Yeah, right, dude. What did you *really* do?"

To what extent does having a politically-charged case affect your treatment by other inmates? When I was arrested I had built up in my head what prison was like. When I arrived, I found something very interesting about convict culture.

Among my first interactions with other prisoners came in Alameda County Jail. I was taken off a bus from San Jose and brought into a standing-room-only holding cell the size of your bathroom, holding 50 guys.

The door closes behind me. The room goes silent. It's like the out of town stranger stepping into the old west saloon.

Finally someone breaks the silence and says,

"What did this motherfucka do, cheat on the SAT's?"

The whole room exploded in laughter. And I thought, "This is it. This is the treatment I'm going to face for the next 20 years."

But that's not how prison was.

What I learned about convict culture was this: when people learned why I was in prison, there was a subtle amount of respect extended to me for being someone who was looked at as having stood up for his beliefs. It didn't matter if those beliefs conflicted in every possible way with those of the other prisoners. All that mattered was that I was perceived as being what they call a "stand up guy."

I've been vegan for 14 years, and I remained vegan in prison. This was very difficult to do. Once a week, in the prison dining hall, they gave out apples.

97

You go through the line with your tray, and they give you an apple. I would hoard these apples. I'd pull them out of the trash. I'd talk to other prisoners, "can I get your apples?" I saved them in my cell just to get me through the week. On these apple days, I'd sneak out of the dining hall with like eight apples in my jacket. Then I'd go to the library or I'd go wherever. And when I came back to my cell at night, I would find on my bed, 8, 10, 15, 20 apples other prisoners had rounded up and just placed on my bed. They never told me who they were. They never came around to say "Hey, did you get those apples we left you?" It was just a subtle gesture of respect.

Whether prison is a very direct threat to anyone in this room or a very indirect threat, I think one of the best things we can do in any movement is demystify prison. To talk about the myths as well as the realities in a very candid way. We shouldn't spare anybody the uncomfortable details, which oftentimes are real. Yet we should also work to demystify some of the myths. Prison has always been a part of every movement. Activists will always be imprisoned. Anytime a movement starts to be effective or starts to be a threat, people will be imprisoned.

As activists, we have unlimited weapons at our disposal. We have a tool box that is bottomless. There is no end to the tactics we can employ to achieve our goals. They — the FBI, prosecutors — have only one weapon. Only one tool they can use, and that's prison, That's all they have. When we demystify prison we have one less thing that stands between us and that world that we're fighting for.

Post-Prison Panopticon

This kind of hysteria continues after prison. If I told you that someone got out of prison on a rape conviction, and I told you they were placed under surveillance by the FBI 24 hours a day, would you say that seems a bit odd? Whether or not it's justified, that wouldn't sound normal to you. Yet that's what they did to me.

They would put a car outside our house with a video camera, not very cleverly disguised, on the dash, aimed right at our front door. Presumably they just wanted to track who came and went. We'd always joke, if we just walked out there with a big bed sheet and put it over the car, what would they charge us with?

When I got out of prison, some people were very nice and hosted a "get out of a prison" party for me in Hollywood. We learned later that a private intelligence firm, funded by the animal research industry, actually sent an agent undercover to the party. For what purpose, I don't know. To see what kind of music eco-terrorists dance to? I don't know.

Something I alluded to earlier: Just a few hours ago I received a frantic call from an old roommate, saying the cops have been harassing her all day, and they are outside the house right now. So if I vanish after this talk, that's why.

Animal Liberation And Misdirected Risk

There is an ALF documentary titled *Behind the Mask*. Somebody pointed out in the film that you have a better chance of dying in a car crash on your way to the grocery store than you do getting arrested for an action to save animals. But most of us would never consider crossing any legal lines to save an animal, while we wouldn't hesitate to drive to the grocery store.

Here is another uncomfortable fact: It takes less skill to liberate a chicken from a factory farm than it does to sneak into a movie. We've all snuck into movies. We know what that's like. There are actually people in movies who are there to stop you. There are people all over the place. I've also been to factory farms at night. There is nobody to stop you. You just walk in.

Another uncomfortable fact: You expose yourself to potentially greater legal consequences carrying a forged ID to get into a bar or club, if you are under 21, than you would just being caught trespassing in the basement of laboratory. I mean that.

In that sense, we are all animal liberators, we just misdirect our risks.

Fighting Smarter, Not Harder

If you are someone who's fighting for a better world, I would encourage you to ask yourself how you can fight smarter, and not harder. How you can fight to achieve your goals in the most efficient way possible.

I've never heard of a struggle that was won by putting a flower in a gun barrel. I know of many that have been won with crowbars and a good pair of gloves. When we released animals from those fur farms, there was no amount of letters in the world that would have saved those mink. When activists went into a laboratory in Minnesota and rescued over 100 animals, there was no legal protest that would have saved them. When activists went into a toxicology lab at Louisiana State University and destroyed every piece of equipment used to torture animals, there were no legal channels that would have accomplished that.

This is fighting smarter, not harder. There are some battles that will be won with a reasoned argument, and there are a lot more that are going to be won with claws and fangs. It is our obligation as activists, and for those animals that cannot speak for themselves, that cannot fight for themselves, to be their claws and their fangs.

The Power Of One

If you're dedicated to what you're fighting for, ask yourself what you're going to do if you wake up tomorrow, and all your friends are gone. To achieve the societal change that we seek, we are going to have to win mass numbers of people over. Concurrently with that, we need to emphasize the power that one person has.

It only takes one person to go to an egg farm with a video camera, videotape the conditions in that egg farm, release it to the media with a press release, and expose millions of people to the conditions of factory farming. It only takes one person to get a job inside a lab, document the conditions in that lab, have a press conference, and expose it to the world. It only takes one person to go down to an overpass at rush hour, hang a banner with whatever message you want, and expose the world to that message.

If you ask yourself if we're going to win in our lifetime and you come to the conclusion that we won't, do not be discouraged. There can be many victories along the way. Every animal you save as a result of persuading a person to be vegan, every one of those lives is a victory. Every animal you can rescue from a farm overnight is a victory.

Remember those images I showed you at the beginning. Don't just get upset, get angry.

And then go out and get active.

Principles Of
Life and Liberation

Lecture transcript
Animal Rights National Conference
"Your success as an activist is in direct proportion to how uncomfortable you're willing to be."

For nearly ten years (as of the time of this writing), I have addressed rooms of newer activists at the Animal Rights National Conference. Titled "Newcomer Orientation," the panel each year is comprised of an eclectic mix of long-time activists sharing their origin stories and lessons for newer activists.

These are edited selections from numerous years on this panel.

Only at the National Animal Rights Conference would a felon who went to prison be asked to offer advice to new activists. I broke into my first slaughterhouse before I went to my first vegan potluck. So that gives you a taste of what you're about to hear. I don't blame you if you want to leave now.

The obligation of anyone at a podium is never merely to talk about themselves, and never merely to talk about their projects. It is to give people the most actionable information they can that they can take out into the world and help animals with. I aim to accomplish that with this talk.

In my years as an activist, I've worn many hats. I've been a protester. I've been an undercover videographer. I've been a burglar, I've been a writer. I've been a fugitive. I've been an author. I've been an "eco-terrorist." I'm proud of each of these, but especially the last one.

If all you want to hear from me is how to pick locks and access buildings through air vents, I may disappoint. If I gave a talk like that, they'd probably charge me with something. So short of that, if I was a new activist, these are the broader lessons and principles I've learned, that I'd like to share.

Nothing is ever as hard as you think it is. Whatever problem you think is insurmountable, you're wrong. I didn't have any burglary training, but years ago there was a lab we wanted to get into. We climbed onto the roof, lifted back the skylight, and rappelled down into this laboratory. We had no idea what we were doing. We had a strong enough "why," and the "how" took care of itself. And I think that's the most important lesson. Anything you think is an impediment to victory, you're wrong.

Have laser focus. Any book on strategy you'll ever read will tell you that victory only comes from repeated, focused action. Focus, focus, focus. Don't focus so narrowly that you're spending a lifetime focusing on a particular animal, or a road side zoo, or something small. Strike a balance between winnable goals that will save animals, while also not being distracted with moving from campaign to campaign. Focus is crucial.

Media matters. I learned early on that whatever activism I do, I'm going to give it a media component. No matter what. Anything you do, no matter what, send out a press release. If you're going to do a protest, send out a press release. If you're going to throw a brick through a window, send out a press release. Everything you do, send out a press release. Just be ruthless. Not to the extent that you compromise the message you're trying to communicate about the animals, but chase a broader audience - and consequently, a broader impact - for all your actions.

Source wisdom and tactics from outside the activist realm. The best lessons you'll get about animal rights activism will not come from animal rights books. They're going to come from reading books about marketing. They're going to come from reading books about communication. They're going to come from reading books about criminals.

I read a book called *The Unsolved Crimes of Phil Kresta*, about a master burglar. What I was impressed with was not just the tactics but how he was able to reverse-engineer man made-systems and isolate loopholes. This offers powerful lessons for activism. Read books about psychology. Read a book called *Influence* (Cialdini). Read books about strategy, like *The Art of War*. These books are invaluable for your activism.

Leverage your strengths, don't spend a lifetime on your weaknesses. If I tried to be a hip-hop artist for the animals, I would totally fail. Everyone knows I can't rap. What I do have that I can leverage are small things, I have a few small stories that bring the media to contact me occasionally, and I'm able to use that platform to deliver a message about animals. If somebody sets a truck on fire at a cattle farm in central California and the media comes to me, I can immediately turn that conversation around to focus solely on the animals. I can say, "This is why someone would set a truck on fire. Whether or not you agree with it, this is the plight of animals. This is what the animals go through. This is what would drive someone to do this."

Most would see having gone to prison as a major liability. Yet I can leverage having gone to prison and use it to benefit animals. Leverage your strengths. Figure out what those strengths are and capitalize on them.

Your success is in direct proportion to how uncomfortable you're willing to be. We do the animals a huge disservice when we tell people to only do what makes them comfortable. Get outside your comfort zone. Move towards resistance.

De-emphasize internet activism. This is the most controversial one. Everyone wants to fight me when I bring this up. It's such a nuanced point that I can't capture this message adequately in just a few minutes. Just understand that animals don't die in cyberspace. Be deliberate and strategic when directing your efforts for animals to the internet. The internet can easily function as a way to accomplish things. And just as easily, it can function as a way to delude yourself into believing you are accomplishing things.

Be content not knowing the full impact of every action. Rewind to when I was 16. I was thumbing through the cable channels. I'll never forget the channel. It was channel 28. It was a public access channel in Seattle. I caught a glimpse — and I mean, one second, if that — of a cow being killed in a slaughterhouse. That image planted the seed that would soon see me become vegan. Whoever played that footage that night had no idea the impact they would have. They did it anyway.

Two years later I had graduated high school. I was vegan. I was skateboarding around town and began seeing stickers on stop signs that read, "eating animals," below the word "Stop." So they read "Stop eating animals." We've all seen these. And I wanted to find out who this anonymous vandal was because I was the only vegan in the town as far as I knew. I began asking around and several people told me, "Yeah, there's this guy named Dave. He's also vegan." I was hearing rumors of a mystery vegan named Dave.

Eventually I found this guy on the other side of the city. I cornered him. I said, "Hey man, was that you who put those stickers up?" He didn't want to admit to it, he's being cagey, but eventually he says, "Yeah, you know, maybe it was me, maybe it wasn't."

This person ended up getting me involved in activism. He brought me to a meeting. He got me involved in protests. He could have never realized the impact his small vandalism had, but it led to me moving from passive vegan to activist.

Quit your job, liberate your time. I want to echo very strongly what was said by someone else on this panel, about being a successful person outside of activism in order to be a successful activist. I am going to offer a different spin on this.

The most powerful thing you can do for activism in your life is quit your job. I don't hear anyone talking about this. The biggest impediment to activism is your day job. Bottom line. Anything you can do to get out of the 9 to 5 lifestyle will be a tremendous asset to animals. There's literally nothing that impedes activism more than selling your time to someone else for money.

At 18 I decided the best thing I could do for my activism was to not have a job. I didn't want to work 9 to 5. I didn't want to have those eight hours blocked out where I couldn't do anything for animals.

I could have become an entrepreneur and made my own hours. That would have been one path. Instead I decided to become militantly unemployed. This meant living with almost no money. Part of this was living in an abandoned house. I lived in a very rich neighborhood at the time. So I found an empty house that was government surplus property. I broke into the back door of this house, and I lived in this house for two years. This empty house gave me the platform to not have to work and to do activism full-time.

To this day I've been employed just a few months of my adult life. That's covered a huge spectrum of things. I've been the guy who's sleeping on your couch longer than you want me to. To the other end of the spectrum where I am today, becoming successful as an entrepreneur. I've run the spectrum.

I look around now at older activist friends, and it's tragic. People I knew from activism in the '90s, their potential now is squandered. They're 40 and work in food service. I want to say to them: Invest your time into building money-making systems such that you don't have to sell your time. You can dedicate it to animals. But they are stuck in an archaic mindset of trading time for money.

For a lot of people, selling their time will mean working for a nonprofit. Groups like MFA could not exist without the people who dedicate their time to carrying out their vision. There are also people whose ambitions or personalities are too big to fit into the confines of a job. Those people need to figure out an alternate plan. Your time is the most valuable asset you have. You must figure out how to use it for animals and not sell it.

That could be entrepreneurship. That could be sleeping on someone's couch. You're welcome to sleep on mine. People don't take me up on that enough.

Liberating your time is the best way to liberate animals.

Demystify a night in jail. Ultimately, the abandoned house I spoke of was raided by the police and I spent three nights in jail. When I was released, I realized this experience had been tremendously empowering. Because as an activist, I had finally demystified what a night in jail was. I knew I could survive it. I knew it wasn't that bad.

There's a huge range of circumstances you'll find yourself in as an activist that may be legally gray, or just outright illegal. Yet knowing you can survive the consequences is massive. It opens up a huge spectrum of possibilities for you to be an effective activist.

Getting out of my middle-class comfort zone and demystifying a night in jail was a hugely important leap for my activism. Finally, I was able to exercise the true range of my options to help animals, not just the narrow ones that fit within legal lines.

There will be a lot in your activist career that's going come up. From an abused dog in a backyard to trespassing inside a lab to obtain footage. A lot will come up that will expose you to a small amount of jail time.

I do not feel like it is our obligation to go to jail. We're not serving the animals by serving time. Yet I do feel it is our obligation, at times, when the situation calls for it, to do things that *might* land us in jail.

There's a tremendous amount that happens to animals where, if we were to act in a way that was consistent with our beliefs, it would bring us into some legally gray areas, or outright illegal areas. It's important we get out of our middle class comfort zone and demystify what a night in jail is.

I had two nicknames in prison, one was "the Fur Bandit," and the other was "Eco-Pimp." There's no lessons to be drawn from this, it's just funny.

The best victories and most triumphs will always come to those who break the most rules. They could be felonies. They could be cultural rules. But those who break the most rules, who create the most friction, who make the most enemies, those are the activists that have the greatest triumphs to their credit at the end of their lives.

Focus on the 20% of your efforts that will have 80% of the impact. When I look at the people I got involved with, I would estimate 80% to 90% of them got involved in one of three ways.

One, a music-based subculture. Two, through someone they know. As in, "I know this person, they were vegan, they got me involved." Three, from seeing a video or image. Many people can cite a specific image or video that they were exposed to that they can never get out of their head. They spend the rest of their lives trying to get that image out of their head.

Personally, I've never met someone who became vegan from hearing a statistic.

When we look at what 80% of our results are coming from which 20% of our efforts, we must focus on that 20%. Figure out what that 20% is, and go after it.

Deliver actionable information. If you're going to give somebody information, give them actionable information. People need to be able to come away from your messages saying, "I know the next step. This is what I can do now," not, "Okay, I know more about how horrible this world is now." They need a next step. If you give somebody information, always give them a next step.

When I got involved, there was a publication called *The Final Nail*. It was a how-to manual on releasing animals from fur farms. What made it more interesting was that it also included a list of fur farms. It was amazing to see what happened when this publication began to circulate. This is before the internet, so this document was passed from person to person. Within two years of this publication coming out, this country went from perhaps three fur farm liberations in its history, to 60 mink liberations in two years. This was because, for the first time, people actually had a "next step." It was, "Here's what you can do and here's where you can do it."

Even if you just gave somebody an address, for example, "Here's a slaughterhouse in your town." I consider that to be actionable information because they can form a campaign around that, they can protest it, they can try to get them on an EPA violation. Whatever avenue they take, it's actionable because it showed them "here's where it's happening." Now you have no excuse. You know it's happening right here at this fixed physical location.

Nothing is more potent than urgency. Once exposed to the plight of animals, I realized immediately that what we do to animals is without question the most urgent and significant injustice in the history of the world. Don't let anyone tell you otherwise.

When I would attend conferences like this when I first got involved, here's what I remember. I used to come to talks like this, and I would sit just where you're sitting. I would look at the podium, and look at the person talking, and I would sit there and roll my eyes. And I would go yeah, yeah, yeah, theory. Yeah yeah yeah philosophy. Just tell me how to pick locks, okay? Just tell me how to break into labs and rescue animals. That's all I wanted to hear at age 18. That's it. And, you know what, I never heard that talk. I've given talks like that, but never heard one.

Ultimately my friends and I decided we had to figure this out on our own. The activism culture I was introduced to was different than most. In addition to making protest signs, we would wander the University of Washington campus with bolt cutters, cutting random padlocks on grates, looking for secret access points into buildings. Instead of going to offices on campus to get a protest permit, we would go to the facilities office and trick them into giving us blueprints to the buildings so we could learn where the animals were.

Because I never heard that talk I so desperately wanted to hear about how to just break into places, we ended up making many mistakes. But the one thing we had that was more important than anything else was a sense of urgency.

The lesson here is: *don't ever let anybody try to quiet that sense of urgency in you.* If you have the impulse to go do something, don't let anyone tell you you're crazy. You might be crazy, but don't let anyone tell you that. Don't let anyone tell you that sense of urgency is something you need to quiet in yourself. Because that's your most important asset as an activist. "Clueless and driven" is 1,000 times better than "educated and patient." My greatest triumphs have come from being in the former category.

Nothing will ever trump a sense of urgency. That is your most important asset as an activist.

Plans are overrated, strategy is not. Plans are overrated. Strategy is *not* overrated. These are two very different things.

Strategy is crucial. Plans themselves are not so important.

In one of our early "burglaries," friends and I put this hodgepodge of tools together that we probably stole from our parents' garages. We went to a pig slaughterhouse. To say that we had no plan was an understatement. We just showed up with bolt cutters and sledgehammers. The biggest amateur burglary tool box ever compiled. We threw some things in our car and showed up. We parked on the road outside this slaughterhouse. So we say,

"What do we do now?" We decided to avoid the driveway and go in from the side. My head touched an electric fence and I collapsed in a field and blacked out for a moment. Finally we got to the rear loading dock. There are pigs squealing on the opposite side of the building. We're looking at each other. "What now? Let's crowbar the door." It's a large sliding door made of wood. It's not budging. We stand there, defeated. A minute passes, and my friend gives the door another forceful tug. It opens. It was unlocked the entire time. We enter the killing room floor. We're looking for equipment to smash. It's a large empty concrete and wood room. We enter the offices. Not even computers to break. We're all dressed up with nothing to smash. "What's the weak link here?" We're shining flashlights around. "There's the captive bolt gun." The device used to kill animals. We can't detach it from the hose. There was nothing about this in any ALF manual we'd read. Minutes go by. We cut it loose with bolt cutters. "Now what?" We look around. There's a set of butcher knives. We put them in a giant tub. But we find it's too heavy to carry across the field. This isn't looking good. At great risk, we get the car and drive up to this slaughterhouse to load the tub. Finally, we have to paint a message. "Where's the spraypaint?" No one can find it. "Did we leave it inside?" We have to go back inside. It's nowhere. We never find it. We disappear into the night. But we did it. Best case, we put that slaughterhouse out of commission, for an hour or a day. But we accomplished it.

Point is, we had no plan. But when you put yourself in a situation where things have to happen, things happen. "How" is never the obstacle. How badly you want it is the obstacle.

Never fall victim to "The Tyranny of How." Which brings me to the next lesson. Something I heard recently referred to as "the tyranny of how." The excuse of "I don't know how" is a 100% fake excuse 100% of the time.

Especially in the age of the internet. If you knew what we had to go through just to get the address of an egg farm in 1997. We had to go to a library. We had to check out a CD-ROM set from the librarian. Then we had to go to a computer. Then we had to page through these giant books to find the correct business code to enter into the computer to look up particular businesses. It was a major production. Today, you have Google.

Focus on strengthening your *why* and don't get caught in the tyranny of *how*.

Leverage your resources. Identify and leverage your resources. No matter how large or how small. Determine what your resources are, and leverage them. There are advantages to having a lot of money. Yet there are also hidden advantages to having no money. Almost no one talks about this.

If you had a full tank of gas and $30, the best way to leverage those resources for animals would be to drive to a fur farm, cut down the fence, and open every cage. If you had $50 million, the best way to leverage that for animals would be to start a mainstream vegan food startup that would make the egg industry obsolete.

The point is to leverage the resources that you do have. Early in my activist career, we made some wise decisions based on the very limited resources we had. We had a lot of time. We had a few tools. We had a total lack of regard for going to prison. Based on those resources and assets, we leveraged them well.

Maximize your effort-to-yield ratio. My first year of activism, we'd stand outside of McDonald's and various other targets. I always held the same sign that read "Meat Is Murder." The whole point was to get people to see the sign and hopefully make a change in their diets.

One night we were like, "the heck with this." A friend and I went to a deli. We threw a brick through the window. Not very strategic. Not very effective. But at the scene of the crime, we spray painted that same slogan: "Meat is murder."

The next night the news broadcast reports of our vandalism to hundreds of thousands of people around Seattle. In this news story, you see the camera panning over to the spray painted phrase: "Meat is murder." This went into the living rooms of every single person in the Seattle area.

We had spent so much time trying to get people to read our sign outside McDonald's, spent countless hours to reach a few dozen, maybe a few hundred people. And in just one hour, we got the message into the living room of everybody in Seattle. Just like that.

That's a lesson in leverage.

Done is better than perfect. There's a phenomenon we see often in activism: "paralysis by analysis." The more you think about something, the less you actually do. Shut your brain off, go out, and do something. Build successes that will lead to bigger successes and onward to even bigger ones.

The most important thing is to start that success ladder by going out and doing *something*.

Break every rule. This is the most important lesson I can offer as an activist. Rules of convention, rules of the law, cultural rules. Whatever rules you can break, break them. The only way you will ever make history is to break rules.

Your only roles as an activist are simple ones. It's two things: be the best possible asset you can be to the animals, and be the animal abusers' worst nightmare. Those are your only two roles. That's it.

Questions

Audience member: Peter, could you talk about The Final Nail?

In 1996, someone had the ingenious idea to assemble a list of all fur farm addresses and put them into a printed document with instructions on how to go into fur farms, cut down the fences, and release the animals *(editor's note: A Canadian activist named Darren Thurston later admitted in court documents to creating The Final Nail)*. Mink and fox are wild animals genetically, and native to North America. There was an animal rights conference in 1996 where people showed up with photocopies of this document called *The Final Nail*, and passed them out to everyone. People returned to their own parts of the country, and within six months, 16 fur farms were hit, with something in range of 30,000 animals released.

Prior to that, there were only three instances of this in the history of the movement. This was the power of the *The Final Nail*.

The latest edition just came out, *The Final Nail #4*. And it has all new fur farm addresses and all new how-to information. There have been quite a few media stories about this latest list. Fur farmers are terrified because they know every time a new edition of *The Final Nail* comes out, fur farms start getting hit almost overnight.

This document was extremely influential to me at an early age. It remains to be seen whether or not the latest edition will be influential to a new generation of activists. I think taking addresses and putting them together with how-to information tends to have a very incendiary effect, you could say.

Audience member: With what you're saying about The Final Nail and farmers being very concerned about break-ins now, has it altered security? And if there is increased security, how is the ALF handling that? From what I have read, there is a strict "no harm" mantra. I would imagine that would be difficult to respond to armed security.

Armed security at fur farms is nonexistent. I've never seen it. As recently as a couple years ago, I drove around and visited almost 200 fur farms. I can tell you, fur farm security is just an absolute joke. These fur farms know they're in our crosshairs. There have been over 90 raids on fur farms in the last 15 years. And the average fur farm is a chicken wire fence with a few sheds in the middle and a farmer who's asleep at eight o'clock at night. So that's fur farm security in a nutshell.

There are many big fur breeding operations. Yet I've never heard of one that had armed security. There are some that have electronic security but that kind of security has been bypassed over and over again and people still are able to get animals out.

What I think is positive about *The Final Nail*, secondary to the actions that it inspires, is that many fur farmers are on the brink. And having their addresses publicized can be the psychological nudge to push them over the edge. Every year they have to decide, "Do I want to continue this one more year?" A lot of times you have older farmers dying. Their kids have to make a decision, "Do I want to continue this family business?" With the media splash *The Final Nail #4* has received in the last two weeks, I like to think they're reading this and it creates a climate of paranoia. Justifiable paranoia, but still paranoia. And maybe they'll decide to go into soybean farming instead.

Audience member: Is there vet care when you take animals out of terrible situations? Or do you just take them and hope that it's a better situation than they were in originally?

I have my own stories, but the only way I can answer that broadly is to look historically at what we know about people who carried out these rescues in the past. What little we can glean from their stories. Historically what we've seen is that communiques come out after lab raids like you describe. And in almost every instance there will be a line in the communique stating these animals were taken to a sympathetic veterinarian. That's all we know. Anyone who is going to risk freedom to save an animal from a laboratory is going to make the animal their first priority. Certainly that would involve veterinary care.

Audience member: I have a question for you because you were saying you were an entrepreneur. I always find that term so vague. How do you actually fund your activism, specifically?

When I was released from prison I was completely unemployable. So that helped. Having your back against the wall is a great motivator.

I looked around at where the most money was being made, and I started a software company. I know nothing about software. I can barely turn on a computer. But I had no other option but to make it work so I figured it out. Big things happen when your back is against the wall.

Audience member: There's young people here, including my son. And I'm a little worried that he's going to take you quite literally and he'll follow your path. But I think that there's a lot of this idealism with the statement, "I started a software company." How the hell did you do that? Give us a little more specifics because otherwise it sounds like a fantasy.

Here's what you do: You find somebody that's done something that you want to do. You ask them exactly how they did it. You do exactly what they say without deviation. Then you'll be successful. That's what I did.

Part III

Research & Investigation

*Because the most damming
intelligence will not be online.*

*Because intelligence can't be
acted on if you can't access it.*

*Because you can't target what
you don't have an address for.*

The Fur Farm Intelligence Project

Article
Bite Back Magazine
"The fur industry is weak. We rented a car, and set out to create the road map to its collapse."

In 2009 I organized a project to make the first major update of fur farm addresses in almost 15 years. The trip took us to 12 states and over 200 fur farms, some which I was seeing for the first time since raiding them over a decade prior.

This is the story of that trip.

In 1997, I left home with a list of fur farm addresses and drove across the country collecting notes on the U.S. fur industry. Those notes were confiscated by the FBI, I was sent to prison, and the notes were never made public.

In 2009, I organized a resurrection: a two-month road trip to every fur farm in the western U.S. The goal: compile the largest collection of raw fur industry data to date.

I drafted a budget. *Bite Back* wrote a check. And the Fur Farm Intelligence Project came to life.

I recruited Amber as a road trip partner. We spent two months scanning satellite images in fur farming regions. We cross-referenced every fur farm address collection. We assembled a binder of maps. We compiled lists of unverified addresses mined from media reports, fur industry literature, and the word-of-mouth stream. Then we left on the Fur Farm Intelligence Project (FFIP): a mission to document and verify every fur farm in the west.

Resurrection

After the passing of twelve years, a return trip; absent the felonies, with an investigative scope never attempted. Our goal: a complete blueprint of the fur industry. Every farm address, its operational status ("open" or "closed"), and every infrastructure target verified and mapped.

In the years since my first trip, the lynx pens of Fraser Fur Farm and sprawling prison of Short's Fur Farm festered in the darkest part of my psyche. And in the years since, I plotted my return. A return to those Iowa dirt roads and Montana trails; a return to the farms. After staring thousands of animals in the eye only to walk away, I would return on their behalf.

This time, I would not be taking their freedom under darkness. And while anything less is to fail them, this mission was nonetheless crucial to winning their freedom.

Operation Bite Back Until Today: Fur Farm Data in the 2000s

The sum of the fur farm addresses we have today are found in two sources: *The Final Nail #4* (2011), and *TheFinalNail.com*; both built from the original fur farm list, *The Final Nail #1* (1996). Yet outside of ALF raids, the "open" or "closed" status of each farm has never been verified. Central to our mission was this goal: providing the first operational-status update of known fur farms in 13 years.

Coordinative Outreach And The Actionability Of The Address
While past fur industry investigations focused on the treatment of animals, this one sought something else: names and addresses. Of all forms of animal rights outreach, the dissemination of "names and addresses" is at once among the most overlooked, and most potent. To understand the power of the name and address, one most accept a distinction between actionable info, and unactionable.

That which is actionable is information that serves as an immediate call to action. Unactionable data is informative, but offers no clear "next step". A "Why Vegan" pamphlet is actionable: the reader can become vegan. Information becomes less useful the further it moves from being something that can be acted on in an immediate way. A philosophical tome on the socio-economic roots of animal exploitation may be informative, but brings with it no call for action. For outreach to be useful, it must incite.

An address gives injustice a fixed physical location, and confronts the reader with the obligation that comes with that knowledge. More than knowing of injustice, it is knowing where. The "next step" could be a protest or undercover investigation, but an address brings the burden of action.

The Parameters
Any breach of property lines to obtain info for a very public project would subject our team to possible criminal prosecution, and defy the instructions of the project's financial backers. All information would be gathered from public space.

To confirm farms the hard way, we brought tools: Soundpro II unidirectional microphone (to pick up sounds of mink from a distance); military grade digital binoculars; old fur farm address lists; a list of new, unconfirmed addresses; digital camera; and video camera.

Scale-Based Strategy and Blueprints as Bullets
Above the equally horrific meat, dairy, and egg industries, intelligence gathering on the fur industry has a special significance. In 2009, the industry has shrunk to fewer than 400 supply-end sites. Fewer than 400 structures and complexes form the architecture of the entire fur industry. We have arrived at the stage the entire industry can be mapped into one concise blueprint. While a blueprint assists construction, it brings equal utility to deconstruction.

The Architecture of Avarice

The current farm and support structure of the U.S. fur industry (numbers approximate):

Processors / wholesalers / etc: numbers unknown.
Mink farms: 274
Feed suppliers: 12
Equipment suppliers (cages, etc): 10
Research farms: 5
Auction houses: 1

That is it. And the end of the industry does not require the erasure of every target, only their support structure. The further one moves upstream, the higher-impact the target. 274 farms are supported by only a very small and vulnerable support-base of research farms and feed suppliers.

The fur industry is on the losing end of the scale / absorption quotient, whereby the effect of any one action is inversely proportional to an industry's mass. In a large industry, rarely does one target takes on major significance in the supply network – there is always another target that fulfills the same role, and quickly absorbs any business from a decommissioned building or bankrupt processor.

The fur industry is in stark contrast. Farms generally have only one choice for specialized feed. Industry research sites number at approximately five. Farms rely on breeding stock with genetic lines that are irreplaceable. From every angle, the fur industry is weak.

We rented a car, and set out to create the road map to its collapse.

Washington

For the first farm of the trip, there was no discussion. Only one was appropriate.

I didn't even have to look at a map. The first farm of the trip was the first mink farm on which I'd ever stepped foot: Beck's Mink Farm in Granite Falls, WA.

What Harvey Beck doesn't know is that we've met. Unlike most farms, the Beck Mink Farm utilizes a photoelectric perimeter security system, comprised of a series of invisible beams broadcast between black boxes affixed to posts in each corner. Break the beam, set off the (silent) alarm. Our first visit in 1996, after five minutes inside the fence, a truck screeched to a halt at the gate. The emerging silhouettes of two men and their shovel inspired our quick exit in the opposite direction.

In the following months, after experimenting with the alarms at a second nearby farm (the nearby Jeff Craggs farm), we learned to circumvent the beam by dropping to the ground and rolling under it. During the FFIP., Amber and I would only encounter such alarms at three other farms.

We dedicated our first night in Washington to the rest of Snohomish County, responsible for nearly half of all mink killed in Washington. Of the six addresses known, two were confirmed closed.

For this investigation, we were giving priority to farms raided by the ALF, to establish an accurate survey of the true efficacy of these actions in not just bringing freedom to animals in the short term, but sparing future victims by shutting down farms forever. We found the numerous small raids at Brainerd's in Snohomish had not (yet) closed this farm. And at the Roesler Bros. Fur Farm (10,000 mink released, 2003)- almost totally enveloped in Evergreens and hidden off a dirt road – one can still hear the cries of mink echoing from the forest.

Government Fur Farm List: Attempt #1
Dale was the head of "wildlife farm licensing" for the Department of Natural Resources. The next day Amber and I were at his office at the Olympia state capitol, testing the counterintuitive theory that the most guarded information can be obtained by asking. Dale wanted to help us get the complete list of fur farms we asked for. He made some calls, and informed us there was no state agency that tracked fur farms. We left with his parting words lingering in our minds: "You want the USDA list. They have the address of every farm, and someone there will give it to you…"

"Twelve Species of Fur Bearing Animals"
Of special interest among our Northwest fur farm list was United Farms in

Graham. The farm, its address only recently made public, was described in an old issue of Fur Rancher as housing "Twelve species of fur bearing animals". There are only four species commonly raised for fur. "Twelve species" can only mean the first person to get inside United Farms is likely to find little-seen species such as lynx and wolves.

We found the mega-farm buried in the woods surrounded by residential housing developments, entirely invisible from the road. Unique to the farm is its level of fortification: the sheds sit behind two layers of barbed wire, chain link fence.

The world is closing in on United Farms, construction cornering it on all sides. They concealed the animals from view, but have not shielded the world from their shrieks, which disturb the quiet night of adjoining tree-lined neighborhoods, telegraphing their suffering to a world that would like to forget they exist at all.

Oregon

The Coast

Hidden in thick forests among the perpetual fog of the Oregon coast is the first, and oldest, cluster of its 18 mink farms. After years of only "rural route" addresses being published (coded addresses with locations known only to mail workers), in the last 18 months the movement had finally identified street addresses of Astoria's mink operations. A total of four farms were listed in close proximity in Svensen, one of which (Tynkila Mink) we found to be closed. Three to go.

The previous year, Final Nail(.com) made public the location of a previously unknown Oregon satellite feed plant of Washington-based Northwest Farm Foods. This vital linchpin in the fur industry was a significant discovery. Located on the waterfront on a dead-end road in south Astoria, we found the combination mink farm / feed supplier to be in full operation. The size of the buildings indicated there was more to this operation than mink. Along with the main Northwest Farm Foods production facility in Burlington WA, this location in Astoria is absolutely crucial to the survival of the Northwest's fur farms.

Day Two: The ALF Wins Again. And Again.

Closure of the Oregon State University Experimental Fur Farm was widely publicized six months after the 1991 arson that destroyed its labs. But our movement is often more quick to claim successes than verify potential failures, taking for granted as fact what could just as easily be deliberate disinformation on the part of a farmer looking to continue their work off the radar. It was established at the outset of the Project: take nothing for granted, and accept as "closed" only that which we saw with our own eyes.

The address for the OSU research farm was reported to be off-campus, at 1510 Brook Lane in Corvallis. We found the property was mostly grassland, spotted with an abandoned poultry research lab and other barns that had fallen into disuse. Two long, gutted sheds, having the general structure of mink sheds, were found empty. After the survey of the property, we confirmed the absence of anything that could house mink. The vacant field and faint outline of buildings long since demolished gave testimony to the power of the only way to give both freedom to animals and life to your words: action.

Still early in the afternoon, we visited our third ALF-raided farm of the day: S&N Fur Farms. This farm felt comfortable enough to forgo even the basic security precaution: a fence. The ALF capitalized on this oversight when it released 100 to 150 mink in 2008. A low number on the average farm, but on a farm as small as S&N (we estimated its capacity at approx. 2 to 3,000 mink) such a release can be high-impact.

High impact it was. Every cage visible from our vantage point was confirmed to be empty. It seemed the Animal Liberation Front had shut down S&N Fur Farm.

Of Farmers, Forests, and Fugitives

On a summer night over 10 years ago, I was doing laps around Drift Creek Road in Sublimity, Oregon, looking for a white piece of fabric in the road – our pre-established signal for "stop here." I had dropped off a team of two to investigate the newly discovered address of Gardner Fur Farm. As I picked them up, the team spoke of finding a farm hidden at a distance from the road, just over a hill at the end of a gravel driveway. The most notable feature of the farm learned for our purposes: no house on site.

The Gardner Fur Farm – to our knowledge never again visited by activists - was overdue for a status update.

In 2009, I was back. In the shadow of the "Gardner Farm" sign, we pulled onto a narrow shoulder. I stepped 10 paces from the car to smell the air for the telltale scent of mink. In a moment, I heard the sound of tires on gravel from a neighboring driveway. Taking cover in the nearest bush, I watched a pickup approach Amber, still in the car, and heard a stern exchange. Both cars drove in opposite directions.

For 8 hours I sat frozen in that bush across the street from the Gardner Fur Farm, watching the ensuing panic: police cars with sirens flying up and down the rural road, and an ATV patrolling the area. At times feet from both, I crouched in silence. With no radio communication, and cell phones strictly banned from the mission, I could only speculate as to the fate of my companion. I spent the evening and night waiting for my rescue vehicle, and carefully digging a hole to bury the camera that held photos of nearly every fur farm in Oregon. At midnight, I had divested from all hopes of Amber's return, and began the 12 mile walk to civilization.

I walked most of the night, traversing dozens of farms, fleeing invisible stampeding cattle in pitch-black ranches, and sleeping for three hours in a field beside a Christmas tree farm. I ate cherries from trees and drank water from barn spigot. And I walked. Fourteen hours after I left the Gardner Fur Farm, I arrived at the Silverton library. Drawing from the $100 kept in my sock at all times as insurance for just such a situation, I made a call to a pre-established liaison, relaying my location. An hour later, Amber arrived.

"I got arrested," she said.

She told the story of stopping to wait for me near the farm, being accosted by neighbors, surrounded by multiple police cars, and placed under arrest. They searched the vehicle without consent, searched it again, and in finding my ID, realized I was on foot nearby and left to comb the countryside. In a case of "hiding in plain sight", there was one place the police and farmer never looked: 10 feet from the site of the original confrontation. Twenty-two hours and many close calls after arriving in Silverton, with the Oregon fur farming community certain to be on high alert, we preempted all remaining Oregon farms and departed for Idaho.

Fugitive-Status Redux

After the official conclusion to the FFIP, five Oregon farms remained un-confirmed after the Gardner Fur Farm incident had derailed our course. In October, we broke from the data-sorting phase, and made the return drive to Silverton, Oregon.

We had changed cars to avoid recognition, while still establishing in advance this stop was to be swift and streamlined: confirm the farm, dig up the camera, and get out.

We made one pass of the farm, and looked back to see a truck at a distance. The road was so rural, I had seen fewer than 15 cars (excepting police and farmers) during my 8-hour fugitive-status on Drift Creek Road, and so any vehicle was suspect. We pulled down onto a dirt road and stopped to wait for the truck to pass. It didn't.

The truck pulled off behind our parked car, stopped, stared, and continued on at snail's pace. This wasn't someone on a Sunday drive. We spun around, returning to Drift Creek just as a second truck approached from the direction of the farm. We made a very unnatural 270-degree turn at a fork. The truck followed suit. There was no room for interpretation: we were being followed.

After following at tailgate-distance for two miles, the truck returned towards the farm. Regardless of the farmers that wanted to harm us, and the police that were likely en route, a return trip to retrieve the buried camera was non-negotiable. We agreed to forgo all finesse and stealth for the only thing that mattered: speed. We looped back to the front of the farm, threw the car into park, and on hands and knees, I dug up the camera from where it had been buried, uninsulated, exactly two months previous. It still worked. We still hadn't visually confirmed animals at the Gardner Fur Farm, but we observed the next best evidence: paranoid vigilance that doesn't come from a farmer who just grows corn.

Idaho

The newest farm reported in Idaho is the so far unconfirmed Ball Brothers farm in Malad. Newspapers reported the farm relocated from Utah to a site in Idaho housing 20,000 mink. This was our most remote destination yet, with blocks a mile in size, often hosting only one or two homes. After miles on dirt roads, we arrived at the newly constructed Ball Brothers ranch, identifying the previously unknown address of 2726 N 5600 W, Malad, ID. There, we found a farm so desolate, it was absent an on-site house. The nearest home sat a half-mile away.

The Hunted

Franklin is a town of 665, where animals outnumbered people one hundred-fold. A large egg farm loomed on a hill overlooking the town. Hundreds of veal calves lined a dirt road. And we didn't have to leave Highway 91 to see the Hobbs Fur Farm was as open as it was large. We took a single photo.

Looking for the library in Franklin's residential downtown, we noticed a single mink shed partially exposed in a backyard. In looping back for a second look, we noticed another, several houses down. And then another. After a cursory lap of downtown, Amber and I had identified six micro-mink farms improbably positioned in very small backyards between crowded homes. Nowhere else would we see farms this small. We parked in a cul-de-sac to take a walk for further documentation. We wouldn't get far.

A red truck lurched to a stop ahead of our car, boxing us in. I hit the lock on the door, knowing whoever he was, he was there for us. A very overweight man charged the car, fists flailing. It was Hobbs.

"Y'all taking pictures of my mink farm!"

He pounded his fists on the glass. The standoff concluded with him reciting our plate number, pointing at me, and saying –

"Yeah, I'll be watching you!"

No matter how severe a confrontation, the nature of our work allowed us the luxury of knowing we were at all times within the law. We continued on course, giving closer look to the backyard mink operations. 20 minutes later, we spotted the red truck again, as Hobbs and a cohort sat outside a church. At the strict direction of our attorney, we made our move. Pulling beside the truck, I tapped the horn, and when they looked – we took their picture. Then we floored it.

They chased us. In clouds of dust, we tore through back roads into the barren hills above Franklin. They cornered us near the veal farm, the passenger leaping from Hobbs' still-moving truck and lunging towards our car. Not content with the blood of mink, they wanted ours. We swerved to miss him, grazed through the gap between their truck and a ditch, and disappeared into the hills. We found sanctuary in the winding driveway of a hillside farm. 30 minutes later we emerged, and in looking for an alternate exit from town, realized the labyrinth of dirt roads winding into the hills had only one exit – the way we came. They were waiting.

Unable to block our path completely, we grazed past them en route to the highway one mile away. With them in chase, we emerged to the residential neighborhood as two police cars wailed by at 60+ mph, sirens blaring. Our rear view mirror told the story of what was to happen next. In a moment, we were on the side of Hwy 91, detained by police.

The cop's extortion attempt was simple: give him the camera, he said, or we were going to jail. I don't give anything to police, and if I did, it wouldn't be a camera with photos of every fur farm in Idaho. I told him to take me to jail. He returned to his car, returning again to ask for the camera. Those that can, do. Those that can't – ask. On the advice of my lawyer, I told him, I neither consented to a search nor questioning, and had nothing more to say.

"This is a farming community," he explained. "There are people who have come here and let loose the mink and chickens, and I just want to make sure you're not one of them".

Local fur farmers were arriving to the scene en masse. They huddled with police, urging our arrest. 20 minutes later, he came to the window with my ID. "Mr. Young, I know who you are, and I know your history. You're here to break into farms. You haven't changed."

He was half right.

"Next time they find you near their property, they're going to shoot you." He gave me a long knowing look.

"And when we find your body, I still have to prove it was them who did it."

Montana

It was the state where the lawless-old-west mentality was alive, well, and reigned in perpetuum. The state of ambiguous property lines, street names unreflected on any printed map, and diner patrons saying things like "put it on my tab" while adjusting their hats on their way out the door.

For our purposes, this off-the-grid culture created the state with the widest gaps in fur industry intelligence. The USDA reported eight mink farms, while addresses for only four were known. Info on possible other locations was vague, such as the sparse address "west of Harlowton", given for the unconfirmed Leppink Mink Ranch. Yet it was these farms where our work was most needed. If we didn't confirm Montana's fur farms, its remoteness made it unlikely anyone would.

Campbell's Mink Ranch: While fireworks exploded overhead, we were celebrating our nation's independence moving silently down Southside Road, towards Campbell's Mink Ranch. Mere yards from I-90, this farm was buried at the end of a driveway, deep in the woods. Elk grazed in the front yard, while squeals of mink could be heard from the back.

Fraser Fur Farm: East of downtown Ronan was in some ways was the most ominous site of the project: Fraser Fur Farm, rumored to imprison more lynx than live wild in the entire state. The information we collected was limited, but one month later we received the following anonymous report:

"In September, 2009, word circulated an investigation was sought for a major fur industry expose. The target: Fraser Fur Farm, largest wildcat farm in the country.

North of Missoula, tucked off a small road east of downtown Ronan, are the cages that may imprison more lynx than exist in the wild in the entire state. Despite its significance, it is possible no one from the animal liberation movement had seen the inside of Fraser Fur Farm. The only recorded account of animal liberators getting close came in a brief mention in Strong Hearts, Rod Coronado's jailhouse zine. We set out for Ronan, MT, to verify the farm was open, confirm the species and numbers of animals, photograph the captives, map the farm's layout, and release the info to the public.

While most fur farms are easily accessed, Fraser's was an exception. It was immediately clear why help was being sought – this was one of the few farms not visible from the road, unable to be investigated without breaching property lines, and once inside: incredibly difficult to gain access to animals without being in view of a house.

A pre-investigation nighttime visit found the farm sat at the end of a dirt driveway off Terrace Lake Rd. The first visit we stayed to the distant perimeter, familiarizing ourselves with the layout. The outline of cages and rattle of large animals hinted at what lay in the shadows, just out of sight. This level of preparation was necessary because to obtain the documentation we sought, a nighttime visit was insufficient. We would have to access the farm mid-day.

The next morning we parked in a residential neighborhood off Timberlane Road, at what we approximated was a point one mile due south of the farm. Our nighttime survey had found two houses on site, making unsafe any attempt at approaching from the front. Gunshots of hunter's echoed in the forest around us, and we entered the woods. In short time we found the faint outline of a trail, following it along a fence for one mile until we came into a clearing. Our shot-in-the-dark calculation had bore fruit: were precisely at the rear of the Fraser Fur Farm.

At the only sliver of an angle not visible to either house, we emerged from the forest at the end of a long shed. We were met with the stare of a large, caged lynx. As majestic as imagined, the lynx seemed to have fallen through the cracks of time, pacing endlessly in its cage, waiting for the freedom just out of its reach. We were now two of the only people in the U.S. to ever lay eyes on a live lynx.

We surveyed four sheds and one long row of lynx pens. Available information put the animals held at Fraser as mink, bobcats, and lynx. Four sheds housing mink were found to be empty, and it is possible the farm no longer imprisons mink. We were unable to confirm the presence of bobcats, but many sheds were not inspected. One long row of pens held approximately 50 lynx; possibly more than exist in the wild.

We heavily documented the farm on video and with still photos. The documentation was submitted anonymously to aboveground contacts. We hope they will make these images – which may be the only existing photos of captive U.S. lynx – available to the public.

A final word on this farm: There would be no easy replacement – if any at all – for lost lynx breeding stock. Only one other farm in the U.S. (Gunnink Fur Farm) is confirmed to house lynx. More than any other animal raised for fur, the loss of irreplaceable lynx breeding stock would very likely be the end of this farm, and perhaps lynx farming in the U.S. Lastly, the person to liberate the captives of Fraser Fur Farm will have one historic accomplishment to their credit: possibly doubling the wild lynx population in Montana.

Thousands of us. Only one Fraser Fur Farm. Do the math.

Anonymous"

Henke Mink Ranch: A seven-hour drive brought us to a region so desolate, the mere presence of an unrecognized car on the road would arouse suspicion. The information available was "10 miles SW of Hobson", and a satellite search revealed possible mink sheds on an unmarked road. While mink farms generally cluster, this one stood alone in the vast central Montana prairie. At the location, we found oddly shaped sheds, but their unique structure obscured view of what was inside. Noting the farm's address (167 Antelope Creek Road) and confirming the presence of possible mink sheds was the sole yield.

Rocky Mountain Fur Company: A court document covering the ALF's Operation Bite Back campaign in the early 1990s transcribes a letter from a reconstructed typewriter ribbon seized during a search warrant. This letter was allegedly used to solicit funds to burn down the Rocky Mountain Fur Company's processing building, and explains the farm / processor's importance in maintaining the Montana fur farming industry:

"After my investigation I discovered that all the fur farmers in Montana use the same company to prepare pelts for auction. The Huggans Rocky Mountain Fur Company is a building I have been in before. It is all wood, with no alarms and no close proximity to animals. The targeted building contains all the drying racks and drums used in pelt processing. If we could cause substantial damage to that equipment, we would cause a serious disruption in the pelting season, and also push the Huggan's family (third generation trappers) into a position closer to bankruptcy."

It is unknown if the Rocky Mountain Fur Company remains the sole processor in Montana. However the small farm itself, housing thousands of mink and fox, was found to remain as it has for years – just out of sight, a stone's throw from Highway 93.

Utah

The terrain in the Northwest was wooded and rural. We ate hash browns at diners next to the mayor, watched the "Frontier Days" parade from library windows, and turned heads writing postcards to prisoners in supermarket aisles at 2am.

Utah introduced a different flavor. In no place other than the area surrounding Lehi could one visit 16 mink farms in one day, and never be more than one mile from a strip mall. So pervasive is the industry in Utah County industrial-size farms merge seamlessly with dense clusters of McMansions, as innocuous a landscape feature as a public tennis court. Zoning ordinances allow farms unrefined room to move, commingling with parks and single-family residences in open-armed harmony.

If Utah County broke records for fur industry pervasiveness, it took it even further with something that caused us to do a triple-take our first encounter. By apparent county mandate, all farms were marked with a 6' x 4' sign reading "Ongoing Mink Operation". To identify operational farms, binoculars or a trained nose were unnecessary, the location of every open farm was spelled out for us. Literally.

The Death Star
Since day one of the trip, one farm had been referred to only as "The Death Star". Curiosity dictated it be our first stop. The Death Star was River Jordan Mink Ranch, reportedly the largest mink farm in the country.

(Note: other sources place the Zimbal Minkery in Wisconsin as the largest)

The elevated view above the farm from Redwood Road gives the best view of its scale: over 100 sheds, housing 100,000 animals.

Common at every fur farm, factory farm, lab, and slaughterhouse I've ever visited is an awe that never dulls with repetition: How a place so significant, that claimed so many lives, could be so accessible.

Two new farms were discovered near Lehi. One hidden feet from Interstate 15, south of the Utah State Prison, on Pony Express Rd. Closed in on three sides by parking lots and office buildings, the farm responded with greater fortification than any other farm we'd seen, with a 12-foot wall surrounding totally enclosed, corrugated metal sheds. The second, at the end of 8170 N in Lehi, was wedged between housing developments on all sides, and so well hidden as to evade our detection until the fifth pass. Arrogantly, the property did not even have a live-in farmer.

Twice Bitten
Among the more significant pillars in the industry is the Fur Breeders' Agricultural Cooperative. The unassuming building, on a quiet street in an industrial

neighborhood just outside Salt Lake City, is the largest and oldest mink feed co-op in the country. After an attempted arson in 1991, and a very successful one in 1997, the building has been rebuilt and its work resumed. The complex consisted of the large feed building, a gated back lot, and several "portable" style buildings concealing the experimental fur farm to its south. Its operational status was never in question. We just wanted to see it. The best info we gathered would not come from that day's visual inspection, but from an employee in the day that followed…

Tailing the Hand the Feeds
The first stop north of Salt Lake City was Peoa, our first "problem child" town. Our attempts to confirm any of the four farms we'd located were unsuccessful. At each one, we sat outside with binoculars, courting confrontation before declaring them "inconclusive" and moving on.

At a park a half block from G-W Fur Farm, we stopped and watched a semi-truck exiting the farm. I stared. There was only one regular delivery to farms: mink feed. As the truck approached too quickly for me to prepare, I angled the camera in its general direction and hit the button. Improbably, I had captured the blurry image of the truck, with a barely visible logo on the cab: "FBAC." I didn't pause to decode, I already knew: "Fur Breeders Agricultural Co-op."

There was one vehicle that went to every fur farm in Utah, both known and unknown, and it was one block away, headed north.

"We're following it," I said.

We watched it pull into the next farm up the street, which we could now check off as open. The truck made it too easy. Every farm where the truck stopped could be confirmed as operational. And it would offer something of even greater intelligence value: a direct path to previously unknown farms.

While we waited for the truck to finish its delivery, we discussed the potential of this developing tactic.

"Following the truck is good." Amber said, "…but having someone inside would be better."

I stared at her blankly.

"Hitchhiking, Peter. I'm talking about hitchhiking."

Without pausing for discussion, she seized a camera, notepad, canvas bag, and said goodbye.

Deep Cover: The Utah Hitchhiking Experiment

Amber took up post 100 yards up Highway 32. My eyes moved between her and the farm's driveway, where the truck would emerge. Less than two minutes later, it did. Amber put out her thumb. The plan rested on one variable outside our control: The driver had to pick her up.

He did.

Regardless of the wisdom or safety of the plan, we had now irreversibly entered into the present circumstance: Amber was in a truck with the man who delivered feed to over half the farms in Utah. I followed. Heading north, I added up every way this didn't rise to the standards of a "plan". We had no cell phone contact, no S.O.S. signal, and if I lost them: no rendezvous point. The only semblance of cohesion in this hasty venture was the suggestion I stammered to Amber as she exited the car: "Copy his delivery list."

She was in one-on-one conversation with among the most valuable intelligence resources in the Utah fur industry. If her questions were calculated, the ride would yield more insight than a hundred issues of Fur Rancher. If she maintained her cover.

I tailed from a distance to Wanship, where they stopped at the Ovard Mink Farm. Later, Amber would describe what she was learning:

The driver's name was Stan. He was a driver for the Sandy plant. He delivered to approximately 30 farms, from Utah County to Coalville. He left the plant each night at 1am, and finished his route at 11am. He had been driving the same route for 17 years.

He was spending much of the conversation in paternal mode, scolding her for hitchhiking and offering advice on getting home (her hitchhiking pretext was "girl from Logan in a fight with her Peoa boyfriend and had no ride home"). Amber focused on reining the conversation in to her subject of preference: information on the Utah fur industry.

The protocol for each farm was to pull up, run a hose from the back of the truck to the farm's feed cart, and give exactly one half-pound for every mink. He pointed to the number "600" on the trucks output meter, saying that Ovard housed approximately 1,200 mink.

"You can't make any money raising 1,200 mink," he said. "This guy is retired. Raising mink is just his hobby."

"Can I see them?" she asked.

"I'm not supposed to do this, so you can't tell anyone, but.... Come on".

He took her into a shed. She asked if she could take pictures. He said yes. While he described the vicious nature of the mink, she was taking rapid-fire photos of them.

"They used to electrocute the mink," he said. "Then the PETA people started hollering'. Now they use gas. PETA don't holler no more."

I watched them pull away 10 minutes later. The truck exited I-80 in Coalville, where after getting caught at a light, I lost the truck. I drove countless loops around town, looking for it at each of Coalville's six mink farms. Three hours later, I drove past Black Willow Mink for the 4th time, and abandoned hope. Moments later on Main Street, in my peripheral vision, I glimpsed arms flailing from the sidewalk. It was Amber.

We took up post in the lobby of Coalville's only hotel where she told me the story: We had caught him near the close of his shift, she said, and Coalville was the end of his route. After lunch, he dropped her off and returned south. She had begged him to take her back to Sandy, where she would aim for a tour of the plant and its experimental mink farm, but he insisted she return "home", to Logan. Before heading back, he took her to lunch at a diner. A man joined them at the counter. Stan whispered the man operated a "big mink farm on Chalk Creek Road". She checked off another one for the "open" list.

"And when he dropped me off," she said, "he gave me this." She held up a $20 bill.

He told her to buy food. He didn't say for who. The fur industry had just unknowingly donated $20 to the jail commissary fund of accused ALF members BJ and Alex. Their alleged crime? Liberating mink from a farm on Stan's route.

Mink Capital U.S.A.

Dethroning Medford, WI in the 1990s, the fur farming capital of the country is now Morgan, UT. We confirmed 13 active farms in the town's core and outlying areas, among them a farm so deep in the heart of downtown you could very nearly reach out and touch a mink from the parking lot of Goldenwest Credit Union. Within days, Morgan newspapers reported farmers had been noticing suspicious activity, including people "seen taking pictures of mink ranches."

Cops, Curses, and Quicksand

Later, while William "BJ" Viehl and Alex Hall were in jail nearby on Animal Enterprise Terrorism charges, we were in Hyrum, UT; at the farm that was the subject of Count Two in their indictment. The charge alleged a "conspiracy" to raid the farm. After reviewing the discovery in their case, I knew the totality of the evidence was being vegan while sitting in a car outside Blackridge Farms. Exactly what we were doing.

We took several photos and went to turn around on a dirt road behind the farm. In perceiving it as a "dirt road", we had been too optimistic. It was a mud swamp. A few pumps of the gas made it clear: We were stuck. As the case of BJ and Alex had shown, there are places where your presence is suspicious. And then there are places where it is arrestable. A dirt road 30 yards from rear gate of a mink farm in Utah was the latter. If there is a curse on surveillance of this farm, it now had its third and fourth victims.

By rule and practice, ours was a 100% legal trip. But we acknowledged in the eyes of rural police and hostile farmers, it at times had the appearance of something else. When outside fur farms, an "arrest first, ask questions later" police response was not only a possibility, it was a probability. When such a confrontation was felt to be imminent, we had an established protocol: One of us announced – "purge the car". The other put the map binder under the seat, the video camera in the dash, the digital camera and binoculars in the console, covered any food package with the word "vegan" on it. Then we braced for the worst.

This was one of those times. We cleansed the car and reclined, waiting for whatever was going to happen, to happen.

Minutes later, a pickup truck pulled up. A man got out, approaching slowly.

"Now now.... what is going on here?"

We were, I told him, prospective students visiting Utah State University. "Well...." He sighed heavily. "...if that's your story".

He threw me a rope.

"Tie this to the back of your car."

He pulled us from the mud. Back on solid ground, I untied the rope, thanked him, and got in the car.

"Let's get out of Hyrum. Fast", I said.

I went to shift, just as a knock came at my window. I rolled it down.

"One more thing" he said. "You aren't mixed up with those..." he stared into the distance with dramatic pause...

..."animal rights people, are you?"

We shook our heads. Then asked why.

"See that right there?" He pointed directly ahead.

"That's a mink farm. They've had problems with people coming here and turning them loose." We nodded with feigned interest.

"The other night I found the farmer walking through this field with his shotgun. He was looking for animal rights people. You're lucky I saw you before he did".

We drove away. The tally of thinly veiled threats on our lives: Now at two.

Lock Down
Every fur farmer in the region would now be on high alert. But we had more farms to see than time, and any break for the alarm to quiet was impractical. We continued north to Logan.

We confirmed several farms in the outlying areas, and at night returned to

Logan for our last stop: Jenson Fur Farm. Just as we were to pull over beside the farm, we noticed a car with its lights off parked at a suspicious angle in an adjacent residential neighborhood, aimed directly at the farm's gate. I kept driving, waited 20 minutes, and passed again. The car was still there. It was an unmarked Crown Victoria, with an occupant.

The police were staking out Logan's fur farms.

We left the state.

Wyoming

Fur farms like WYO Furs exemplified our mission. This address in Eden, Wyoming (pop 97), had appeared in all three editions of *The Final Nail*, while being so remote it had never been publicly visited or confirmed. A several-hour drive confirmed the farm was no longer in business. By all available fur farm lists, Wyoming was now void of fur farms.

Nebraksa

We stood at a barbed wire fence in Scribner, in high winds, listening to a tortured cacophony of howling animals echoing from the metal sheds of John Smeal's fox farm. It was the only fur farm we found open in Nebraska, and the largest fox farm we would see all summer.

South Dakota

After a second 2006 state charge for a mink release to which I had already plead guilty, prosecutors agreed to drop the charges under one condition: that I never return to South Dakota. Ever. Under threat of prison, South Dakota was barred from the investigation, while the farm I was charged with (Turbak Mink Ranch) was put out of business. We hoped the Fur Farm Intelligence Project's financial backers considered the trade an acceptable one.

Iowa

By every measure, Iowa is the hardest hit state in the ALF's war on the fur industry. It has the most farms hit (eight) and most numbers of animals released (27,401).

In continuing to update the status of ALF-visited farms, we surveyed old satellite images to locate the Scott Nelson Mink Ranch near Jewell (the communiqué listed a street but not address). This farm was raided twice in one week, after which the farmer announced the farm would be forced to close. Whether this was a genuine admission of defeat or lie to deter against future raids had never been confirmed.

We located the site of the farm on a dirt road NE of downtown Jewell. Where the farm once stood, was now a field of corn. The farm had been closed by the ALF Now passed from history, the only traces left are blurry satellite images, and if you looked closely, a break in the grass marking the turnoff that once led to the sheds of the Scott Nelson Mink Ranch.

The Lost Farm

For years I was tormented by a reoccurring nightmare. Driving down a dirt road in Iowa, I pull over, as though directed by an unseen hand. The compulsion brings me to push through a wall of thick roadside bramble. I come to a small clearing, with a single row of fox pens. The pens lay just feet from the road, concealed by thick, dead foliage. The foxes stare up with looks of both anticipation, and betrayal. Looks asking how so many had passed within 10 feet and never seen them, and never stopped to help.

So vivid were those images, I spent my drives in Iowa looking for that farm. My eyes never on the road, always to the side, afflicted with the fear I would pass this undiscovered farm of my nightmare, hidden feet from the road, never noticing their eyes staring back, waiting to be discovered.

We never found that fox farm. But the vigilance it inspired brought us another. Set back from the road, on Highway 9 in Osage, I glimpsed a fox pen in a side yard. We pulled over and approached the fence. At midnight, the only sounds were the crackling of the electric fence and the howls of hundreds of caged foxes. It wasn't the farm of my nightmare. It was the farm of a nightmare I had yet to have.

Then came the losing streak.

The Iowa Mink Farmer Mobilization

We had taken over 400 photos of farms across the West. And many of the hurried photos, when reviewed, showed an agape farmer staring back. Despite our efforts, we were being regularly seen outside farms, taking photos, counting sheds, and fooling no one while taking "after dinner walks" down dirt roads where no one goes for a stroll.

Most farmers submit any such suspicious activity to the Fur Commission USA's "Incident Report" – in the "members only" portion of the FCUSA site functioning as a nationwide log of suspicious fur farm activity. The log lists thousands of entries going back to the mid-90s: transcripts of threatening emails, license plate numbers of cars passing farms a little too slowly, descriptions of trespassers wearing night vision goggles being chased from farms, and even tail numbers from low passing planes. A review of any page of the Incident Report, makes one thing above debate: fur farmers are paranoid, and spend their entire lives in fear of the ALF

We weren't the ALF, but after our third day in Iowa, it was clear that Iowa's farmers were waiting for us. Moving into eastern Iowa's succession of fox farms, we would barely raise our camera before finding a car gunning its engine, pulling from the farm, and chasing us. Iowa's farms had been raided so many times; farmers didn't run to their computers first, they ran to their cars.

A yellow Datsun tailed us across town when we were seen photographing sheds in Mystic. After losing the car, we found it again, now joined by a police car on the shoulder of Highway T14. Not seeing us after our well-timed U-turn, the police car turned on its lights and sped south. In Union, after three photos, a car left the Andres & Sons Fur Farm and followed us north on Highway D67. And we hadn't been out of the car long enough to take a photo of Schmuecker Fox Farm before a farmer boxed us in, pulled open our car door, and leaned in with the words "I know what you're doing. And I have your license plate". All in one day.

Our final day in Iowa brought a reversal of fortune. The final stop of the trip - Hidden Valley Fur Farm, raided by the ALF in 1998 - was found with its sheds gutted, and a mountain of empty fox cages seen decaying at the rear.

Day after day, we were looking fur farm prisoners in the eye, only to walk away. Every one was a broken promise.

Wisconsin

Wisconsin is the largest fur farming state in the country. Before concluding our nine days there, we would lay eyes on the prisons and cemeteries of over one million mink.

The farms in Wisconsin were massive on a scale we had not seen. Northwest Mink Ranches, Brecke Farms, Patrick Fur Farm, and others each imprisoned tens of thousands of animals.

Klinger Farms was once among the oldest mink farms in the country. At the address in Chippewa Falls, we found instead a small country market swarmed by a Saturday crowd. With satellite images clearly showing 14 sheds at this address, we slipped around the back of the building, believing the benign storefront to be concealing something much more sinister. And behind the store, we found 14 sheds. Each one imprisoning hundreds of decorative potted plants. We returned to the front and entered the store. The address of the former fur farm was now an all-vegetarian farmers market.

On our list of new data was a cluster of farms in the town of Polar. Previously we uncovered new addresses for 3 farms, and satellite images revealed 2 more in close proximity. These mink and fox farms stood as the largest cluster of newly discovered farms of the Project.

Plymouth was home to three farms on our list, and one of the largest feed suppliers. After a successful arson destroyed United Feeds in 1999, the president vowed to rebuild. And he did. We made one pass on Highway 67 and knew the next nighttime saboteurs to visit United Feeds will find it a greater challenge than their predecessors: The buildings were rebuilt entirely of metal.

Some days in Wisconsin the number of farms we found closed were greater than those found open. Altogether, we confirmed the closure of over 30 Wisconsin farms.

Of ALF visited farms: Otts Mink Ranch: open. Smieja Fur Farm: open. Zimbal Mink Ranch: open. Krieger's Fur Farm: open (Krieger may have found evidence his farm was approached from the north when it was raided in 1999: A 15-foot barricade of cages has been constructed along the farm's rear). And there was one more, saved for last.

Closure

Half of my two-year prison sentence was served for what happened at 5226 Perkins St, Medford, Wisconsin in 1997. Ed Dittrich awoke the morning of October 25th to find his fence stripped away, and 2,500 of his mink gone. Among the several farms I was accused of, my lawyer had speculated this farm was hand picked for the subject of my plea bargain because the farm had been forced to close, and the FBI wanted a body. The alleged closure had never been confirmed.

The farm had been chosen that night solely because of the shed's distance from the farmer's house. That night we watched 2,500 mink evanesce into the countryside, as we, too, made our own escape – every one of us on the run.

13 years later, I had come full circle. We turned off Hwy 13 onto Perkins St, and one mile later came to a stop in front of a field. The farm was gone.

We drove away in silence. Just past the farm, in my peripheral vision, I noticed motion in the grass. I braked abruptly for a small animal darting from the field, and watched it scurry across the road.

It was a mink.

On the site of the now-closed Dittrich fur farm.

Researching Your Targets

Lecture transcript
Portland State University
"A burglar alarm may be difficult to bypass. But if you can talk your way into a building, you don't need to know how to bypass that alarm."

A short transcript from the only surviving recording of a talk I gave many times (usually in much greater detail) on guerrilla tactics for accessing information on animal abusers — where they are, what they're doing, and how to stop them.

With this talk, I will give a thumbnail version of tactics we can repurpose from other fields and apply to the animal rights movement, specifically as it relates to investigating targets.

Let's talk about finding out what's happening to animals in your neighborhood. What you choose to do with that information is up to you.

Given the limited time we have, what's most important is not an exhaustive look at each tactic, but rather that you know these tactics exist, and are possible. Once you know what's possible, you can go off into the world with this information, expand on it, improvise on it, and apply it.

The best tactics that we can apply towards investigation come not from animal rights literature, but from books that are written by experts in other spheres such as private investigators. This workshop is designed to address the fact that information is power. Actually, information is not power. How well you act on it is power. Still, it is power in that animal abusers thrive on "out of sight, out of mind."

B2B Directories
Most people don't even know these exist. These are directories for businesses that don't sell to consumers. They sell to other businesses. An egg farm does not need to advertise themselves to a general audience. They don't sell to you. They sell to stores. They sell to distributors. They sell to other businesses.

The largest database I know of is called Reference USA. It's available for a price online, and also in most libraries. It's a database of over 15,000,000, businesses. And you can search by subject. You can search for everything from egg farms to slaughterhouses. They offer a 30-day free trial.

Vehicle Tailing
One tactic we used to employ to great effect was to physically tail vehicles. This works well to determine a source of anything for which either the destination is known but not the source, or the source is known but not the destination.

There was a free-range chicken slaughterhouse in Seattle. We wanted to know where the chickens came from. We wanted to know if, in fact, the farm was free range. So we simply staked out the slaughterhouse, and when the trucks would come and drop the chickens off, we would follow these trucks back to the farms.

Take another industry. There's wide speculation of numerous fur farms existing that are so far undiscovered, and not present on existing fur farm lists. Fur farms go to great lengths to hide themselves. In theory, if you were to simply follow the fur feed vehicles from the local fur feed supplier — and there's one up in Burlington, Washington — for a couple days, you're going to get addresses for most fur farms in the entire state, possibly the whole Northwest.

Another example: Most research labs are not registered with the USDA, so these labs can be difficult to find. Yet if you know where a vivisection breeder is, you can tail the trucks to find out where they deliver.

Social Engineering
The next tactic is a crucial tool in any investigator's arsenal. It is something called social engineering. This tactic originated in the hacker subculture. I once read something by a private investigator who said that most of their cases that were not solved through publicly available sources were solved through two tactics: Social engineering and dumpster diving.

To put it simply, social engineering is a collection of techniques that are used to persuade people into divulging confidential information or carrying out specific acts with the outcome of confidential information being divulged. It's generally done over the telephone. You can also do it in person. But the premise is gaining compliance to any kind of request that results in the revealing of information that person is not supposed to reveal. To put it crudely, it's a form of smooth talking to get people to divulge information they're not supposed to share.

Let's say you want to call a laboratory and find out where their secretive satellite facility is that nobody knows the address of. You can call an employee, use a simple social engineering pretext, such as being from UPS trying to deliver a package with an illegible address, and socially engineer the employee into sharing that address.

There's a book entirely on this subject called *The Art of Deception*, which sounds sinister but has endless righteous applications. It's a how-to book on getting people to tell you things they're not supposed to tell you.

The premise of this is that the human element of security is the weakest link of security. A burglar alarm may be difficult to bypass. But if you can talk your way into a building, you don't need to know how to bypass that alarm.

There have been people with, let's just say, illicit intent, who have obtained things like door keypad access codes using social engineering. The sky is the limit. There's nothing that you can't get someone to tell you with the right psychological tools.

Common pretexts used by social engineers include posing as a fellow employee and getting another employee to divulge certain information. Posing as a vendor. Posing as someone in authority. Posing as a new employee who's requesting help, such as, "Hey, I'm driving around here. They just hired me. Where's this particular facility? I can't find it anywhere." Employees like to help each other out. And then, using various insider lingo to gain the target's trust.

Here are the three elements in the cycle of a social engineering campaign.

First, research open source info, such as trade journals and so forth. Then you know the lingo and some basic information.

Second, make the call or make contact with somebody and develop rapport and trust.

Third, exploit that trust by getting them to tell you what you want to know.

You may be thinking, "How could this be relevant to any animal rights campaign?" The reality is this is relevant to every campaign. You can get anybody to tell you anything with the right amount of finesse.

What I like about low-tech tactics such as this is that as security gets more intense and businesses get more security conscious, low-tech tactics become all the more effective. When they shift their attention over there, suddenly this big gap opens up over here. Their guard is down. They're not thinking so much about low-tech methods like social engineering. They're concentrated on infrared sensors and face-recognition perimeter access. When they go high-tech, we have to go low-tech.

Being A Mole
Another tactic I am not at all qualified to talk about is obtaining employment inside of a facility. Some of the best ammunition we have against vivisection

in particular has come from the people who have obtained jobs inside labs. There are people at this conference much more qualified to talk about this than I am, but it's worth mentioning this as an advanced option.

Courting Whistleblowers

One of the investigative tactics we employed in Seattle involved a simple flyer. We wanted to know what was happening to animals inside labs at the University of Washington. We made a flyer that said. *"If you know any information about anything happening to animals on this campus, please call us and leave an anonymous message. We would love to hear about any information you have about what's happening to animals in laboratories on this campus."* And we set up an anonymous phone number with voicemail. People could call and leave messages. And we saturated the campus with these flyers. And we received several calls a week from people leaving anonymous messages saying, "Hey, I work in this lab. This is what I see. This is what's going on."

Spy Satellites For Dummies

I'm specifically avoiding internet research with this talk, but I have to mention a powerful tool is Google Earth satellite images. It's absolutely staggering what you can see on Google Earth satellite images. The question is: what can you use this information for? In particular, fur farms have a very distinct layout. You can now effectively use Google Earth images to visually scan an entire state to find farms that would have taken us literally years of driving around aimlessly to find in the 1990s.

I did a talk on this subject at Hampshire College recently. I tried an experiment. I had a laptop hooked up to a projector. I wanted to do a live search for a mink farm. I had never done this before. This was a risky experiment and could have totally failed. In front of an audience, I got on Google Earth and typed in "Medford, Wisconsin." Medford used to be known as the fur farming capital of the world. At one time, there were something like 30 fur farms in this one small town. So I clicked to view satellite images and sure enough, you could see in that first shot three fur farms in downtown Medford. These are farms that may or may not be publicly known. But it took me 30 seconds to find them.

Dumpster Diving

Last tactic is dumpster diving, There's nothing you cannot find in a dumpster. If you think that furniture and bagels are the best things you can get from a dumpster, you're thinking way too small. Most of what's in a building ends up in a dumpster at some point. That includes paperwork with every amount of information you can imagine on it. You really can't overstate the wealth of information you can find in the trash.

As an example of what you can find in the trash, one time we were dumpster diving at a lab. We found blueprints for the whole building in the dumpster. Animal bedding is another thing. If you speculate there's a place that has animals, such as a lab, you would look for animal bedding in the trash. Paperwork, obviously. Information on research protocols. Quite simply, most of everything you'd ever want to know ends up in the trash at some point.

You'll also find things that you don't want to know or will never use. When I was dumpster diving in high school, I remember I found a whole set of keys to the Tower Records in Bellevue, Washington.

No Excuse For Ignorance
I'll just close this out by saying that we live in the information age. If you don't know something, it's because you don't want to know. It's not because the information is not available to you. While the internet is a great resource, there are gaps we have to fill. The most important information will require us to get our hands dirty. But if you want to know about what's happening in your neighborhood, and the information you need to stop it, the information is out there. So, go get it.

Part IV

The Animal Liberation Front

*The history and tactics of those who work outside the
law to save animals.*

History of 1980s Lab Raids

Article
No Compromise Magazine
"Let us look back at their story, and now, pick up where they left off."

Of all the content in this book, this entry is the oldest, and has the backstory most worth sharing.

In early 2000, I was 23 and in my fourth year on the run. Along my string of safehouses, I found myself occupying another room in the home of another sympathetic host. In this room was a file cabinet containing a trove of ALF history. Photocopied ALF-themed newsletters from the 1980s I'd never seen, legal documents from past ALF investigations, and newspaper clippings of past ALF raids. Lots of newspaper clippings.

From hiding, I had continued to follow ALF actions closely. After a long period of dormancy, I had watched the reemergence of ALF lab break-ins. In my abundant idle time, I set out to preserve the early history of this tactic by distilling the file cabinet's contents down into one brief history. For weeks I pored over the file cabinet contents, took notes, and wrote the brief history that follows.

To give the story an audience, I made a Hail Mary move and submitted it anonymously to No Compromise Magazine. I put on rubber gloves (on the distant chance all incoming mail was forensically analyzed), put the article on computer disc, mailed it with a short unsigned note, and waited.

The article ran several months later. They had no idea the anonymous author was not just an ALF fugitive, but a fugitive mentioned elsewhere in that same issue.

Blast From the Past - '80s Lab Raids

1999 saw the return of the quintessential ALF action: the lab raid. After seven years of dormancy, the Animal Liberation Front has resurrected its laboratory liberation campaign, and in the last year has broken into four research facilities, liberating nearly 200 animals. These actions mark the return of a daring high-risk, high-skill operation and reintroduced an urgent "get-in-and-get-the-animals-out" approach not seen since the 80's.

Decades of legal anti-vivisection campaigning, including letter writing and sign waving, failed to effect change for animals in laboratories as swiftly as a few active bands of the ALF in the 1980s. These selfless individuals, wielding crowbars, brought the American public its first glimpses of the horrors committed on animals in laboratory torture chambers through the huge media exposure the early lab raids generated throughout the '80s.

The achievements and victories of these few bands of caring warriors must never be forgotten and must never be understated. And though we may have failed the animals in labs for a dark era of inaction, let us look back at their story and now pick up where they left off.

Breaking Down the Doors

The 1984 raid of the University of Pennsylvania marks what may be the ALF's greatest lab raid success.

On May 28th the Animal Liberation Front picked the lock to Thomas Gennarelli's head injury research lab at the University of Pennsylvania, smashing every piece of equipment in the lab and confiscating over 60 hours of Gennarelli's own research footage depicting head-smashing experiments with live primates. Gennarelli, who had for years hidden behind a laboratory door and thumbed his nose at animal advocates, had just met the animal rights movement's new answer to vivisection secrecy: the ALF

The footage revealed the most horrific glimpse inside a vivisection lab ever seen before or since: 60 hours of inadequately anesthetized primates plastered into restraining devices receiving blows to the head at up to 1000 times the force of gravity. The video brought the evil of animal research to the attention of the nation and its "reallocation" became the ALF's most publicized action ever.

The ALF of the 1980s found its greatest voice in PETA, who acted as a mouthpiece for the ALF following the raids, holding press conferences and distributing videos and seized documents to the media. The PETA press conference following the Gennarelli raid set off a media-wildfire surrounding the confiscated footage and sparked a fierce standoff between the compassionate public and the animal researchers. The biomedical research PR machine swung into motion, reassuring an outraged public of the "necessity" of head injury research. They said the choice was simple: the baboons or their children.

The ALF responded two months later by breaking into the University of Pennsylvania Vet School and liberating one dog.

A witch hunt was already underway for the ALF raiders, introducing to the movement the now-routine grand jury. High-profile animal rights activists and PETA employees were subpoenaed to answer questions before a panel closed to the public. The ALF's answer to these attempts at neutralization and to the blatant lies of vivisectors came four days after the previous break-in: UP Vet school raided again - four cats, one dog and eight pigeons were liberated. The ALF strikes again.

When the smoke cleared it was a victory for the ALF and the animals: NIH funding was revoked and Gennarelli's lab was shut down.

From one lab to the next throughout the '80s, the Animal Liberation Front saw the suffering, the torture, the legal means ignored, and implemented their timely and direct reaction to the slaughter - break down the doors, smash the labs, get the animals out. The U of P break-ins displayed what best characterized the ALF raids of the '80s - a sense of urgency. And the ALF never rested long.

City of Hell

By the end of 1984, the East Coast had seen 10 lab break-ins compared to the West Coast's three. In the east were NYU Medical Center (1 cat, 2 dogs, 2 guinea pigs), University of Southern Florida (55 gerbils, 35 rats), University of Massachusetts (2 rabbits), University of Maryland (42 rabbits), Howard University (30 cats), US Naval Medical Research Institute (1 dog), US Naval

Medical Research Institute (3 dogs), John Hopkins University (6 rats), University of Pennsylvania and University of Florida (many rats), and in the west were UC Berkeley (3 cats), UCLA Harbor Medical Center (12 dogs), and Cal State Sacramento (23 rats). December 1984 would put the West Coast ALF on the map and mark the first in a wave of high profile, expertly planned and executed lab break-ins in California during the mid '80s.

Tips from an inside whistleblower filtered down to ALF operatives during 1984 and led to the highly publicized raid on the City of Hope cancer research labs in Duarte, suburban LA.

The ALF's source inside the lab allowed the band pre-raid entry into the facility, where the ALF noted numbers and varieties of animals, allowing time to arrange homes for the freed prisoners in what would be the ALF's largest lab liberation to date.

During the early morning hours of December 9, 1984, the Animal Liberation Front gained access to the City of Hope labs via a door left open by the inside hand, destroyed over a half-million dollars in research, and loaded up 13 cats, 18 rabbits, 21 dogs, 50 mice and dozens more. The score that night: ALF — 115; City of Hope — zero.

The City of Hope raid showcased the 1980s' expertly orchestrated media campaigns where the highest importance was placed on projecting a Robin Hood-image to the public, and releasing confiscated research documents and video to the media to expose the fraud and lies of animal research. Through post-raid media coverage, the ALF brought vivisection to the forefront and expedited its demise swifter than the hundred years of legal protest that preceded them.

A crucial realization led to this approach - the animals that they liberate always seem to get replaced. The ALF never lost sight of the importance of individual lives, but it was the ripple effect of the ALF raids during the '80s that proved to save the most animals in the long term. Job #1: Liberate. Job #2: Expose. It was the ALF's steps to "expose" which would ultimately be the vivisectors' biggest threat and what would bring the ALF and the animals their greatest victories.

Video documentation and seized research logs from the raid had the most damaging effect on the City of Hope. When it was all over, City of Hope lost $700,000 in research, many experiments were permanently ended and, citing Animal Welfare Act infractions, the NIH suspended $1 million in funding.

Another victory, but the ALF was only getting started.

"This Is Only the Beginning"

By 1985, the West Coast had an active, expertly skilled ALF cell coupled with safehouses and a highly efficient underground railroad. ALF cell members were closely linked with known aboveground animal rights groups. Underground activists had positions inside such groups, intercepting whistle blower tips about research facilities and utilizing the help of sympathetic volunteers at mainstream groups who passed down information gained from such calls. The West Coast cell was quick to utilize the information from concerned employees, research assistants, students and vet techs passed to them, often warming up to and nurturing whistle blowers for their assistance in gaining access to the labs. It was through one such inside hand that the ALF pulled off what would be it's most ambitious raid yet, and left authorities wondering, "How did they get in?"

During the early morning hours of April 20, 1985, the Animal Liberation Front gained access to the psychology labs at the University of California at Riverside, removed laboratory doors from their hinges, and liberated nearly 1000 animals. When vivisectors arrived the next morning, they found their labs trashed and animals gone. Property damage exceeded $700,000. "Research," vice chancellor of the university said, "has been set back years."

It was the ALF's largest liberation ever - 21 cats, 9 opossums, 38 pigeons, 70 gerbils, 300 mice, 300 rats, 300 rabbits, and a baby monkey named Britches.

Britches was an infant macaque, the subject of a sight deprivation experiment since birth. When the ALF released video footage of Britches - only slightly larger than a human hand, an electronic implant taped to his tiny head, eyes sewn shut - it was a PR disaster for the biomedical research industry. News coverage of the UC Riverside raid and Britches, the baby monkey, elicited an emotional and outraged response from much of the public, forcing the vivisectors to answer for the unjustifiable cruelty revealed by the raid - starved pigeons, mutilated opossums, cats with eyes sewn shut, and a showpiece in the war against vivisection - a baby monkey named Britches.

News coverage and public response to the ALF rescue missions of the '80s contrast sharply to "terrorist" portrayal in media reports of the contemporary ALF The public and media, it seemed, were in love with the ALF

That the ALF affected permanent change was undeniable. Eight of the 17 experiments interrupted by the ALF at UC Riverside were never begun again. The psychology department no longer allowed baby monkeys' eyes to be sewn shut. Heat was installed to the outdoor primate colony. And one vivisector quit animal research forever.

Above The Law

During the early morning hours of October 26, 1986 the Animal Liberation Front entered the Science I building at the University of Oregon in Eugene, broke into 3 labs and rescued 264 animals from certain torture and death. Damage exceeded $120,000. There was no sign of forced entry.

The ALF released a statement following the rescue stating, "This is just the beginning of our efforts to liberate those oppressed in research concentration camps in Oregon. We will not allow the slaughter to continue without resistance. You will hear from us again soon."

The raid brought into the spotlight the until-then-unknown bloody career of Barbara Gordon-Lickey, a researcher at the University, who for over 17 years had tortured over a hundred kittens in pain research experiments and was the stated target of the break-in: "This freedom raid, which included the destruction of instruments inside these torture chambers, was directed at a butcher known as Barbara Gordon-Lickey, and in retaliation for the hundreds of innocent kittens she has murdered in the name of science."

The communique went on to explain the finer tactical points of research equipment destruction: "(a) $10,000 microscope was destroyed in about 12 seconds with a 36-inch steel wrecking bar that we purchased at a Fred-Meyer store for less than five dollars. We consider that a pretty good return on our investment." The statement continues, "the primate stereotactic device... (is) one of the most sinister instruments of torture ever devised by the human mind. We took particular delight in destroying it."

The University of Oregon raid showcased what has been proven in break-in after break-in to ultimately be the ALF's most damaging tactic - the confiscation of damning documents and photos. The U of O raiders seized veterinary logs, cage notes, and over 400 photographs - many of the most graphic ever obtained by the animal rights movement. The photographs revealed the callousness of the vivisectors and the barbarity of their "research." One photo-series contains a gruesome "staged cesarean delivery," showing a clearly terrified baby monkey being "delivered" from the stomach of a female researcher. These photos, taken by researchers of each other as they abused and made fun of animals, were released to the media at press conferences in Eugene and LA following the raid.

The confiscated photos proved, once again, to be a PR disaster for the researchers. The University quickly moved the "evidence" of such violations as seen in the photos - the remaining primates - to a secret location elsewhere on campus.

Once again the ALF exposed, in a high profile raid, absolute proof of blatant animal abuse inside vivisection labs. And once again the researchers repeated form-response after form-response that the raided facilities were "isolated instances," "an embarrassment to all research," and "not the norm." To alert members of the public, this was becoming difficult to accept.

The University of Oregon brought the movement its second ALF-related arrest. The night of the University of Oregon rescue, Roger Troen, a known animal advocate, received an anonymous phone call. The caller asked Roger if he could drive to Eugene without mentioning it to anyone and take some animals in desperate need of a home. No details were offered as to the animals' origin, though as Roger put it, "I didn't need to ask."

Weeks later a veterinarian who had been asked to examine the animals led the police to Roger. The court case that followed put the University of Oregon and its vivisectors on the witness stand where the "scientists" were forced to describe their careers and the barbaric research protocols taking place inside their labs, bringing the vivisectors out from behind the walls of secrecy where they would prefer to hide.

Roger Troen received six months home detention and was ordered to pay restitution for his role in the ALF's Underground Railroad. 10 rabbits were recovered and returned to the University labs. 254 animals were never located by investigators. Each one is an ALF victory.

The Flames Of Justice

The next lab attack brought to America the ALF's most effective tool against animal abuser Naziism, introducing a strategy of "maximum destruction, not minimum damage," and setting the direction of large-scale ALF actions for much of the next 15 years.

On April 16, 1987, the under-construction Animal Diagnostic Lab at UC Davis was firebombed. The animal research lab designed to cater to the needs of the food-animal industry burned to the ground. Damage was at $4.5 million. It is the most expensive ALF action to date.

It was on that night the American ALF gave birth to its most functional tool to directly render the instruments and structures of animal torture permanently inoperable. Circumventing the effort, risk, and limited damage of a nighttime live liberation after the lab's completion, the ALF simply erased the Animal Diagnostics lab from existence.

After Davis, the fire bombings continued throughout northern California with further actions claimed by the Animal Rights Militia including a $10,000 fire at the San Jose Veal Company warehouse, followed by a $230,000 fire at the Ferrara Meat Company. Two days later a poultry warehouse was set on fire and sustained $200,000 in damages. The ALF took credit. The arson campaign continued into 1988 with the firebombing of the San Jose Meat Company, burning the building to the ground, and the torching of a fur store in Santa Rosa. The store never reopened. But the ALF, as they say, was only "warming up."

"Nowhere To Hide"

Using bolt cutters, crowbars, and blueprints retrieved from laboratory dumpsters, ALF freedom fighters systematically raided four buildings at the University of Arizona in Tucson on April 3, 1989, setting two fires, burning one building to the ground, doing nearly $300,000 in damages and liberating over 1,200 animals. It was the largest live laboratory liberation to date and arguably the most monumental ALF action ever.

The raid began in the early morning hours when ALF operatives broke into a ground floor door of the Bio-West building, took an elevator to the sixth floor, and wheeled out 965 animals before destroying the labs. Simultaneously across campus at the Shantz building, a second team removed an air vent cover approximately 12 feet off the ground, entered an airshaft and broke into a ground floor laboratory. Soon after, raiders broke into a ground floor door at the Microbiology/Pharmacy building, took an elevator to the sixth floor, and rescued additional animals.

Once the animals were out, one lab and one autopsy room were destroyed, the walls soaked in gasoline and the entire area torched. The team then moved off campus where an incendiary was placed under the building housing the office of the UA's director of animal research. The building and all contents were destroyed. Damages neared $300,000, and 1,231 animals were out of the vivisectors' lethal reach.

National news articles after the rescue called it a "Rambo-style remake of the story of Noah's ark."

A police report following the raid testified to the precision of the action. In the ensuing investigation, the UAPD "found little or no physical evidence left behind." The police found "the organization... prepares extensively for its strikes, leaves little or no evidence for police purposes, and operates at peak efficiency."

Investigators estimate the animal rescue and incendiary attacks took less than 90 minutes. "The ALF," the report stated, "had thoroughly prepared for this attack." The police had no suspects.

A crucial and intended effect of ALF actions, large or small, is the increase in the cost of killing animals. Following the rescue mission, campus police announced that as a direct result of the break-in, the University of Arizona had "to divest $1 million into animal research protection." By 5:00 PM the day of the raid, 24-hour security by off duty police was ordered at 11 campus research sites. This 24-hour security coverage continued for 6 weeks following the raid at a cost of $40,000 a week. Animal research labs scattered in 11 separate buildings throughout campus were consolidated into two secured facilities. The University of Arizona spent half a million dollars on new security following the raid to prevent against another ALF break-in.

With the University of Arizona raid, the ALF's statement was clear - the cost of torturing animals just went up.

Into The '90s

Direct action in the '80s ended with a break-in at John "Gorem" Orem's Texas Tech lab with five cats liberated and $70,000 damage to equipment. Less publicized raids took place into the early '90s with six rabbits liberated from a lab in Florida; 100 guinea pigs liberated from Simonsen Labs in Gilroy, CA; 750 mice, rats, and hamsters from a lab in Buffalo, NY; and 11 rabbits and 10 guinea pigs from Cook County Hospital in Chicago. These and the four-state "Operation Bite Back" campaign to end the fur industry would be the ALF's final lab raids for several years.

Fast forward to 1999. Modern labs were perceived by many as being impenetrable. Lab liberations had been non-existent for 7 years. Then, on April 5, 1999, ten years and two days after the University of Arizona raid, masked liberators broke into two separate buildings at the University of Minnesota rescuing 116 animals and using wrecking bars and sledgehammers to inflict a $2 million blow to vivisection.

It was the ALF's most triumphant comeback, setting off a small-wave of lab liberations and sabotage lasting through the end of the year. 1999 saw the liberation of 193 animals from medical research, more than the previous 9 years combined. Small-scale property damage of the early-mid '90s has given way to mink releases in great numbers, large scale arsons, and now, thanks to small cells of masked liberators with crowbars, the return of the lab raid.

The ALF of the 1980s brought the horrors of vivisection from the shadows and formed the first true threat to the demons in their torture chambers who chose to murder the innocent. Month after month, throughout the 80s, many of these monsters found the Animal Liberation Front coming through their door.

To those demons who were not stopped and still continue - lock yourself inside, because the storm is brewing again...

The Enemy Within

Article
Earth First Journal
"In times of peace, everyone talks a hard line, it is in times of conflict that our true resolve is revealed."

In 2006, I was in a federal prison cell in Victorville, California. The evidence that had put me there was incriminating, but in a courtroom, still negotiable. Yet I had opted to avoid trial. What made a trial impossible was the promised testimony of my codefendant, Justin Samuel.

The fiery article that follows was inspired by two things.

One, his betrayal. Two, my realization while on the run that people move primarily in the direction of social incentive, independent of their rhetoric. With no social incentive to do otherwise, I had watched visible figures in activism say nothing as Justin re-assimilated back into the movement after his release from prison. Only when I was arrested and regained a voice, was their stance suddenly unfashionable, and only then were they inspired to publicly condemn him.

This article was a small attempt to maintain a culture of intolerance towards those who implicate others to save themselves.

Security's weakest link is not the forensic threat of a hair left on the laboratory floor, nor is it the technological threat of a wiretap. Security's weakest link is the human element. And the weak links have arrived.

Josh Ellerman. Roger Troen. Geof Kearns. Justin Samuel. Billy Cottrell. Jacob Sherman. Stanislas Meyerhoff. Kevin Tubbs. Jacob Ferguson… The enemies we must work around are those with badges. The enemies we must fear are those among us—the enemies within.

On August 28, 2000, my co-defendant, Justin Samuel, entered the grand jury room and implicated me in six major felonies that could have earned me more than 10 years in prison. For this assault, his punishment was the open arms of many animal liberationists, complemented by the silence of nearly all.

As a case study, it speaks volumes: a column about Samuel in an established activist publication calling for forgiveness, movement elders giving him sanctuary, widespread repetition by activists of lines like "he didn't tell them anything they didn't already know," and even updates on Samuel's legal situation from the former Animal Liberation Front Press Office. As the directly affected party, I remained on the FBI wanted list, and the movement erred on the side of harmony.

Before we take collective comfort in any self-perceived hard stance on informants, first consider my experience. Consider with whom you might side if your good friend were to inform on another, and where the movement would stand if one of its high-status scene darlings were to inform on you. In times of peace, everyone talks a hard line, It is in times of conflict that our true resolve is revealed.

Our most grievous error is to see this issue as somehow separate from that which unites us—the fight for all life. To take one from active service is to condemn to obliteration and death all they could have saved, just as if the slaughter were brought by the snitch's own hand. Lives are on the line, and not just the lives of humans

For the sake of clarity, let us be uncomfortably honest: to snitch is to take a life. By words and by weapons, each day lives are taken in the most egregious of crimes. When this happens in the courtroom, we call it "cooperation." I call it violence, and I call anything done to keep an informant out of the courtroom "self defense."

"Let's not squander our energy on those who have turned," I have heard it said. But is there any greater energy drain than cleaning up the mess left by snitches and their apologists?

The small perk to the snitch's betrayal is that in the wake of their deed, the cooperators of the future are revealed. We excuse those with whom we identify and behavior that we can imagine from ourselves. As the case of recently-jailed ALF operatives unfolds, watch closely those apologists for the cooperating parties. Then read between the lines.

If only I could say there was a fix for the damage done post-deed. That when the weak link breaks, there is such a thing as damage control. But talking is a one-way door. Our only hope comes at the front end—through education, observation and intolerance.

The forsaking of the most sacred of vows, to remain solid in the interrogation room in defense of something much higher than ourselves, has as its origin one thing: the fear of prison.

Thus, snitching prevention comes in these forms:

1. For ALF actions, research federal sentencing guidelines to understand the range one faces in advance.
2. Collectively demystify prison—the fantasy is often worse than the reality, and it is the fantasy that induces the crime of collaboration.
3. Work alone when possible.
4. Give immediate attention and assistance to anyone subpoenaed to a grand jury.
5. As a movement, teach not just tactics but the fortitude needed to move from arrest to prison unbroken.
6. Never allow an informant reentry into our ranks—this sends a message that breeds a climate fertile for collaborators. The costs of harmony and forgiveness are more indictments and stolen lives.

It is the wise saboteur who knows the high-risk categories and avoids them: drug users, the emotionally unstable, snitch apologists, braggarts and others who will not be tagged "high–risk" here to avert violent uproar from this readership. Suffice it to say, entering into partnership for commission of a felony is no time to be polite. While generalizations are dangerous, so is crime....

"No one talks, everyone walks." In the end, the truth of these words may be our best defense, and in fact—our only defense. And when the weak link breaks, let us never fail in our duty to those whose lives were stolen and to all they could have saved.

How To Raid Fur Farms

Interview
War Machine
"The only measure of whether something is 'smart' is if it gets the job done."

A small vegan straight edge zine from Europe put to me some of the most important questions I've been asked to answer.

Everything there is to know about freeing fur farm prisoners, step by step.

How many Midwest farms did you surveil during the fall of 1997?

Between 35 and 50. We traveled eastward across Montana, South Dakota, Iowa, Minnesota, and Wisconsin. We spent the daytime driving past farms and the nighttime on them. We walked the sheds of every manner of farm, from single sheds to farms imprisoning 80,000 mink. We walked the Fraser Fur Farm compound and stared in the eyes what may have been more lynx than existed in the wild in the entire state of Montana. We encountered masked scarecrows with signs reading "ALF Stay Away". We were chased from farms on foot on more than one occasion and by cars from several more. We looked at a lot of farms, many of which have been hit in the years since. It brings me immeasurable pleasure to read of farms I visited, whose captives I had to leave behind, being raided years later. I hope I'm alive to see the day one or both of the Zimbal mink farms (WI) has every cage opened.

We received a tremendous amount of information on the farms we surveilled via the discovery process of my legal case. Dozens of pages of confiscated notes we had taken on farms were turned over; in addition to numerous police reports listing often detailed information on, and addresses of, fur farms in areas where we were accused of actions. I believe all the fur farmers who wrote my judge asking for the harshest possible sentence were not aware photocopies of their letterhead and (unpublished) return addresses were turned over directly to my lawyer. Again, as with raids that are carried out in the wake of an arrest, we see it doesn't pay for an industry to encourage the imprisonment of animal liberators.

What was your intention with this campaign?

To get as many animals out of those cages as we could before pelting season. The fact that some of the farms shut down was an unanticipated yet welcome side effect.

Describe this period (1996 to 1998) of underground activism against the fur industry.

An anecdote to illustrate the pace at which farms were getting raided from 1996 to 1998: We had discussed surveilling farms in Idaho, including one in Preston, Idaho. We decided against it and did not visit any farms until Montana. We would later read that literally the night we were to have visited that farm, every one of its 5,000 mink were released by individuals unknown.

Later, when we received the various police reports from that period it was revealed there were others surveying farms in the same three-state area, sometimes visiting the same farms we had only a day apart. That three groups were out simultaneously seeking farms to raid illustrates the momentum at the time. Had we sustained this pace, there would be no U.S. fur industry today.

Talk about how you located fur farms. Were all farms you visited listed in *The Final Nail?* Did you draw from other sources?

The Final Nail was a starting point. To this day it is the best resource for fur farm addresses, although it has many gaps. To locate unknown farms and find street addresses for those where only a "rural route" address was listed, we had to call on our creativity. This pre-dated the internet as we know it, and hard-copy material was our sole resource. The sources from which we drew the most info: local phone directories, business directories at the library, and agricultural survey maps at university libraries. Above them all, fur industry trade publications like *Fur Rancher* provided the most leads. And then there were those farms we found by turning down "Fur Farm Road." Sometimes they hide in plain sight.

What did you look for in choosing one farm to raid over another?

We looked at many farms and couldn't hit them all. There were features we looked for which disqualified some farms and beckoned us to others, which I will leave unmentioned to avoid giving the fur industry insight into the workings of those working to rid them from this earth.

We should be reminded there have been farms raided with everything from perimeter security to guard dogs. Activists should take from this that "security" is only a deterrent if you let it be. Farmers should take from this that when animal liberators have you in their sights, cash in your chips because you're getting raided either way.

What did you do with the car while you were surveilling or raiding farms? Did you have a driver, or did you park?

Parking is an exercise in creativity. Cornfields, farm service roads, nearby non-residential buildings, and any place that will not arouse suspicion are all options. Our most desperate parking incident was the time we parked directly in the farmer's driveway, behind his personal vehicle. The only measure of whether something is "smart" is if it gets the job done.

Having a driver would be sensible in an extreme case where parking was an impossibility. There are too many variables that could necessitate quick and premature flight from the premises to chance having to wait for pickup from a circling driver. We parked every time.

Talk about removing fencing. How did you remove the fences surrounding a farm to allow the mink an escape route?

There is no correlation between the apparent fortitude of a fence and the ease with which it can be dismantled. Often the most intricately constructed fences are held together by only a few pieces of wire affixed to posts. When the wire is cut, the entire fence falls. Generally a small pair of wire cutters is sufficient, with larger bolt cutters sometimes being necessary. We took down 400 feet of fence in Medford in less than 20 minutes with fewer than 50 cuts.

What equipment did you bring to the farms?

Dark clothes, facial covering, gloves, headlamp with red screen (making it barely visible at a distance), bolt cutters, and wire cutters. That's it.

Is there anything you wish you had used which would have made the action safer or more effective?

With all actions, as in life, I believe low-tech and streamlined is best. Trust your senses and work with the absolute minimum needed to accomplish the goal.

That said, the complications that came from our policy to always be in eye-shot of each other on the farm could have been avoided with radio contact. For that reason, I would see no good argument against using radios during an action. We never procured radios for the simple reason that we were short on money and the animals were short on time.

Describe a mink shed.

One to four rows, partially walled, with a very crude saloon-style door, if any. There is not much to it. When you've made it that far, the hardest part is behind you.

Are there any security precautions you encountered at the farms (security guards, cameras, alarms, etc)?

In the 35 to 50 farms we visited during the fall of 1997, I saw one video camera and no alarms. In the farms I've visited in the Northwest, I've seen over 10 farms with perimeter security and several with video cameras. Thus there are serious regional differences in security. The perimeter alarms I've encountered are invisible beams, which, most of the time, can be rolled under. I would suspect there is close to zero chance cameras on a farm are monitored overnight, and would not consider them a deterrent.

Is the opening of the cages self-explanatory?

It's always self-explanatory but never consistent. Latch styles are numerous. In addition to simple latches, there are nesting boxes which are most often removable and provide the best option for mink to escape. Occasionally cages are wired shut individually, easily remedied with wire cutters. Snip, then twist.

Other than your over-arching conspiracy charge, you plead guilty to an explicit perpetrator role in releasing 2,500 mink from a Medford, Wisconsin farm. What can you tell us about this action? How long did it take, and what were the obstacles?

Medford, Wisconsin was at one time known as "Mink Capital USA" (while still a contender, the title today would likely go to Morgan, Utah). There are several farms in or around downtown, and at least a dozen in Medford and outlying areas (some may have closed in the years since). The house was a safe distance from the sheds, and altogether there were no obstacles to speak of. The entire action took one hour.

In light of the numbers you give in your university talks, that 2 people can release 1,000 animals in 15 minutes, what do you feel are the reasons behind the abundance of small mink releases in which only 1 to 200 mink are freed?

I know exactly what this is because I almost fell victim to it. None of the available literature forewarned of the decibel level created by even a few dozen mink given their first taste of freedom. When you're in someone's backyard at

1am, and being detected means going to prison, if you're not prepared for the wall of noise it can be an immediate cause for flight. The fear dissipated the first time I left a farm and became aware that what is deafening inside a shed is almost inaudible just 25 yards away.

There are certainly other reasons for aborted raids, such as discovery by farmers, which has been known to happen. Relative to just 20 years ago, there are only a handful of farms left and I would hope animal liberators would invest the preparation time to ensure they release 10,000 animals over finding themselves unprepared and leaving after releasing only 10.

What lessons can we learn from the past 10+ years of fur farm liberations? What have been our mistakes?

Mistakes: Not maintaining the momentum of the mid-to-late-90s that would have brought the end of the U.S. fur industry. And squandering risk-exposure on periphery targets (such as fur stores) in areas where farms or infrastructure targets are within a day's drive. A mink release on the right farm will be a much less risky endeavor than breaking the windows of a fur store. This is less a criticism than a call to cater every action for maximum impact.

Did you issue communiqués for your actions?

We issued no communiqués. There are pros and cons to issuing communiqués, and for live liberations, I see more pros than cons. Generally I think communiqués are a necessary element to any large-scale, successful action. Whatever our reasons at the time, we did not make any claims of responsibility and were focused solely on getting to the next farm. There was a plan to issue a communiqué after leaving the Midwest, making public all the intelligence gathered during our investigation of farms - from unknown addresses to farm layout and more. These notes were confiscated by the FBI during the seizure of our vehicle, and this information was never made public.

Among fur industry actions you were not a part of, which stand out as most impressive, and what can we learn from them?

The examples of multiple raids taking place back-to-back, such as the 5 raids that took place in 10 days during August of 1998. Anyone who thinks fur farmers are on too high alert now to successfully empty their farms should take note that there is no farmer on higher alert than one within three hours drive of a farm that had been raided the night before. Yet still liberators have still slipped in, released animals, and slipped out undetected. We should have an evidential basis for our fears, not vague assumptions rooted in a default-bias towards the path of least resistance.

Offer your analysis of the direction mink and fox releases should take in the future.

Bigger raids and more of them. There's nothing more to say.

Animal Liberation: How Far Is Too Far?

Lecture transcript
Animal Rights National Conference
"Actions that generate negative feedback now are actions you'll be praised as a hero for in the history books."

This is an unscripted conversation that emerged from a group discussion around the subject: How far is too far?

Welcome. I was invited here to serve the role of unbiased moderator in this conversation. I'm not going to do that because I have biases.

How far is too far? This is definitely one of the most contentious issues in the movement. I will frame this discussion around these questions:

- What's better: education, or a more militant toolbox of tactics?
- How do we know we're being too extreme?
- How do we know when education is making us feel good but not being effective?
- What is the "right" approach?
- How far *is* too far?

I spent the first couple years of my activism essentially waving signs outside of buildings. I had been fed this model as "this is what activism is." I was too young to adequately question it, and I just deferred to the people who were older than me.

Soon I examined whether we were actually saving any animals and realized the answer was, "no." And I adopted the belief, which I still stand by, that only in the two extremes were we saving animals. The one extreme, where we were educating people about veganism, number one. This had an indirect, and not necessarily quantifiable, benefit to animals. And the other extreme - breaking laws.

In regards to the tactics in between, we were a voice for animals, but it wasn't strategic. I'm not saying there are not strategic ways to go about that type of activism. I still do that form of activism. But we began to realize there are ways we can complement our education-based activism, the one extreme, with the other extreme. I can tell you that until I began to act in this other extreme, I had never felt truly effective for animals.

I remember many times after these actions, thinking that I had just done more for animals in one night using "extreme tactics" than I ever did in years of legal activism. I have not changed my opinion on the value of the two extremes.

One point I'll throw out to get the conversation going is, I feel like this debate is a false dichotomy. Education versus direct action is an artificial construct and we've created an artificial dichotomy.

Framing the conversation in this way is problematic in two ways:

One is that you can take action in both extremes. You don't have to choose. You can do both. This whole conversation presupposes that you have to choose. We would go out leafleting during the day and literally be breaking windows of butcher shops in the dark just a few hours later.

The other false dichotomy is that a tactic is either educational or direct. In fact the best confrontational tactic is also an educational tactic.

I learned this lesson early on when some activists broke into an egg farm near Seattle and took 11 chickens. They took a video of them breaking in and cutting through cages in ski masks, putting chickens in carriers. They also videotaped the conditions of the egg farm. They then dropped the VHS tapes off at every news stations. This is before YouTube, before Mercy For Animals, well before this kind of footage was accessible. Every single news station that night played footage taken from the raid and gave hundreds of thousands of people their first glimpse inside of an egg farm. That activists could carry out an "extreme tactic" and also use it as an outreach tool, illustrates my point.

More recently on this point, does anyone here know what the Iowa Butter Cow is? The Butter Cow is an iconic deity at the Iowa State Fair each year. It's literally a cow made of butter. People wait in line for hours to see this thing. It's kept in a locked glass case. It's like a state mascot. This is a big deal in Iowa.

Several years ago someone broke in to the building and the glass case at night and splashed red paint on the Butter Cow, then issued a statement declaring it was done to bring awareness to the plight of animals on Iowa's factory farms. It became a national news story. The activists who did this sent out an anonymous press release, a communique. The media literally copied and pasted quotes directly from the communique. Quotes that were published in large outlets like USA Today. Quotes like how this was done to bring attention to the plight of dairy farm cows on factory farms. You couldn't get better press than that. They literally just took our slogans and inserted them into these articles. You could not pay for that kind of media. It was priceless.

This conversation brings up another important point, which is just how one-sided this debate about "extreme" tactics is. We consider tactics debatable when we apply them to saving animals. But it would never be debatable if we were talking about humans. Because of the privilege of not being oppressed ourselves, it becomes a big college debate.

<commentary from audience member>

There's two important things I got from what you just said. One is that people tend to scale their actions to the options you give them. If you say, "Just eat meat one day a week," yes, you can quantify and say that saves a lot of animals. But people generally will adjust their actions to what's asked of them. So why ask for so little.

The other thing is the question of: When a beagle is rescued from a lab, do the animals just get replaced? That's a valid consideration. Not that it undermines the merits of those actions, but when the ALF carries out these actions, they should work into the action ways that will prevent those animals being replaced as quickly. For example, damaging equipment, to the extent that they are able, without getting caught.

All of us have to be comfortable, no matter where you are in the spectrum of activism, with not being able to quantify your results. We all want to be able to hold up an animal and say, "I saved this animal." Yet it's very rare that you can do that. So you have to be comfortable just saying, "I tried."

Another question was just raised: Does the ALF's use of ski masks make us look bad? There's no reason you shouldn't make your actions more palatable to a larger audience. But we should never let our actions be defined by people who don't share our goals. Because then they're in control and we'll never get anything done.

Also based on what you said, you understand the concept of leverage. This is an important concept I didn't fully grasp until about a year ago. I run a couple of online businesses. I've launched several others in the past. And there are businesses you can start where you sell one thing, like a used book, and then you have to go out and replace that thing before you can sell it again. Then there are businesses where you can do work one time, like publish a book and make money from it indefinitely. The latter is the "leveraged" option.

It's the same thing with activism. There are actions where the impact ends

175

with that action, like projecting slaughterhouse footage on the side of a Burger King. And there are actions where the impact continues indefinitely, like taking footage from inside a slaughterhouse and publicizing it. We can take actions that just have a defined end to their impact and strategically work to make sure they have an impact that extends indefinitely, such as working media into an animal liberation, where we educate large numbers who then become vegan, influence their friends, and so on.

There is much potential to generate mainstream media using "direct action" tactics. If you snuck into a factory farm, took footage of the factory farm and sent it to the media, that's not a news story. Yet if you went in there and took footage and even did something as small as spraypainting the side of the shed so it's visible from the nearest road, so it's something a reporter or blogger can take a photo of, then *that's* a news story.

There are so many ways you can take something that is not news and turn it into news. It would be awesome if animal abuse was newsworthy. But unfortunately, business as usual is never newsworthy. It comes back to breaking people from their trance. You have to understand how the media works and provoke them. That's leverage.

Our job as activists, fundamentally, is to break people from their trance. We're all in a trance, whether it's induced by television, organized sports, or going to bars, we're all in a literal trance at this point in our society's history. If what you do breaks people from their trance, that's the most important first step. Communicating raw facts, unfortunately, doesn't often jolt people from their trance.

With "extreme" tactics, I look at it like this: if someone in line in front of me at Starbucks is having a heart attack, I don't want them to tap me on the shoulder and say, "Excuse me sir, I have something important I have to tell you." I want them to flop on the ground flailing so they get my attention, because it's an urgent situation.

With activism, we need to impart that same urgency with our tactics.

To end on a related point: Be careful as activists not to internalize negative feedback when you live in a totally insane world. Actions that generate negative feedback today are actions you'll be praised as a hero for in the history books.

Tribute To
Underground Magazine

Book introduction
Underground: The Animal Liberation Front in the 1990s
"Underground is a chronicle of those who fight for animals under the radar, and above the law. Read their history, and then make your own."

My activism would have taken a very different turn were it not for the guidance and inspiration of Underground: The Newsletter of the North American ALF Supporters Group.

Years later I had the good fortune of publishing a collection of Underground in book form and offered this introduction.

(Spliced into this piece are related excerpts from a second book introduction I authored for Until All Are Free – The Story of the Swedish Animal Liberation Front.)

At 18, I walked into my first meeting for an animal rights group at the University of Washington in Seattle. I was ready to be more than just a passive vegan - I wanted to be an activist. And I had found just the right group. They had set up a literature table, and one item immediately had my full attention: issue #3 of *Underground: Newsletter of the North American Animal Liberation Front Supporter's Group*.

I was learning about the ALF before I had attended my first protest.

There are times in your life you recognize as a dividing line, after which your life is forever divided into two parts: "the period before," and "the period after." That first meeting, and in particular reading my first issue of *Underground*, was one of those moments.

I turned directly to the first article: "The Story of the Swedish ALF" – which I consumed (rather rudely) during the meeting while the rest of the group discussed an upcoming protest. I will always find stories of breaking into labs more interesting than meetings about waving signs in front of them, and I had read this story start to finish several times over before the meeting had finished.

That night was my first exposure to the world of activism, and as I juxtaposed the conversation in the room (about chanting outside the UW labs) with the story of the Swedish ALF (about breaking into them) I knew which direction I put my faith in.

That story – a mere three pages in stark black-and-white – was a short account of how one small group formed and launched a 10-year campaign, carrying out dozens of high-impact yet elegantly simple raids of labs and farms. It is quite possible my life would have gone a vastly different direction had I not opened that magazine to this short, powerful story. It offered the right lessons at the right time.

The prose was simplistic, the anecdotes under-embellished, and the message implicit: We did it, and you can too.

This story had many messages which have stood the test of time. Some of these I understood but failed to act on. Some I can see now only after the passing of nearly 20 years. And others can only be truly understood by those who put themselves in a laboratory basement at midnight.

Perhaps sensing my interest in *Underground*, which I carried with me for weeks and re-read zealously, one of the group's founders took me aside at the next meeting and asked my feelings about direct action. He said he had an action planned and needed help.

Having received no further details, I met him late one night at his house in Seattle. He handed me a pair of gloves and took me into the bathroom, where we spent the next two hours filling light bulbs with red paint. As per his instructions, I had brought a backpack with disposable, dark clothing.

As we filled paint bombs, he went over the plan: Walk the three miles to a large taxidermy warehouse in Seattle's industrial neighborhood (we had no cars, and taking the bus, he explained, would present the risk of a bus driver remembering us and giving our description to police). I would unleash a half-dozen paint bombs on the building's front, while he spray painted animal liberation messages on the warehouse before we disappeared into the night.

It was my first illegal action for animals. Although we did not claim it as an ALF action (or report it to *Underground*), we followed the model first introduced to me by that copy of *Underground #3*.

For over a year we continued these small-scale attacks around Seattle. Although most went unreported, they eventually grew too numerous for the media, or police, to ignore. The latter began staking out my friend's homes, in a hunt for the ALF saboteurs who had hit dozens of meat distribution companies and other businesses. Soon we were finding ourselves pulled over at 2 a.m. under "suspicious circumstances" near recent ALF targets, and the media was labeling my home an ALF "safe house."

With the stakes raised and an arrest appearing imminent, I began to question the strategic value of small-scale ALF "smash attacks." If I was going to prison, I wanted to go down for something that made a real difference for animals. Any action aiming for less than maximum impact was to fail them.

With greater victories in mind, soon I would be pulling back shed doors to enter chicken farms and cutting through fences to access local mink prisons. As I strove for more effective tiers of ALF activity, *Underground* was both instructional and catalytic.

Underground came early in a line of U.S. ALF-focused publications that continues to this day. In the 1980s, a smattering of small, limited-circulation publications made appearances, including *The Liberator*. The first (to my knowledge) sustained U.S. direct action publication came in the form of *The Militant Vegan*, which published 8 issues in the early to mid-1990s. *Underground* debuted in 1994, followed soon after by *No Compromise*. *Bite Back* published its first issue in 2002, and at the time of this writing has published its 17th issue covering ALF actions worldwide.

The combined issues of *Underground* serve one important end: offering the most comprehensive look at ALF activity in the 90s available. Much of the history documented has never been covered anywhere but the pages of *Underground* and would be lost forever had *Underground* never existed.

Notable articles from *Underground* included "Raiding Arizona" - the story of the ALF's largest U.S. lab raid to date, the extensive debate over Rod Coronado, a history of the splinter-group Justice Department, and a first-hand account of a raid on the University of Alberta. With an explicit willingness to publish anonymous articles (and offering guidelines for making forensics-free submissions), the ALF's otherwise muted voice finally had a platform in the pages of *Underground*.

After losing my personal copies in the frenzy of my fugitive life, I eventually reunited with a complete archive of *Underground*. Reading these magazines for the first time in over a decade, I was reminded of the power of print. There is an organic energy to printed matter somehow absent from a website or PDF. I know my first issue of *Underground* was a greater motivating force than anything I've since read on the internet. While no one has isolated what is lost when information is digested from a digital medium, I know that one piece of printed matter has greater impact than a thousand "website hits." The internet strips a document of its analog electricity, something vital to any book worth reading. When I want someone to merely know of something, I give them a website. When I want them to feel and act on it, I give them a book.

With *Underground* inextricably tied into my personal history, reading became a reflective journey. Through the process, I confronted how many of my life's experiences had a lineage that could be traced directly to the early issues. Had I chosen more conservative periodicals, I may never have dropped through rooftop hatches, obtained IDs at DMVs with forged documents, traveled miles through woods pursued by farmers, or gone to prison.

While legislative "victories" mandating extra cage space in puppy mills get national media, the history of those who strike blows to animal abusers under darkness goes largely unrecorded and uncelebrated but for small publications like *Underground*.

Underground is a chronicle of those who fight for animals under the radar, and above the law. Read their history, and then make your own.

Rescuing Animals: ALF Style

Lecture transcript
Animal Rights National Conference
"Learning lock picking takes mere days."

The how's, why's, and more how's of illegal animal rescue.

(Also included, spliced-in excerpts from other, related material.)

There is a silent, mostly unwritten history of a type of rescue that hasn't been covered here today: people acting on behalf of the Animal Liberation Front rescuing animals illegally from labs, farms, and anywhere animals are imprisoned.

I don't think any of us here are promoting individual animal rescues as a sustainable, long-term strategy for ending animal exploitation. But they are very successful in the short term. Because every liberation matters to that one animal. And making that difference for one animal, or a hundred, takes very little time and even less skill.

I give the other panelists here credit for showing up at abusive situations, dealing with animal "owners," negotiating with police, and having to navigate laws. That's hard work.

Everything I have done has been in the middle of the night where we can avoid those things. It's much less work. There are no abusers present, no negotiation skills required, and you are essentially above the law.

ALF actions I would argue are the easiest way to rescue animals, because you're showing up in the middle of the night when the only obstacles are physical, eliminating all the middlemen and directly saving an animal in need.

I've been to egg farms in the middle of the day. There are employees there who will stop you before you're 10 feet into the property.

I have also been to egg farms at night. There is no one there, and you can move through the property and into the sheds undetected.

The simplest option is clear.

There are so many animals that need us every second that anyone in a position to house an animal or who has access to homes needs to expand their options to allow for things that are legally gray. Or legally…. *illegal.*

Risk Assessment & Animal Liberation

Part of this is accurately assessing the risks and consequences of animal rescue.

I received an email recently from a woman who had a problem. A problem that wasn't really a problem – a problem in her head. She contacted me to say that there was an alligator someone had abandoned at a pond behind a shopping center near her home in Florida. She said there were kids who were abusing the alligator, and that animal control was going to take the alligator and kill it any minute. She said she had alligator-handling experience. She said she had a home for the alligator. It was every obstacle removed: access, skills, and a home. But she said she couldn't save the alligator. Why? Because she was afraid she might be "caught."

I'm reading this email thinking this is the most benign crime in world history. I don't even know what they would charge her with. And on the slim chance she were arrested for relocating this "problem" alligator, I could not imagine it being an offense that could possibly warrant more than a night in jail. Yet because this woman had not demystified lawbreaking, she had not practiced risk-assessment. And because of this, that alligator was probably killed.

We must deflate the simple act of prowling in someone's backyard at 2am. You accomplish this by developing habits and rituals where you put yourself in places you're not supposed to be regularly to build tolerance. These obstacles are things we can condition ourselves to tolerate. Barriers to entry to animal rescues in all forms are more psychological than anything.

The Raid Actualization Framework

I want to repeat this: physical barriers between you and an animal are really psychological barriers. They are impassable because you believe they are. When professional thieves want to get inside a hotel room where there are jewels, they rent the room next door and smash through the wall. When they want to circumvent alarms, they cut through the room and drop in with a rope.

Like much in life, imagination inflates the complexity of rescues. Imagination creates the belief there is something prohibitively complex about getting inside a facility or farm, removing an animal, and giving it a home.

When I read a story of an ALF raid, my first question is always: How did they get inside? How did they infiltrate the building to gain access to the animals?

Looking at the limited information available, we can get an uncomprehensive, but still long list of the tactics the ALF has employed to get inside: Picking locks. Hiding inside buildings and emerging after hours. Cutting through walls. Cutting through air vents. Stealing keys. Circumventing motion sensors. Unlocked doors. Breaking through windows.

Of those that require any skill at all, none of these couldn't be learned in an afternoon.

So ask yourself whose interest it serves to cling to false beliefs about the ALF possessing skills outside your ability. Tell the animals you "could never do anything like that," when you have never once put yourself outside a mink farm or a lab at midnight, when you've done nothing to give any basis to your beliefs.

Our limiting, baseless beliefs provide animal abusers with a level of security no alarm can offer.

If you believe it is impossible to rescue animals by entering these horror chambers because of a belief based assumptions and not evidence, then you have condemned every animal in that building to death.

Tell it to the people who got inside the University of Minnesota and got over 100 animals out of the building. Tell it to those who broke through an air vent to get inside labs at Louisiana State University, rescuing 21 mice.

You may not know anyone you trust who can house animals. You may have legitimate reasons for not participating in a live animal rescue. But "it's impossible to get inside" is not among them.

Even with no skills, opportunities are abundant if you create the circumstances where opportunities show themselves. Put yourself outside of a building with no expectations, with a blank mind, and just observe. You'll see someone come out of a back door and notice it didn't close all the way behind him. You'll notice a pipe to step on that leads to a ledge next to an unlocked window. Things happen. But you have to turn off the computer and go there.

When I learned about the hidden world of enslaved animals all around me, I began to parlay my youthful "sneaking around" skills into getting access to animals. And I got good at it.

One of the first and simplest examples was a breeder of rabbits specifically for labs. They were kept in a fortified structure in the middle of a field. The doors were locked, yet we were able to open them using the crude method of jimmying the lock with a credit card. Of course, the doors were not alarmed.

Another was a large laboratory, large enough to have several floors and balconies and levels to the roof. There was a fire escape stairwell leading up two floors, both with heavy metal doors. In an unnecessary design flaw, it was just barely possible for the person among us with the longest arms to reach under each of these doors, and push the lever from the inside, thus opening the door. Confident the roof was secured, of course this facility left several windows unlocked.

Later myself and several friends were on the roof of a lab that experimented on rabbits. Again, this is the kind of place most activists file away as "impossible to get into." We noticed an entire skylight of this one story building was loose and were able to remove it entirely without the use of any tools. We then climbed down off the roof, went to Target, bought a collapsible fire escape ladder, returned, hung the ladder on the rim where the skylight had been, and dropped right into that lab.

Because of the access that came with this creativity, I was seeing horrible things. I saw mice with horrific head implants, chickens packed seven to a small wire cage, and injured animals on the killing floor of slaughterhouses.

Finding Homes

There is a visceral "I have to get these animals out of here" response to seeing animals in those conditions. We had access to many animals. The missing link was finding homes.

We began canvassing people in our area who had land. Almost every one of them slammed the door in our face – figuratively, and sometimes literally.

I remember having to go back to an egg farm after this, having to look at those birds, and not being able to explain to them why we had to walk away without taking them with us.

The best way you can support people who rescue animals is to offer a home. The best way to support animals, if you are offered such an opportunity, is to give them a home. Whether the animals were obtained legally or illegally. If you want to support these actions, and you want to save animals, give the animals a home.

We couldn't find more than a couple people willing to take more than a couple of animals. We were able to rescue a few here and there, but if we wanted to do anything on a grander scale, we had to transport animals across state lines. There were just no homes.

I set my sights on networking with people who knew people who could home animals. This became my priority.

We did some things during this period that were very hasty and unplanned. I can't say I would advise against them, because they got the job done, but they were outside the bounds of conventional wisdom. Specifically I'm recalling two occasions where we took animals from places having literally no idea where they were going. No homes lined up. We decided to take the animals first, and figure the rest out later.

Those particular situations were so dire we felt we had to act. And there is something interesting that came from that: We always found homes when we had no choice but to find homes.

This is in direct conflict with everything you'll read about animal rescues. Conventional wisdom states you must always find homes for animals in advance.

My experience is such that when you have an animal in your custody, and you have to find homes, you always find homes.

Where Do Animals Rescued By The ALF Go?

With many rescues, such as mink, fox, deer, and game farms, the animals are released directly into the wild. No homes required.

For the rest, the info we can draw from ALF literature is limited. If we knew where the animals went, so would the police and FBI.

Simply put, animals are homed wherever there are homes. There is no ALF sanctuary. There is no one-size-fits-all answer. Ask yourself if you know someone who fits these parameters:

- Can give a lifetime home to an animal.
- Has the fortitude to not talk to police, and who will be willing to go to jail before giving your name to police.
- Can house the animals in a way that they will not be noticeable to visitors or neighbors.

-or-

- Are distant enough from the action that visitors will not have heard of the rescue in the news (actions that receive nationwide attention excluded)

If you or someone you trust knows someone who fits these guidelines, then you have your answer – that's where the animals go.

Architecture Of Animal Rescue

What of the animal rescue learning curve? Were you, tonight, to say - "I'm ready," how long until you are standing inside a laboratory at 1am, lowering rabbits into duffel bags?

In truth, the barriers to entry are small and easily cleared. Here they are, in order:

1. Acceptance
Jail will not be a likelihood, but it is a possibility, and liberators accept that the necessity of their actions exceeds the risk of prison.

2. Skills
The range here is vast. Rescuers for the most part have fewer laborious skills to master and a cheaper toolbox than the average criminal, and for greater ends. Learning lock picking takes mere days. And while not necessary, that may be the most complex skill you ever learn.

3. People
Required are those who are driven, composed under pressure, willing to go to prison before talking to police. If you know such a person, you have a partner in your first liberation.

4. Resources
The actions that run best can be those which use the least. The actions that run best are carried out by those who don't overestimate the tools needed to accomplish the goal. Where there is no car, one might use a bike. Where there are no expensive radios, there is the will to stay within eyeshot of your co-conspirator and do it anyway. A tank of gas costs $30. Resources should never be the obstacle.

5. Empowerment

Start with the safe assumption that even the largest rescues were carried out not by trained operatives, but compassionate people who simply dedicated themselves to the mission.

6. Homes

A place for the animals to live out their lives at peace.

Those rescuing wildlife are relieved of this burden.

Animal Liberation In Seven Steps

That is the architecture. What is the process in linear form?

Criticisms have been directed at some of the few existing in-depth ALF narratives (see *Free the Animals*) accusing them of oversimplifying animal liberation actions. Those who find discomfort in the rather inornate truth of animal rescues fall prey to the impulse of disbelief – a psychological safety device keeping animal liberation safely out of reach, in the untouchable realm of the superhuman. These limiting beliefs bring the comfort of excused inaction, yet none of the available windows into animal liberations support these notions of prohibitive complexity.

To put in more focused terms, let's draw from existing accounts on significant actions, as well as personal experience, and examine the anatomy of an animal rescue:

Choose A Target: Resources from trade journals to *FinalNail.com* are utilized to locate a target – from a quail farm to a research lab.

Find People: A determination is made on the absolute minimum needed to accomplish the goal, and trusted people are recruited on a strict as-needed basis.

Identify A Point Of Entry: In pre-raid visits, points and methods of entry are determined. Methods used have ranged from cutting fences to drilling through walls.

Action: The raid is executed.

Post-raid: Communiques are sent (if applicable), evidence disposed of, and animals homed.

The work of the ALF animal liberator does not end there. Any factors which contribute to the potential for police interactions should be examined. Above all, the mission continues through silence: knowing that the weakest link in an illegal act is the threat of loose talk, and the raider never speaks of their actions to anyone, ever.

For The Win

You don't learn to free mink by reading ALF stories. You learn to free mink by going to a mink farm at midnight. You don't learn to raid a lab by watching ALF footage. You learn to raid a lab by going to a lab. There is always a way in.

During my time in prison, I saw countless people who had risked more for money than you and I ever have for animals. I knew a professional burglar who would cut through skylights and repel down inside to get his hands on expensive items. I knew a man who rented a semi, backed up to a Wal Mart distribution center, and filled it with hundreds of thousands of dollars of expensive electronic equipment.

It was fascinating to see how people we call "criminals" were willing to apply more creativity in the pursuit of profit than you and I have in pursuit of animal liberation. I look at this as a challenge to all of us.

Next time you're asking yourself: "I want to rescue this animal, but I don't know how," or "I don't have the courage," or, "I don't know where to start." Just remember: if that rabbit was a bag of money, there is someone a lot dumber than you who would figure it out.

You can do it.

Applying Direct Action

Lecture transcript
Animal Rights National Conference
"The ALF knows the best way to respond to increased security is to go around it."

For nearly a decade (as of the time of this writing), I have participated in an annual panel at the Animal Rights National Conference titled "Applying Direct Action."

The term "direct action" is ambiguous and evolves across generations. Each year the panel is an eclectic mix of activists with their own definitions and angles.

Mine is always the same: Breaking the law, anonymously, to achieve direct results for animals.

What follows are excerpts from nearly ten years of these panels.

When I started down the path that ultimately led to me breaking the law for animals, it followed a predictable lineage. One I believe is followed by most who carry out ALF actions.

People start by becoming vegan. Then they decide that's not enough. Then they get involved in entry-level activism. Then they decide that's not enough.

That was the point where I began to ask myself, "Am I actually saving animals by following the classic protest model?" I knew it wasn't saving animals fast enough.

At that point I began to look around my neighborhood and ask myself, "Well how can I directly intervene in animal suffering?" Not just protest and make a symbolic effort, but actually throw myself between animals and their killers. To get animals out of these places and directly save their lives.

So we began to look around our neighborhood in Seattle. It's amazing what you'll find if you look around your own neighborhood. What's happening to animals just under the surface will blow your mind.

It began being young and not having any intention of doing anything illegal, but just investigating my neighborhood to see what was there.

I remember taking a small road trip to investigate an animal research laboratory. We were just very interested in learning what they were doing to animals inside. Zero plan whatsoever. We were able to access the roof. On the roof, there was a maintenance room. The door to it was unlocked. They had not anticipated anyone getting access to the roof, so in all likelihood it was always unlocked. Inside this room was another door, which opened to a staircase that descended directly into the top floor of this lab. With minimal effort, we had full access to this laboratory at two o'clock in the morning.

I remember crawling through a chute that led pigs to the killing floor slaughterhouse, to gain access to the killing floor.

Again, it was curiosity-driven at this stage. This is the phase I was in when I was trying to figure out how I could have a serious impact for animals outside of the formulaic protest model.

There there was a point after looking around my neighborhood, where we decided to set our sights on fur farms. We were able to release many thousands of mink and fox before I was caught and went to prison.

The Power of the ALF

What was most inspiring to me about crossing that threshold from legal activism to illegal activism is the results we achieved. There were six fur farms where I was charged with releasing mink. Of those, two had to shut down forever.

This success was as much credited to the ineptitude of fur farmers to install even basic security measures as it was my skill as a liberator. But to me the only argument I need for direct action is that it can close farms down. The only argument I needed is that it saved animals. For the first time, I was watching caged animals run free.

At the end of the day results are all that we answer to. All we answer to are those animals. It's not the person on your left, or the person on your right. It's not law enforcement. It's not a judge. It's only the animals. That's it.

Here is an equation to highlight how high-impact stepping outside the law is. I'm going to talk about this conference. You have here today 1,500 people who come to this event. Many of us took time out of our jobs or school. We put a lot of resources into being here. We put money into hotels and travel. I'm in no way condemning this. I did exactly what I described in order to be here today. We're all going to benefit greatly from this event in the end.

But consider this for a moment. What if every single person here, instead of coming to this conference, dedicated the same amount of time and resources into pairing off and visiting a fur farm today. If we bought some small tools, and a tank of gas, and raided the nearest fur farm. And then if every single person paired off and visited another fur farm tomorrow, I would argue you would effectively have no fur industry in this county by the end of the weekend. Think about that for a moment.

Let's continue this thought. What if every one of the 1,500 people here, instead of being at this conference, paired off and went to a veal slaughterhouse tonight and burned it down. You would effectively cease veal production in this country. If every person here today paired off and went to a farm that breeds quail for hunts, hundreds of thousands of animals would be saved. That is the power of direct action.

While it is great that we come together to network and learn, the question is what do we do with that. The power of direct action is so massive, we can destroy most animal abuse industries that exists, even with our current numbers.

There are some battles in this movement that will be won through a reasoned argument, or a, "Please and thank you." And there are many that will be won through crowbars, through drills, and through lock picks. We must accept this if we're going to be effective as a movement.

The Education Of Liberation

Direct action at its best, when you look at history, is not just liberation, but also education. Recently there was a large-scale mink release in Utah. Myself and local activists got together and said, "The media is grossly misrepresenting this action. They're giving fur industry soundbites to the public verbatim. How can we capitalize on this? How can we turn something bad into something good?"

So we put out a simple press release. It read, essentially, "I, Peter Young, offer $2,500 to the legal defense of anyone arrested for this raid."

The media devoured this. It was incendiary. I had an hour on the biggest conservative talk radio news show in Salt Lake City, where I kept most of the conversation off of fur, and on things that were actually more directly related to people's consumer choices like eating animals. It was in every major newspaper. Again, this is capitalizing on the ALF to obtain priceless media coverage.

As an endnote, two people eventually were arrested for this mink release, and I had to pay the $2,500. Which I was not expecting.

We have an obligation as above-ground activists to leverage ALF actions to bring attention to animal suffering. Every time you hear about an ALF action in your area, contact the media. We have an invaluable opportunity because the media almost always covers ALF actions. The hard work has been done. And we totally drop the ball in the above-ground by not using this coverage to draw more attention to animal suffering.

I can tell you from being involved in actions, I would often shake my head when above-ground activists failed to speak for us, and more importantly the animals, after a raid. Nobody would use our actions and the media coverage they generated to give the animals a voice. We didn't have a voice either. We were underground. We couldn't contact the media beyond a single anonymous communique. Understand that obligation.

Maximizing ALF Impact Through Superior Strategy

In the US we have not maximized the power of the ALF because our application and strategy has been imperfect.

I want to propose a new model for the ALF. And I know none of us here are ever going to do anything illegal. Yet if the ALF is out there listening to me right now, this is what I would suggest as a new model for ALF tactics.

The first element of strategy is to avoid small-scale sabotage. Go only for high impact actions. Because I promise you if you're sitting in a jail cell, you want to know that you went to prison for something that truly saved animals. Not for something that had mere symbolic value.

My opinions on this have changed over the years. When I began carrying out ALF tactics, I was reading various ALF reports in animal liberation publications at the time. And I decided, okay, I'm going to do the things I'm reading about. I'm going to break out the windows of a McDonald's, or spray paint a fur store. Very small-scale sabotage.

I had a naive faith at the time in the power of militant vegans carrying out widespread yet small-scale sabotage tactics. I felt like we could be a true threat, even at this scale. My opinions have dramatically changed.

Part of the mistake I made, part of the mistake that most of us make, is that we have not demystified large-scale ALF tactics. We think they are the domain of the elite few who are smart enough, and clever enough, and crafty enough, to figure out how to get inside buildings. That's not the case. I learned these actions are simple.

I learned this after breaking countless McDonald's windows, when I eventually concluded, "This isn't getting the job done."

It did not take me long to get very good at getting into things. I remember going to an egg farm one night. And there was a padlock on the door. Most people at that point would turn around and walk away. But I realized if I could pull the shed door back far enough, I could slip inside. That's what my friends and I did.

These aren't superhero moves. This is all very basic. Again, the learning phase for me was as young as 18, 19, and I'm simply just very driven to find out what is being done to animals, and then driven to do something about it. So I decide to make that happen. These are tactics my friends and I were teaching ourselves, and all of it was incredibly simple.

The second strategic element is that ALF actions should always go after weak links and vulnerable industries. Not merely soft targets. A soft target is something that you hit opportunistically. Because it's easy, because you know no one is around, because it's in the middle of the country, because it's on a street without street lights.

But good strategy would dictate that you focus on the weak links in the chain that are going to have a high impact. Actions that deal a significant blow to a certain industry.

Direct action as a tactic is best applied to weak links in the animal abuse chain. Industries like foie gras. The fur industry. Niche industries that can realistically be taken out by a few people committing to risking anything to bring them to an end. Going after weak links should be the primary focus of the ALF.

Take an industry like foie gras. A very small industry. When you look at the infrastructure of the foie gras industry, it's shocking how small it is. Same with fur.

There was a man named Jonathan Paul who has been released from prison. He burned down a horse slaughterhouse. It closed down forever. And there is now effectively no horse slaughtering industry in this country to speak off, in part because of this actions. This is what just one or two people can do when they effectively execute ALF tactics.

The next element of strategy I would offer is the ALF should target the infrastructure of industries, not the retail end. You can think of this in terms of "upstream versus downstream." For every 100 McDonald's there's probably one meat distributor. For every 10 meat distributors, there's probably one slaughterhouse. Think about how you can move up the chain and go to the source. How you can go after an industry's infrastructure.

One example of note: I've long been obsessed with the fur industry. I read a lot of fur industry literature. When you read their literature, it's fascinating how candid they are. I read something the other day in a fur industry publication, stating explicitly that if one fur processing plant in south-central Wisconsin didn't exist, the entire fur industry in the US would be unable to function. That's amazing. This is an example of the targets to consider when shifting your thinking to what the vital linchpins are in weak industries.

The last strategic improvement would be to choose low-risk yet high-yield targets. It will come as a surprise to most people that it's actually riskier to break the windows at a fur store than it is to go to a fur farm and release thousands of animals. I've been to fur stores in the middle of the night. There's street lights, there's cars driving by, there's often people around. I've also been to fur farms in the middle of the night. There's nobody around. It's just you, those animals, and a sleeping farmer. The chances of getting caught are almost insignificant.

Unless you make some hasty mistakes. Like I did.

If the ALF optimized its strategy, we would see amazing results. Much greater than we've seen. Saving individual animals is always something to celebrate. In addition to saving individual animals, we can also take out whole industries. But only if the ALF's actions are strategically applied.

Always ask how you could fight smarter and not just harder.

The Psychology of Infiltration

Let's talk about a false dichotomy that exists, that of a divide between "the ALF" and "everyone else." This is exemplified in things people say, like,

- "Do I want to join the ALF, or do I want to be an above ground activist?"
- "Do I want to leaflet, or do I want to go out and save animals?"

197

There is a myth we've perpetuated as a movement. A myth that there's the ALF, and then there's everybody else. It's as though there's an illusion that by carrying out ALF actions, you cross a threshold into an alternate world. Almost like you join the Mafia. The language that people use when they describe the ALF is very telling. It's as though you're crossing a line, past which your life is never going to be the same.

It's not necessary to make an elaborate production or identify around carrying out an ALF action. You don't need to do soul-searching. You don't need to meditate, take deep breaths, and say, "Okay, I think I'm going to do it." Instead, it's something that you can just decide to do one night, and it's possible you'll never carry out an ALF action again.

People have frequently said things to me things like, "I would love to carry out ALF actions, but I'm just not ready yet. I'm just not there. Maybe one day."

Can you imagine somebody in high school who is 17 years old saying, "You know what? I would love to slip in the back door of the movie theatre so that I don't have to pay $8, but gosh, I'm just not ready yet. It's going to take a couple more years of psyching myself up."

Doesn't that sound silly? The fact is most ALF actions are no more complicated than sneaking into a movie. And sneaking into a movie is something most of us at some point have done without even thinking about it.

In this way, we tragically misframe direct action as something ominous. But you don't have to be a Jedi.

The Myths Of Direct Action

Here is one pervasive myth about direct action: That carrying out direct action equals going to prison. That is a falsehood. Practically speaking, almost nobody gets caught. We need to apply sound risk-assessments, not fear-based hysteria.

Let's talk about common myths about the ALF. Specifically, disempowering myths that we hold about the ALF as a movement that keep people from working outside the law.

Among the largest is that the ALF is sole the domain of well-trained warriors. That their tactical toolbox is the stuff of ninjas. On some level, most of us believe ALF tactics require specialized skills.

Humor me for a second. How many people here have gone to school for four years? Okay. How many people have gone to school for two years? Okay. So that's almost everybody here. Studying something even for two years is a long time.

How many people here... Actually don't raise your hand if this is true... How many people here have spent even just four days learning how to pick locks? Okay. Nobody of course.

The point is that picking locks is something that would give you essentially a universal key to many facilities that imprisons animals. Yet we don't even spend just four days out of our life to learn it.

Many of the tactics used in ALF actions are tactics we believe are more complicated than they are. When you strip away the layer of mystique, almost nothing is as complicated as you think it is. This is true across the whole spectrum of activism.

In an interview, a jewel thief is asked how he learned to bypass burglar alarms. He answers that he had the most elaborate system available installed in his home, and spent months experimenting with it. We know vegans among us who spend months learning to properly bake vegan donuts, yet so few who dedicate even a small portion of this time to learning the craft of animal rescues or sabotage.

I have an update to a story I told here last year. Forgive me if you've heard this story before. I'm repeating it because it has an update that offers a powerful lesson.

The FBI searched my house ostensibly because they believed that I was involved in a raid of a laboratory at the University of Iowa a number of years ago. After the FBI raid, myself and my roommate were driving around talking about this Iowa lab action.

He remarked to me, "You know the ALF rescued 400 animals at this lab, and by some estimates they did around $750,000 in damages. That had to be an inside job."

I said, "Okay. Well, why do you think that? Let's explore this." And he said, "Well, the reason I think that is because labs these days are impossible to get into. So for anyone to get inside a lab it has to be an inside job."

And I said, "OK. Let's go into this a little more. How do you know it's impossible to get inside of a lab?" And he said, "Well, everybody knows it's impossible to get inside of a lab. After all the labs got broken into in the 80's, all the labs increased their security, and you just can't do that anymore."

And I said,"Right. Okay. But how do you know?" And he said, "Come on man it's just common knowledge. Everybody knows you can't get inside labs."

We went back and forth a little and the discussion devolved into, "Look man, everybody knows this is true. What's your problem?" But he eventually admitted he had no evidence to support his belief.

My whole argument was, "You don't know one way or the other whether a lab is impossible to get into. You lack evidence because you've never gone to a lab to find out."

So here is the update: This conversation stayed with me for a while. Then last month I was driving westward from Chicago to visit friends in Des Moines, Iowa. I found myself driving through Iowa City, where the University of Iowa is.

I thought, "If the FBI is going to raid my house and take everything I own because they think I had something to do with the break-in at the University of Iowa, maybe I should go see this building they're accusing me of breaking into." So I pulled off the freeway, and found the laboratory right away. It's in the heart of downtown in a small college town. It was about 11:00 o'clock at night.

And I'm standing outside this lab and I'm thinking, "Okay, so if I was the ALF, how would I get into this lab?" This is the exact building the ALF broke into in 2004, rescuing 400 animals. I'm looking at this lab, looking up at the top floor, which is usually where they hide the animals. Either there or the basement. This building looks fortified. I'm sitting back thinking, this very impressive. How did they get into this building? There's only a couple of doors. It is a very small building. I took a lap around the building and it looks like a fortress. And I thought, "Wow! This may in fact have been an inside job like my friend theorized. It does seem pretty close to being impenetrable as far as buildings go." And I thought, "You know, let me just try something here." And I walk over to the front door of the University of Iowa psychology building. I tug on the door. It was open.

And I thought, "How ironic that the FBI would take so much effort to get a search warrant, and raid my house, and take my belongings. But the lab itself won't even lock its own front door."

Then I thought, "How fascinating is it that anybody, including myself, who would think of breaking into this lab, would step back and say, 'This is a difficult target - how would we even get through the front door?'" Especially a building that has been broken into before. You would assume it would be impossible. Certainly they would at least lock their door. But no.

I expect there were more locked doors between the front door and the animals. Of course there's more to an ALF raid than getting through the front door. Yet I think this highlights so clearly how many of our assumptions are just manufactured out of psychological convenience. Their grooves run deep out of sheer repetition. In that way, lies can become "truth." That was a lesson I was reminded of that night.

The ALF knows this. The ALF knows the best way to respond to increased security is to go around it. The ALF knows the best way to respond to the threat of prison is to not get caught.

I'll just give a couple examples. University of Arizona, 1989. There were 1,000 animals taken out of the labs. An anonymous article was written by someone who organized that raid. They dressed up like construction workers in the middle the day, went to the laboratory looking like school maintenance staff, took a drill to the door, removed the plate that locks the door into place, then replaced it with a plate of their own. That plate had been rigged so that when that door appeared to be closed, if they gave it a harsh tug, it would pop open. That's how they got inside this lab.

No One Is Against The ALF

I would assert that nobody in this room is against direct action. How many people who get so upset over the rescue of animals from a laboratory would have the same position against the June plotters in Nazi Germany who conspired to kill Hitler? How many people who are so upset by the burning down of a slaughterhouse would be upset over somebody rescuing a dog from somebody's backyard? Or rescuing a baby from a burning building for that matter? Any arguments you hear against direct action are internalized speciesim. Plain and simple.

This subject somehow become debatable when the suffering is not happening directly in front of us. The more physical distance we put between ourselves and what's happening to animals the more the subject of the ALF becomes debatable.

So if you have an argument against direct action, ask yourself if you could look an animal in the eye and give that same argument. Don't ask yourself if you could convince the person next to you, or your parents, or a debate audience. We only answer to those animals. That's it.

It is a myth that the general public does not support illegal animal liberations. When it comes to live liberations of animals taken out of abusive situations and re-homing them, or raiding farms, the public by and large supports these actions.

I estimate 30% of the mail I received in prison was not from people who would ever come to a conference like this, but average people from Middle America who read about my case, found me on the internet, and just wrote to say, "Great job. I think what you did is fantastic." Even prison guards in prison were vocally supportive.

When it comes to tactics like arson it becomes more dicey in terms of public support, but the common argument that people are alienated from our movement or alienated from becoming vegan when they hear about direct action is false. It totally misunderstands how people make decisions.

Lessons From The ALF

I haven't talked about this publicly but I've been quietly compiling material for a book on the secret history of the ALF during a certain period of history.

I've documented the stories of people who've chosen to share those stories with me. These are people who, over the past many years, have felt somewhat legally less constrained, and can share their stories with certain people in a certain context for the first time. I've compiled those stories into a book.

This book is primarily an action piece. What I'm going to cover here is the lessons I have distilled from speaking to these anonymous liberators. People who have put themselves on the line year after year to save animals, at great risk to themselves. People who risked prison, and more, to save animals.

Lesson one: Everyone had a deep sense of urgency. When I began to look at the patterns that emerge in the stories the ALF shared with me, one big one stood out: every single person that carried out these actions had a tremendous sense of urgency when it came to animal abuse.

This is something much more powerful than "motivation" or a "driving force." This is the primary factor that separates people who carry out ALF actions from the people that do not. It is a sense of urgency.

Lesson two: It is a myth that ALF tactics are the domain of highly-trained people.

No one I spoke with went to burglary school. No one I spoke with went to locksmithing school. No one was trained in any kind of clandestine tactics. They simply had a strong sense of purpose, they sized up the obstacles, and they taught themselves how to overcome those obstacles to save animals.

There's one person I spoke with who learned how to pick locks for the purpose of rescuing animals. I had all these questions for him. I said, "How did you learn how to pick locks? Who taught you? Where did you get the lock picks?"

He said, in effect, "I don't even remember many details. I just knew that I had a mission, I had to accomplish it. I knew that there was a lock between me and these animals, and I taught myself to pick locks."

Lesson three: The ALF learns by doing. They did not learn through book research. They learned by putting themselves in a situation where they had no choice but to learn, and they learned.

There was a story that I heard from activists involved with removing animals from a laboratory. The people that I spoke with told me that they did not have any idea how to do this. Remember, essentially we're talking about burglarizing a building. They said, "We had no idea how to do this."

But they put themselves in the building and looked for opportunities. They learned by putting themselves physically in a place where they wanted something to happen, and let the necessary path unfold. In this particular instance, they found an unlocked door with a set of keys in it.

How many of us sit back and think and think about raiding a lab, and think, "I wouldn't know how or what to do." We get locked into "analysis paralysis." Consequently, we never put ourselves in a situation where "what to do" will become clear.

Lesson four: People who carry out ALF actions have dispelled the myth that carrying out an illegal action equates to prison. This is very different from being prepared for prison, although that is an element. It is understanding how to manage and mitigate risks.

I think most of us consciously or subconsciously have an equation in our heads that goes, "If I do this thing, I will go to prison." So we ask ourselves the question, "Am I willing to go to prison?"

Everyone I spoke with did put that question to themselves. But what I thought was an interesting twist is, they didn't have the belief, "We're willing to do this because we're willing to go to prison." There was a sober assessment of the risk and how to mitigate it, and they decided the chances of going to prison were very small. Much smaller than we've been led to believe.

Everyone I spoke with was comfortable with going to prison, but they also did not believe it would happen. That may seem reckless, but more accurately I would say it is having a sober assessment of risk.

Lesson five: Nothing happens until you get out of your house and start trespassing. These ALF members were obsessed with doing research on foot. If they found out about a lab, they would go there. If they found out about a slaughterhouse, they would go there. If they found out about a factory farm, they would go there.

The greatest insights and advancements in a plan only happen when you get out of your house, get off the internet, and do the footwork.

Lesson six: People who carried out these actions were not fearless. They used their fear as fuel. Someone I spoke with, when I asked him, "What is one thing you really want to come across in this story?" He said, essentially, "Please highlight how calm we were when we were carrying out these raids." He said, "The people that I worked with, we were always very calm. We were so on purpose that it transcended the fear."

It was not the absence of fear, but it was fear used as fuel. Fear used to motivate.

Lesson seven: The people I spoke with were far too humble to ever say this in this exact way, but I extrapolated something from what they told me. There is a tremendous chasm between the doers and the critics. Between the talkers and the critics. The people I spoke with are very unassuming. Most of the time they did not wear radical t-shirts. They had few tattoos among them. They weren't terribly outspoken. They weren't people who you would identify as being a fist-waving radical.

I liken it to how you identify the poorest person in the room. It's always the guy who talks about how much money he has. These people were unassuming, and never the big talkers. They were focused on what they were going to do about the problem. Not focused on getting an audience. Not focused on creating and cultivating an image of being somebody that was willing to take action. They were simply people who actually took action.

This humility was evident in this rough quote said to me by an anonymous ALF operative:

"We're not terrorists." He said, "We're not even freedom fighters. When you see suffering and you have the ability to do something about it, that's just being a decent human being."

Out Obligations

Consider how the first generation to achieve animal liberation is going to look back on us right here, right now. They're going to ask how we stood by and had a friendly college debate about animal suffering when it was happening right under our nose. These are the same questions we put to the citizens in Nazi Germany. We ask them, "How did you let this happen right under your nose?" We will be asked that same question ourselves one day. A large part of the conversation is going to be how we sat by and acted so well-behaved and so obedient to the law when mass-murder was happening all around us.

We are the servants of animals. That's all we are. We're not the servants of judges, of courts, of cops, of the people around us. We only serve the animals. That's our only obligation as activists.

We have an obligation to act in their service. That means to be their guardian angels when the situation calls for it. But it also means when the situation calls for it, to be their claws and fangs.

That's what the ALF is.

I'll end with a quote that captures the spirit of the ALF more than anything else, from a book titled *Frogs Into Princes*:

"When you hesitate you're acting as though you are immortal. And you ladies and gentlemen, are not. You do not know the place and hour of your death. And so the one thing you can do to remind yourself not to hesitate is to suddenly glance over your left shoulder and remember that death is standing there, and make death your adviser. He will always tell you to do something representative of your full potential as a person. You can afford no less."

Questions

Audience member: When you talk about going to places and breaking into places to get a lot of animals out. I'm just wondering what do you do with them? Where do those animals go? I'm wondering about logistics.

The "top two" obstacles when it comes to executing an action are these: One is, where do we put the animals? And the second one is, where do I find people to work with?

You have to draw from your immediate circle of people you trust. First assess who can house animals without asking outright and implicating yourself before an action even happens. Then approach those you trust.

This is among the weakest links in an action. Because the person who takes in animals is not just someone exposed to risk while they're carrying out an action, as you are. It's somebody who is exposed to risk for the life of that animal. Because you're essentially in possession of stolen property.

It's up to each person as an individual to ask themselves: Who do I know? Who can house animals? Who is not going to talk freely about where the animals came from?

To anyone here who supports the ALF yet will never carry out an ALF action, the best thing you can do to support the ALF is offer homes for animals.

On this subject, I would like to highlight the option of carrying out animal rescues where no homes are required. This is overlooked and massively significant.

The scale of wildlife farming in this country is huge. I think we know about fur farms. There's a lot of those. And you can release mink directly into the wild. You can release fox directly into the wild. And the addresses for those farms are widely available. You can go to FinalNail.com for example.

Yet there is also a huge, massive, invisible empire of wildlife farms out there that house and breed quail, woodchucks, squirrels, and much more. I've been to a skunk farm. There's tons and tons and tons of these niche industries that you don't even think exist that imprison animals you can release directly into the wild.

It's up to every individual to figure out where these places are. There's no directory to speak of for wildlife farms. But I guarantee you can do a public record request to state wildlife or agriculture departments. This would leave an incriminating paper trail of course, which could be an issue. But you can do a public records request to your local US Fish and Wildlife Department, or the Department of Agriculture, and just say, "I want to know where all the chipmunk farms are in my state." And you will get a stack of papers back. I've done this. You will get a stack with hundreds and hundreds of addresses. It's amazing. And these are farms that can be raided, and you won't even require homes for animals. They can be released directly into the wild.

Audience member: What do you do in small countries like France where you can't release thousands of animals because there's nowhere for them to go?

The one thing I would say is that you have to work with what you have. There is always a way. Work with the circumstances that you have available to you. We can't release certain animals in the wild here because they're not native, yet they could be released in other countries. The bottom line is, I don't care what country you live in, there's never a shortage of things to do.

Anyone who thinks, "There's no good targets in my town," is out of touch. You just work with what you have. I don't know about mink in particular when it comes to habitat in France. I can't speak to that. But there's always a way you can target that industry in other ways, or save animals in other ways.

Audience member: What's the best way to report my actions so that you guys can know what I'm doing? The second part is how can I find like-minded individuals to join me?

This is a really important lesson for everyone in this room. If you have something you've done that is legally sensitive, you should never ever, ever tell anybody that you've done this legally sensitive thing. Especially a room full of people like this, that is probably peppered with feds.

Loose lip sink ships. Nobody talks, everybody walks.

The Communique: Voice Of The Underground

Article
Animal Liberation Front: Communique Collection
"The communique is the story of the ALF, in the only way available to them to tell it."

An excerpt from a limited-run document I released (and soon took out of circulation), compiling two decades of communiques from the ALF and other groups who work outside the law to save animals.

When compassionate raiders break down the doors to a university lab and spirit animals to freedom, they have only one opportunity to deliver their message: the communique.

Issued anonymously (and untraceably) in the hours or days following an ALF action, these dispatches from the animal liberation underground offer activists their sole chance at managing public perception, educating the public, admonishing animal abusers, and inspiring others to take up crowbars and make animal liberation a reality... *tonight*.

Pre-internet, news outlets and above-ground groups would tell of receiving packets of info via the mail (or doorstep) in the wake of high profile ALF raids - packets containing various combinations of typed communique, copies of confiscated documents, photos, and video of the raid.

Today, they tell of communiques arriving to inboxes, via disposable accounts and public computers surely never to be touched by the raider's hands again.

Once disseminated, these snapshots of history often fade from view and memory, evading the history books through the hyper-transience of the digital age. Yet history was meant to be told, and ALF communiques are the history of a movement – history as told by those who made it.

Unavailable to explain themselves publicly by the very nature of their work, the communique is the press release of those without a call back number, the stage for those in hiding, the microphone for those without a voice.

Of all names claimed by those who work above the law for animals, the Animal Liberation Front holds the title of most used, and most recognizable. When the guidelines of the ALF are found to be too confining – or the pressures of its history too great – there are those who do their work under different banners. Included in the history of the animal liberation communique are dispatches from the Animal Liberation Brigade, Justice Department, and others. Common to them all, the understanding that in some battles, working within the law will win you favor from the police, and little else.

The communique lends itself to the Who, What, When, and Why. The How is more elusive. On occasion, anonymous "how it was done" narratives will surface, offering a step-by-step tactical breakdown of a chosen ALF action in which the author took part.

Outside these pieces, and the occasional ALF arrest, the communique is the only unfiltered glimpse we ever have into the minds and motives of "the animals' last hope."

Communiques serve the under-appreciated purpose of forcing visibility upon abusers. When animal exploiters thrive on staying under the public's radar, their response to a large scale action is often to pretend it didn't happen. And when impossible – deny it was animal liberators (*see E-L Labs, 3- 89, University of Iowa, 11-04*). The communique puts exploiters in a rare defensive stance, an uncomfortable place for those guilty of the indefensible.

With the communique, the necessary conditions of their composition bring all the mystique of the prison-scribed memoir or message in a bottle from a lost ship at sea. They bring up images of road-worn liberators, the morning after in an obscure rural town, fighting sleep over a note pad, debating the finer points of style and message before disseminating the final product and living to fight another day... and night.

The general communique adheres to the who/what/when/where/why formula, but the tastes of the anonymous authors varies slightly more on the issue of tone. Most consistent is the utter seriousness and sense of urgency that is requisite to any ALF action. But some offer undertones of humor, while others do not stray in the slightest from a staunch battle-cry. On either end of this spectrum, no matter the taste of the audience, their words cannot be reduced to mere rhetoric. Inherent in the communique is the integrity of the authors – integrity in their willingness to put action before their words.

The communique is the story of the ALF, in the only way available to them to tell it.

Unconventional Liberator

Article
Bite Back Magazine
"Our mission is not only nobler than the safecracker, our short-term gains are more easily achieved."

The tactics and psychology that drives profit-motivated criminals are written of in explicit detail, available to all. Their secrets are practiced, honed, and recorded. And their application to activism is obvious and direct.

But these books won't be found on the "animal rights" shelf of a bookstore. And these books are off the radar of most activists. Yet most often they offer more inspiration and instruction than any-thing originating from within the animal liberation movement.

This is an article about looking outside the movement for tactics that produce results.

It is not from animal rights books that we will find the tactics that will bring the next phase of animal liberation. Rather, it is from less convention-al sources that these advances will be sourced.

In my reading, I am often both inspired and disappointed that there are people employing more ingenuity in making money than you or I ever have in helping non-human animals. I am inspired by the creativity at work in both legal and illegal pursuits of profit, and disappointed that the plight of the billions slaughtered does not push our ingenuity far beyond that of those who work from less benevolent motives. It is this history that those who win the next major achievements for animals will draw from, to move us ahead towards total liberation.

The struggle for animal liberation will not be won the way other move-ments have won. This struggle is more different than we admit. Many of the greatest strategies for animals have come not only from history or polit-ical science books, but rather from the stories of those who have fought for much less noble reasons. The unconventional liberator has read *Long Walk to Freedom* (Mandela). She has also read books on police science, persuasion psychology, and no-tech hacking. The unconventional liberator has read books on the histories of liberation struggles. He has also drawn selectively from *The Spy's Guide: Office Espionage* and *The Big Con*. The results-oriented activist draws from those who achieve results.

We should be much more driven than the subjects and authors of these books. More driven than the autograph hound who takes improvisational act-ing classes to fine tune his infiltration skills for getting backstage at a concert, when getting inside the Seattle Fur Exchange would yield so much more. And we should be much more driven than the Arizona burglars who recent-ly shimmied through an air duct to steal purebred dogs from a pet store for resale on the black market, when removing abused animals from a laboratory would be far more virtuous.

The books on liberation struggles and those who have achieved long-term change are both invaluable as well as well-studied. Overlooked but no less valuable are those books with hidden gems of strategy and methodology, those books which at first glance appear irrelevant to the issue at hand, but from which comes a wellspring of innovative and applicative material.

We will achieve our ends by both education and liberation. And I see overlooked and underdeveloped approaches in each path. For education, it is primary we understand the basic psychological principles that govern influence, as marketers have done in selling their products for decades. And for liberation, learning the tactics used by those who throughout history have pursued less noble goals.

I will give attention here to both, highlighting books that showcase strategies that can be re-contextualized and applied towards helping non-human animals.

The Art of Deception (Kevin Mitnick)
Private Investigators will tell you that of the cases not solved through publicly available information, the vast majority of their cases are solved through dumpster diving and a tactic known as *social engineering*.

Social engineering is a collection of techniques used to persuade people into performing actions or divulging confidential information (primarily over the telephone, yet often in person). Using anywhere from crude to advanced psychology, the skilled social engineer has the power to finesse information out of anyone, anytime. From persuading a police officer into performing a warrant search over the phone to talking a crucial computer password out of an office clerk, no information is off limits to the skilled social engineer.

Utilizing tactics such as pretexting (creating and using an invented scenario to persuade someone to divulge information) to "credibility props" and more, this is an invaluable tactic to achieve gains in any above or underground campaign.

Some information that can be obtained through social engineering:

* Locations of unknown sites
* Obtaining home addresses for people of interest
* Security protocols

…and quite simply anything anyone knows which he or she are not supposed to tell you.

Some of the most fantastic stunts in history have been performed not through physical force but verbal finesse. As the opening chapter details, the largest bank robbery in history was performed over the telephone.

And we can no doubt assume companies will guard wire transfer codes for 10-figure bank accounts more vigilantly than they will the location of their unlisted satellite research facility.

Access All Areas (Ninjalicious)
By the editors of the zine *Infiltration* ("The zine about going places you're not supposed to go"), *Access All Areas* is a thorough look at urban exploration. It should need no explaining the myriad ways in which these tactics for expanding freedom of movement within our landscape can be applied toward animal liberation campaigns. Subjects include everything one can imagine under the banner of "going places you are not supposed to go," from bypassing front desk security to obtaining roof access. While the writing is less than stellar, the content is solid and applicable to countless goals and campaigns.

Influence (Robert Cialdini)
As a marketing book, this is not immediately apparent as a title offering anything that will achieve victories for animals. *Influence* is a classic work on the psychology of gaining compliance, and details the principals at work in many of the titles described in this article. The book looks in depth at the six principals of influence, and how they can be applied in communications. It is a must read as a supplement to books like *The Art of Deception*, and anyone wishing to improve their success in anything from leafleting to being stopped on a farm at midnight.

Confessions of a Master Jewel Thief (Bill Mason)
Overlooking the less-than-charitable aims of its protagonist, the reader of *Confessions of a Master Jewel Thief* finds what is certainly a rarely-used model for the animal liberator: working alone. In light of increased surveillance, repression and informants, this title offers the incredible story of one of the most prolific and low-tech ventures in history. *Confessions* is the story of one man, using only a grappling hook and flashlight, capitalizing on unlocked 2nd-story-and-above doors and windows and becoming the most successful jewel thief in US history. What nearly every reader may overlook is the hidden lessons in this otherwise mainstream mass-market crime story: solo can be best, and low-tech does not mean low-yield.

Art of Intrusion (Kevin Mitnick)
Super hacker Kevin Mitnick's follow-up to *The Art of Deception*, *Art of Intrusion* ("The Real Stories Behind the Exploits of Hackers, Intruders & Deceiv-

ers") showcases numerous high- and low-tech exploits. Much of the material is arcane and specialized, yet there are crumbs of valuable advice to be found within. Follow the front-to-back workings of a "penetration test," in which a group of hackers are paid to test a company's security for every imaginable weakness: from perimeter security to document disposal. Stimulates thought on what is possible with a little confidence and a lot of passion.

The Burglars Guide To The City (Geoff Manaugh)
An instant classic in the unintentional genre of "how-to manuals disguised as criminology texts." The author promises to show "how any building transforms when seen through the eyes of someone hoping to break into it." In a lightning-round analysis of overnight art heists, tunnel jobs, and bank vault infiltrations; we learn how high-level burglars reverse-engineer structures for their weaknesses, and get whatever is in the building - out of it.

You can't have burglary without architecture, and this is the guide to understanding loopholes of design and how they yield great victories for burglars of *all* kinds.

Conclusion

The tactical toolbox of the animal liberator was assembled less by the animal liberators before them than by criminals with less noble motives. Our mission is not only nobler than the safecracker or penetration tester, its short-term gains are more easily achieved. It is the new wave of liberator who knows that only through tactical innovation will we achieve animal liberation.

From Obstacle To Opportunity: Security and Surveillance, Reframed

Article
North American Animal Liberation Press Office Newsletter
"As a movement, survival demands that what they package as 'obstacles,' we must redefine as opportunities."

I've watched the conversation on advanced ALF tactics turn from empowered to defeatist. While the ALF has repeatedly gotten inside and raided labs, sentiments like "Security is too tight to get inside labs anymore" are rampant. Apathy will always find an excuse.

The dominant belief in the movement is that increased technology has rendered old tactics impossible. You miss 100% of the shots you don't take, and the people who believe this are the ones who have never made the attempt.

Upon publication, this article was criticized for putting an unrealistically positive spin on something (increasingly sophisticated security and surveillance) that presents a genuine threat to activists. Soon after this saw print, an animal research lab trade publication published an article by a security consultant paid to audit lab security by trying to get inside. At every lab he visited, he found -

"…an over-reliance on security technology. This reliance had diminished the security program in its entirety."

This point - from the vivisection industry itself - vindicates the precise message of this article.

To respond with surrender to a perceived obstacle is to lay down and die, and thus fail the animals. I believe every perceived obstacle presents an opportunity.

This is an article about that mindset.

The increasing advance of the "crime deterrent" is uneclipsed in human history. Cell phones have become their roving microphones, cameras their outsourced eyes, and the silicon chip Big Brother's all-knowing brain. As a movement, survival demands that what they package as "obstacles," we must redefine as opportunities.

Many books cover counter surveillance and security circumvention. Eclipsing the need for a tactical checklist is a paradigm-shift - from that which frames advancing technology as the *loss* of options, to that which frames advancing technology as the *introduction* of new ones.

The re-framing of those things we deem "obstacles" infuses the power necessary to carry us forward when these obstacles would otherwise have us cower in despair.

Victory comes to the versatile, conquest to the fluid.

When does security increase, and when does it merely change forms? The beat cop of a century ago, once patrolling Main Street on foot, today does not leave his patrol car. As such, movement outside eyeshot of the road becomes invisible, and low-level noise at any distance – inaudible. The proportionate numbers of law enforcement have not increased dramatically, just their ability to increase selectivity and speed of processing data. There are not more human eyes, just the refining of what they see. When examined from this angle, many blind spots are revealed.

Survival in the face of increased security and surveillance requires a new approach. Will we perceive a ruined landscape of lost options, or see the unintentional introduction of hidden advantages? Acknowledging the subjectivity of new controls is not just necessary for morale, but for survival of the underground movement.

In a paradigm that holds increased technology as synonymous with decreased options, this blind faith often brings with it a blind spot. For a shift in attention *to*, is also a shift in attention *from*.

The Art Of Misdirection

The purchaser of high-tech security pays for the luxury of inattention. With this false sense of comfort, and blind faith in technology, she who circumvents an alarm finds herself in a much easier position to do a complete job once inside. When one pays for an alarm to tell them if all is not well, the un-tripped alarm translates to all being well. I have seen the fur farmer who invests five-figures in a perimeter alarm system, developing an arrogant confidence in that technology such that he suddenly feels comfortable moving to a house off-site. This creates a condition in which one knowledgeable in evading such alarms enjoys a much easier time emptying a farm than had the system never been installed. And so their perceived advantage becomes their actual demise.

The sinister byproduct of the social networking phenomenon is the revealing of one's entire social grid: "who knows who" is but one step from "who knows what." Investigations, typically hobbled by the laborious task of compiling lists of names, now have their lists compiled for them. Most preliminary investigation methods, from isolating a suspect's list of friends, to a list of those subscribing to a certain ideology in a given geographical range, are now accomplished not just warrantlessly, but from a desk. Today, an internet presence for almost all is a given. As emphasis for intelligence gathering by law enforcement shifts to the internet, the non-participant in social media becomes all the less traceable; with law enforcement all the more inept at employing alternative investigative methods, and all the more likely to omit non-digital strategies from their toolbox. The social networking abstainer thus becomes the unseen.

Increasing in rate are prosecutions based on placing suspects at crime scenes via cell phone signals. Cell phones are in constant transmission of their position to towers. The ubiquity of cell phones increases law enforcement's certainty in their use as a reliable tracking device. The person who leaves their cell phone at home is all the less suspect, and the person who does not own one at all is all but visible.

For those who commit legal transgressions, the early days of video surveillance brought a fearful paralysis of a new technology. Today, cameras are an idle threat, having reached such ubiquity there is a vastly diminished fear of any one camera being monitored in real time. Through their proliferation, cameras have rightfully devolved to the limp threat of the "no trespassing" sign. Assumptions in their deterrent value makes the undeterred liberator an even greater threat.

The permanent record of internet browsing history is well-understood. Yet even public computers have proven to be a liability, with records from such – in conjunction with visitor logs from a university vivisection website – being used to bring an indictment in a recent animal liberation case. While this appears on the surface to be a disturbing trend, it can be re-framed as an encouraging testimony to their emphasis on computers to solve crimes. The wise liberator who rejects the false promises of technology and the allure of their convenience achieves room to move within the invisible blind spot of trade journals, books, and analog resources.

If it is forensics they want in the courtroom, then they just may get what they are begging for. It should come to them as no surprise when there are those who respond to forensic threats by taking a page from less noble organized crime syndicates, and source forensics from animal abusers own trash - from hairs to objects laden with fingerprints - and plant them at the crime scene, to be recovered by forensics teams. An animal abuser's false conviction for insurance fraud is vastly more just than an Animal Enterprise Terrorism charge for those truly responsible. All the better for the saboteurs, and with one less abuser roaming the streets - the world.

Looking at the increased high profile use of informants and snitches in movements, there are those who do not respond with more despair but with better tactics, reformatting their work to be carried out alone. When their greatest weapons are the enemies within us, lone-liberators achieves greater freedom and stealth while insuring against defection from within their ranks. Shedding blind faith in "strength in numbers," we shift emphasis from the "cell" to the "self," render their most potent weapon useless, and stay free to fight another day.

With the technology we fear comes blind faith in its power – a truth to be exploited by both sides. The nighttime saboteur tracked via cell phone mails it to Tucson for the weekend to carry out a nighttime raid of a transgenic mice breeding facility in Hollister – serving not just the cause of suggesting innocence in a courtroom, but deterring suspicion entirely. Supreme faith in "supreme" technology introduces an increased sense of comfort, as in the laboratory which installs a state of the art security system and fires the security guard. The freedom fighter who has studied the system's flaws suddenly finds herself in a better position to enter undetected than with the presence of a guard, and their advantage becomes ours.

With this angle, there is opportunity in security and surveillance, when it brings their attention one direction while you operate in another. Attention re-directed is attention denied.

Simplicity Revisited

As security becomes increasingly technologically complex, low-tech methods become all the more effective. With the increase of confidence in technology, large gaps open on the spectrum's opposite end. And even where the gap is not large, some wiggle-room remains.

When they go high-tech, being effective can mean us going low-tech. The infiltrator deeming an alarm system beyond his ability to circumvent, instead hides in plain site, entering the building in disguise during business hours under the guise of a UPS delivery. High-tech methods of bypassing keypad-based security are forgone for a social engineering move that coerces an access code from a staff person over the phone under a "new employee" pretext. When techno-fetishism increases, so does the power of low-tech methods.

When they monitor our computers, it is because they expect us to use computers. When they track our movements through cell phones, it is because they take for granted our use of cell phones. Their power is dependent on our cooperation. Without it, we are not just under their radar, we are outside their paradigm. The well-compartmentalized life, in which computers are never used for the important work, and cell phones are never present during its planning or execution, brings a level of invisibility in the present day which the same behavior would not have brought just 15 years ago. As usage of technologies increase, their confidence and emphasis in tracking people with them increases at pace. One thing about living in a cell without bars: when you know which way to aim, you can exit anytime.

To misrepresent increased security as a decrease in options is movement suicide. While we are given no say in the advent of new technologies, ultimate control remains in how we respond. While we are never asked permission for cameras in public places or how communication tools will be used against us, we can claim control over whether we classify this shift as "defeat" or "advantage." Will we respond with surrender, guaranteeing failure for us and death for those we fight for; or instead bring life to a changing landscape with the application of creativity and reinvention?

The Leveraging of Strengths

On the front of resources and physical might, we can never win. Our weapons are circumvention, invisibility, surprise, and justness of purpose.

Previous ALF writings have cited Roger Taber's book *The War of the Flea* ("The Element of Surprise," *Bite Back Magazine*, 2003) offering necessary direction to a materially out-resourced resistance.

"The guerrilla fights the war of the flea, and his military enemy suffers the dog's disadvantages: too much to defend; too small, ubiquitous, and agile an enemy to come to grips with."

So begins Taber's work, emphasizing that any resistance that by most measures suffers a disadvantage, must focus on leveraging its strengths. A movement's more disempowering members would have us direct our energies on the opposition's strengths, and attack on fronts which we can not compete. If we can not compete in our numbers, we can only ask what advantages lower numbers offer. If we are not competitive in our resources, we can only ask what tools we do have that may strike a fatal blow. Wait a lifetime for a moment of random opportunity which may never come, or stand up and leverage our strengths today.

From Force Fed Distractions to Net-Losses

Their obstacles become our opportunities. In this art of reversal, those things packaged as roadblocks become their weaknesses. We can look to the history books for the volumes of stories offered as lessons on their dictates being turned against them – to their greater detriment than had they never been imposed.

This reversal is carried out to great effect in every struggle every day. Concerned people respond to inefficacy of spoon-fed protest models and act outside the law to achieve progress for non-human animals. Activists are sent to prison, and when their cases are publicized, the effect for many is not fear, but galvanization translating to more illegal actions carried out in their name. They send one of ours to prison, the slack is picked up threefold by inspired activists who respond with raids. The opposition yields a net loss as it suffers more blows against their machine than were ever carried out by the fallen liberator.

Advance

It is either momentum-reversal or defeat, tactical jujitsu or the end of the underground. We can not win this on the playing field of resources or legal standing. Only by capitalizing on their obstacles do we seize their power and make it ours.

How They Got In

Article
Unpublished
"Being effective most often means making your own doors."

The ALF's methods of entry are so shrouded in mystery, in some raids the police have announced publicly they are at a loss to explain how activists got inside. I drew from the limited information available to answer that question for numerous high profile ALF raids.

This is an article about how the ALF gets in.

Missing from much coverage on, and communiques from, the ALF's most expertly planned break-ins and live liberations are any mention of how the activists gained entry. And perhaps for good reason: revealing the method of access to the FBI and the action's target can provide clues to aid in the investigation, as well as alerting the facility and others to loopholes in security which could be patched, impeding future actions. Yet both the aspiring raider and academic voyeur reads of skilled raids on fortified facilities, and ask every time: *How did they get in?*

Compiled from communiques, "how it was done" articles, media reports, and ALF raid videos, a brief look at the most innovative surreptitious entry tactics, and what can be learned from them.

Action: 47 rats liberated from Scripps Hospital. San Diego, CA. February 10th, 2008.
Method of entry: Vivarium accessed via an unlocked door.
The lesson: It is more fruitful to find opportunity than to wait for opportunity to find you. Liberators make their own luck.

Action: 1,500 mink liberated from a fur farm. Astoria, OR. October 17th, 2008.
Method of entry: None needed. The farm, which spent its entire existence without its address made public, was comfortable enough in its anonymity to never have installed a fence. Within a month of its location being released publicly, the farm was raided.
The lesson: Forethought is not requisite for a farmer entering the fur industry, but it just may be necessary for them to stay in business.

Actions: The 90 recorded fur farm raids in the U.S. since 1995, seeing the release of hundreds of thousands of animals.
Method of entry: Activists report bypassing occasional photoelectric beam sensors by dropping to the ground and rolling under the beam.
The lesson: The low-tech can often defeat the high, and tricks from art gallery heist films do sometimes work.

Action: 21 mice liberated from Louisiana State University. New Orleans, LA. April 22nd, 2005.
Method of entry: Activists broke through a vent in a side door of the biology building.
The lesson: While doors may still be known as the worst way in, they can

never be ruled out.

Action: 88 mice and 313 rats liberated from University of Iowa. Iowa City, IA. November 14th, 2004.

Method of entry: While the lengthy communique reveals no clues as to how they bypassed alarms for the psychology building's security system, the video of the raid shows masked activists accessing doors with what appears to be key cards, and picking the lock of a secured elevator. Photos released post-raid also show activists reaching through a door to unlock it via a hole they had cut through the wood. Post-raid media coverage reports rooms were accessed via employee key cards which accessed more rooms than the card's issuers intended. Speculation centered around the raid being an inside job.

The lesson: Sophisticated security is only as secure as its most accessible key card.

Action: 115 chickens liberated from Merial Select Pharmaceuticals. Berlin, MD. February 27th, 2003.

Method of entry: Animal house accessed by cutting through the windows and wire mesh covers, bypassing the door alarm.

The lesson: Like most amateur burglars, animal abusers assume everyone goes through the front door. The wise liberator looks elsewhere.

Action: 14 beagles liberated from Huntingdon Life Sciences. East Millstone, NJ. March 31st, 2002.

Method of entry: Activists cut a hole through the ceiling to gain access to the animal house.

The lesson: Walls and roofs are less physical barriers than psychological ones.

Action: 179 birds liberated from Genesis Laboratories, a contract wildlife toxicology lab. Wellington, CO. August 28th, 2000.

Method of entry: Using a high-speed drill and 3/8" drill bit, activists drilled several holes into the lab's metal siding. Using bolt cutters, the holes were then used to begin cutting through the corrugated metal. Fiberglass insulation was stripped away, and an additional hole was cut into the drywall giving them direct access to the lab.

The lesson: With ALF actions, Europe knows best. This was the first recorded incident of U.S. activists importing the tried-and-tested UK tactic of drilling through walls.

Action: 116 animal liberated from the University of Minnesota. Millions of dollars in damage done to equipment in one building. Minneapolis, MN. April 5th, 1999.

Method of entry: The FBI was never able to determine how activists gained access to the two labs. Their best guess: the ALF free-climbed the wall of a five-story building and gained access through the roof.

The lesson: There is always a way in. And it's best if they never find out what it was.

Action: 31 animal liberated from Western Washington University. Bellingham, WA. October 24th, 1999.

Method of entry: Activists entered the basement of the WWU psychology building via unknown means. A set of keys was located in an unlocked office, giving them direct access to the labs and vivariums.

The lesson: Sometimes it is that easy, and you'll never know until you put yourself in a laboratory basement at midnight, prepared for anything.

Action: Break-in and sabotage at Washington State University Poultry Research Laboratory. Puyallup, WA. November 20th, 1999.

Method of entry: In the video released post-raid, activists are seen smashing through a first-floor window, and crawling through to access the lab.

The lesson: Aim for graceful, and settle for whatever works.

Action: Two days after the torching of its trucks, the San Diego Meat Company building is set on fire. San Diego, CA. January 30th, 1994.

Method of entry: Access gained via a boarded up window.

The lesson: Those who know have said that achieving maximum damage through arson means locating the structural center of the building. And this is totally unrelated to getting in.

Action: Break-in at animal researcher Frederick Knowlton's Utah State University office. Files taken and the office set on fire. Millville, UT. October 24th, 1992.

Method of Entry: Aluminum trim removed from a window, and suction cups used to remove a pane to gain access to the researcher's office.

The Lesson: Going through the window doesn't always mean dangerous decible-levels and excessive debris.

Action: Oregon State University Experimental Fur Farm has files confiscated, building set on fire, and equipment destroyed. Facility closed as a result of this action. Corvallis, OR. June 10th, 1991.

Method of entry: Unlocked window.
The lesson: Careless mistakes leading to the demise of labs don't find themselves, they need our help.

Action: Washington State University Fur Animal Research Facility has two buildings broken into and 6 mink, 7 coyotes, and 10 mice liberated. Two offices had extensive damage done. Pullman, WA. August 13th, 1991.
Method of entry: Myth and legend tells of ALF operatives dressed as maintenance workers entering the university building during the day, unscrewing the lock plates which hold the door closed, and replacing the screws with dummy replacements. These filed-down screws hold in place only during casual use, yet are so short as to pop out of the frame with a forceful tug. Activists returned to the lab at night with easy access to the building. Once inside, the fur industry researcher's office was accessed by pushing through the ceiling in the building hallway, and using a keyhole saw to cut away the thin drywall above the ceiling tiles.
The lesson: If you look like you belong, and you act like you belong – you belong.

The action: Over 1,200 animals liberated and two fires set at the University of Arizona in the largest laboratory liberation to date. Tucson, AZ. April 2nd, 1989.
Method of entry: According to the post-raid article detailing the raid, a diverse palette of tactics were used including opening building doors "with a few small hand held tools which left no telltale sign of forced entry," and cutting through an extractor fan on the psychology building loading dock with tin snips. Activists video taped the raid, which shows vivariums being accessed by liberators in lab coats smashing holes through glass door windows, reaching in, and unlocking the doors from the inside.
The lesson: The over-arching lesson from this action and others: Being effective most often means making your own doors.

Action: 264 animals liberated and $120,000 damage done to University of Oregon. Eugene, OR. October 26th 1986.
Method of entry: Undetectable.
The lesson: Well-researched raiders know the layout and structural nuances of a lab better than the university staff themselves.

Action: Activists enter SEMA Corporation (now called Bioqual) overnight, video-taping the conditions and liberating 4 chimpanzees. Rockville, MD.

December 6th, 1986.
Method of entry: Usable key made from a photocopy of the original, accessed by the ALF momentarily by a contact on the inside.
The lesson: It can be as much what you do as who you know.

Action: Nearly 1,000 animals liberated from UC-Riverside, equipment sabotaged. Riverside, CA. April 20th, 1985.
Method of entry: Video released post-raid shows masked activists loading animals into trucks via a basement door. Inside the lab, activists pry door hinges from walls to access labs and vivariums.
The lesson: Locked doors are always negotiable, and not always alarmed.

Action: University of Pennsylvania Head Injury Laboratory raided, equipment damaged, videos of experiments confiscated. Philadelphia, PA. May 28th, 1984.
Method of entry: Building accessed via ladder to unlocked second floor window. Lock to lab picked.
The lesson: She with the greatest range of skills yields the greatest results.

Action: 12 dogs liberated from UC-Harbor Medical Center. Los Angeles, CA. December 25th, 1983.
Method of entry: Sledgehammer taken to door hinges, doors removed.
The lesson: Brute force is not always elegant, but sometimes effective.

Action: 35 cats liberated and equipment damaged at Howard University Medical School. Washington, DC. December 25th, 1983.
Method of entry: Building accessed with glass cutters to window. Lab doors pried open with crowbar.
The lesson: Multi-layered security requires a multi-layered toolbox.

Action: U.S. Naval Medical Research Institute has 1 dog liberated. Bethesda, MD. December 28th, 1982.
Method of entry: Walked in during daylight hours.
The lesson: When intuitive tactics fail, go counterintuitive: e.g. "raiding in plain sight."

Liberate

Part V

Media Manipulation For Activists

The guerrilla playbook for generating massive publicity without PR firms or media connections.

How To Get Mainstream Media For Animals If You Have No Name Recognition, No Media List, No Money, And No Story

Lecture Transcript
Animal Rights National Conference

"Create a polarizing and attention grabbing story. Seed the blogosphere with that fake controversy. Trade it up the chain to bigger blogs. Gather documentation of the buzz and send it to mainstream media. That's the formula."

This the poor-man's blueprint for effectively marketing your message.

I'm going to share exactly how I've turned simple stunts into mainstream news, using a simple model that's known to very few people.

We're going to cover engineering virality and leveraging it as an outreach tool. To illustrate the power of viral stunts as outreach tools, there was a recent story of a comedian who wheatpasted posters of funny slogans all over the LA Zoo. This story went viral. The only thing he did was put up posters all over the zoo. That's it. He wanted to promote himself as a comedian. There was no activism element to this. He became mainstream news overnight with this simple stunt.

I was talking to somebody about this, and we were both saying, "If this guy had just posted a message with actual meaning, such as anti-zoo slogans, this would have been a viral media story that would have benefited animals." This stunt follows the classic elements of a viral story.

Everyone has their opinions about the most effective kind of activism, in terms of leverage. As in, how do you get the biggest yield for the least amount of effort? For me, my top three have always been undercover footage of farms and labs, media coverage in any form, and the Animal Liberation Front model. By my analysis, those are the top three. I used to do the last one, and now I've dedicated my efforts to generating media.

To be clear, the ideal method to generate media is to actually have a real story about real animal abuse that the media will pick up on. But we're not all in the privileged position where we have access to a breaking story about animal abuse documented in a way that will be appetizing to the media.

Then the question becomes, what do you do if you don't have a story? We are going to talk about how to do that.

We're going to cover how to use a secret back door to the mainstream media. I will break down the elements of a viral news story. Then I'll give you a blueprint for creating a story and taking it from nothing to mainstream news.

The one disclaimer I have to give: use this for good and not evil. This is a very powerful model. If applied thoughtlessly, it can be detrimental to animals. Be careful.

I won't offer my entire resume applying this model, because most of what I've done has been anonymous. I've also been exposed a couple of times while attempting to be anonymous. Most of what I've done to generate media has been using anonymous email accounts, burner TracFones, fake names, doing everything anonymously, and just letting the media cycle snowball effect take over after I set it into motion.

Here's the formula:

Phase one, create a Trojan horse in the form of a sensational story. It doesn't even have to be a real story.

Phase two, the agitation phase. You drum up a buzz about your story. I'll tell you exactly how to do this.

Phase three is to deliver this manufactured story to mainstream media.

Phase four, leverage that Trojan horse to spin the issue back to the animals and educate.

To understand why this works, you have to understand four facts about modern media, and how the modern media has changed, especially in the last five years.

Number one, legacy media no longer controls the conversation. If you think the New York Times or CNN drives the public conversation now, that world is dead. It doesn't exist anymore. The biggest outlets are ones you possibly haven't even heard of. Sites like Breitbart, Infowars, Vice. Each one of these gets more traffic than CNN.com or the New York Times. Most people don't even realize this. The mainstream media is essentially dead.

This is fantastic news for those who have no resources and are trying to generate coverage. Because these sites have very low journalistic standards. Oftentimes, they don't even masquerade as news sites. They are essentially gossip sites, but have a broader impact than CNN.

Number two, it's no longer about delivering news. It's about generating clicks. There's a massive amount of psychological research around what drives engagement on the internet.

Number three, what drives traffic. The #1 thing that's they found that generates traffic is outrage. Anything that elicits outrage will get clicks and drive advertising revenue. Outrage is what drives the news now. We all contribute to this. They call it "outrage porn." People spend all day online outraged about everything. Activists are the worst offenders. Full time outrage junkies. That's the psychology websites have tapped into to, compelling us to repost their content and generate advertising revenue. Your opinions are a product. Your outrage is a product.

Number four, large media outlets now rely on blogs and social media for their stories. This creates a back door by which we can use small blogs and low-barrier-to-entry channels to infiltrate mainstream news sources.

Your job as a media manipulator is to create a polarizing story. Then give that news story to blogs. Then send links to those blogs to bigger websites until it becomes mainstream news. They call this "trading up the chain."

In the last week, I have a friend who had an anonymous blog post about her surface. She is a journalist, and was seen hanging out with an FBI informant. I've known her for years. I hope its not true. But the point is, this blog post was anonymous. It was posted on Medium.com, a site that anyone can post on. This "news" was on Breitbart within 48 hours. We're talking about an anonymous blog post with possibly total bogus information and it was able to hit mainstream news. Breitbart is considered mainstream news now. This is how powerful this model is, when used with a story that will generate clicks. These websites have a strong incentive to disregard fact checking and publish false news because it drives clicks.

Let's get into a very specific example you can put into practice right away.

Let's say you want to screen an animal rights documentary at your university. Here's what I would do. Book the room where you're going it show the film in an auditorium inside a building where animal research is done. If it is a large school, this will be easy.

A lot of films where I live in Boulder, Colorado are screened at the University of Colorado in an auditorium inside the Psychology Building. Where, presumably, they have animals. Perfect example.

Set-up ten burner email accounts. Buy a burner TracFone or set up a Google Voice number attached to your phone. Call and email the police, the university department, animal researchers, the Chancellor, the Young Republicans Club, whoever you can think of. Say, "I'm completely outraged at this serious security threat to our campus. These radical animal rights activists being allowed access into this building after hours. This is an outrageous security concern!" Whatever you want to say. Just sound an alarm in the form of a two or three line email how scared you are that animal rights activists are going to be running loose in this building at night freeing animals.

They will be forced to react. They'll probably relocate the film to another building because most schools are scared of their own shadows. Now you have a story.

Then you email the college newspaper and tip them off to the story. They will salivate at the potential headlines. "Animal Rights Activists Forced to Relocate Film Due to Threats to Research." "University Shuts Down Animal Rights Film Due to Security Concerns."

So, what have we done here? Very simple. We sent a few emails. Presuming this is a film you're going to screen anyway, you might as well take a few minutes to generate this kind of buzz.

What you've accomplished first is that you've put the spotlight on animal research. Second thing you've done is created publicity to get 150 people to attend your movie screening instead of the 15 people that would have showed up otherwise.

How do I know this works? I used to lecture at schools. Before I would go to a college campus, I would find out what building I was speaking in. If it was anywhere near the animal research building, I would anonymously email anyone I could think of and say, "I can't believe you're allowing this terrorist, this felon, this horrible person to come to our campus within proximity of buildings that house animals for research." Multiple times I received coverage. All I did was generate totally fake outrage that didn't even exist.

Whatever you're trying to generate coverage for, step number one is to create the Trojan horse. Create a story. It has to be totally unique and totally polarizing. Those are the elements of a viral story. You have to break people from their trance. You're in the business of capturing attention.

Two books about this that are essential reads are "*Contagious*," and "*Captivology*." Remember the story does not matter. It's just the Trojan horse. We all wish the truth about animal abuse was enough. We should be able to send out a press release and say "the University of Nebraska is torturing animals." That's not news. So we have to create a Trojan horse.

We'll take a hypothetical stunt to illustrate how this would work in a real world application. Let's say you set up a quick website where you post the home addresses of slaughterhouse owners in your area. Maybe screenshot Google Street View images of their homes. It could be anything, but this is just controversial enough that it might work.

The next phase is agitation phase. So this is where you inflame the controversy and make it seem bigger that it is. You seed the blogosphere with your story to give it legitimacy. You might have a story that's so good the media will jump on it immediately without this phase, but probably not. Remember the media subsists on stories from blogs and uses them for plausible deniability. Blogs rarely have any journalistic standards. That's how the media works.

Identify blogs or sites with no journalistic standards. Sites that have a low barrier to entry. A site that relies primarily on gossip. Set-up burner email accounts. Email conservative blogs, pig farming sites, agricultural blogs, other people who are easily excitable. Get them buzzing about this fake controversy that you totally made up. Send them simple one or two-line emails saying, "I'm outraged about this website! Have you seen this? What the heck are you doing about this? Why aren't you covering this?" They will cover it. Do this fifty times, and you will get coverage.

The next phase is to go for the prize. You've created a story, you've generated small-scale buzz. Next step is to contact bigger media sources and send them links to those smaller blogs who just covered your totally fake story. Also send them any material you have, like a photograph, anything that legitimizes the story.

You email them and do the same thing. "Listen, why aren't you covering this? This is crazy." Send five or ten emails from different burner accounts. It gives the appearance there are a lot of people who are interested in seeing this story. Chances are they will cover it.

To recap, you create a polarizing and attention grabbing story. You seed the blogosphere with that fake controversy. You trade it up the chain to bigger blogs. You gather documentation of the buzz and send it to mainstream media. That's the formula.

The final step is to leverage this attention to bring the message back to the animals. It's not just about getting your name in the paper. It's about bringing attention back on the animals. Remember that story we created was just the Trojan horse. If you don't handle this part very carefully, your message will get lost. You have to have this carefully planned out.

You're going to be contacted by the media at this point. Your job is to leverage this attention and bring the story back to the animals through your soundbites, and the general message you've crafted in advance.

To accomplish this strategy effectively, study what goes viral. Look at BoingBoing.com. Reverse engineer their biggest stories. If you really want to understand know the media works, read "*Trust me, I'm Lying.*" It's by someone who carried out campaigns like this for American Apparel and other clients.

Use this for good not evil. It is very powerful. I hope you all go out, apply this model, and generate as much media attention as you can for animals.

"How This Left-Wing Activist Manipulates The Media"

Interview
New York Observer
"If you've built a career around creating – or spreading – fake drama, then you're fair game."

After hearing I was a fan of his work, and learning I had applied his playbook to great effect in the activist realm, author Ryan Holiday (author of Trust Me I'm Lying) and I had this conversation for The New York Observer.

Since the interview, faux-activist "outrage" culture has only become more rampant, more bold, and devolved even further into self-parody, making this blueprint even more effective now than when this was published.

So tell us, are you really on the TSA watch list and how did that happen?

In 1998 I was charged with Animal Enterprise Terrorism for my role in freeing foxes and mink from fur farms. This amounted to cutting fences and opening cages at six farms. Under the weight of an 82-year maximum sentence, I became a fugitive for 7 years, lived under several aliases, and was arrested at a Starbucks in 2005. I served two years in prison.

Because of the "terrorist" label, in the years since I've had my house raided by the FBI twice, been named as suspect in several animal liberations, found laptops with dead batteries fully charged when removed from storage a year later (do the math), had my garbage stolen by the authorities, and learned a woman who took me on trip to Moab was working for the FBI.

Of all it, the TSA attention is among the least intrusive.

Now, how does that differ from what got reported in the media and what you put up on your blog? Is there any part of the record you can clear up for us?

Before my anonymity as "the jetsetting terrorist" was compromised by Forbes, I described the crime that put me on the TSA's watch list as an "activist-related property crime." Animals are considered property in the eyes of the law, so this was accurate.

As for the rest - It wouldn't be possible to untangle all the misinformation reported in the media and elsewhere over the years. I can't complain. I probably planted half of it anyway.

Tell us how and why you decided to make this something the media would pounce on? What did you do? How did it work? How much traffic / attention did it get?

The Jetsetting Terrorist was launched with the stated goal of going mainstream within 2 weeks. It took about 8 hours.

The specific end-goal was The Alex Jones Show. While culturally considered fringe, he has a larger platform than most websites and TV shows. And he hates the TSA. (Spoiler alert: Alex has yet to call me.)

(To get this out upfront: All stories on the site are 100% true.)

My blueprint – straight from your *Trust Me I'm Lying* playbook – was as follows:

- Set up an anonymous burner email account.
- Identify people (leftist / libertarian-leaning celebrities & public figures) with large Twitter followings, get their personal email addresses.
- Email them a link to the site and a two-line email about how this is the best site ever and how "surprised" I am they haven't tweeted it yet. Pretty simple.
- Trade it up the chain until hitting something big.
- Leverage my anonymity to offer Alex Jones the exclusive on my identity reveal, for an interview.

Why Twitter? Better credibility-to-ease-of-penetration ratio. Here's what I mean:

Writing a blog post is a time investment. Bloggers are selective of what they dedicate a post to. A prolific blogger might post once or twice a day.

A Tweet is copy, paste, done. A prolific Twitter user might post on Twitter 20+ times a day.

But for the purpose of leveraging mentions to receive larger mentions, they are the same: A single tweet has a unique URL that can be sent to larger platforms needing some social proof before running a story.

In short, baiting John Cusack into tweeting a link is lower-effort, higher-yield than coverage on a low-level libertarian blog.

Hipster jetsetting terrorist

to clover hope ▾

Clover

This was on the front page of Boing Boing over the weekend, but they just did a weak copy/paste job. Would like to see Jezebel cover this properly

He's getting tons of internet love right now, but no one is highlighting what an entitled, pompous douchebag this guy is.

http://bbs.boingboing.net/t/jetsetting-terrorist-blog-from-a-guy-who-is-branded-ssss-by-the-tsa/42788

A white hipster writing stories about verbally abusing the TSA (including women) because he's on the "terrorist watch list"

I didn't have to go far. Within a few hours of going live, I anonymously sent a link to Sean Bonner. Sean and I had spoken at the same conference once and met afterwards. I was a fan of his email newsletter, and he had a decent Twitter following. More importantly: He was a former contributor to Boing Boing.

As a major driver of virality, Boing Boing was a prized target. Going through a current contributor was like storming the gates. Going through a former contributor was sneaking in the back door.

Sean tweeted it within minutes.

With the anonymous burner account, I sent a link to the Tweet to Cory Doctorow at Boing Boing. A few hours later, it was on Boing Boing.

From there I set up ten more burner accounts and carpet-bombed the internet with this email:

> *"This is on the front page of Boing Boing right now but they just did a weak copy/paste job. Would like to see _____ cover this properly.*
>
> *A white hipster writes hilarious stories about TSA encounters, and flying while on the terrorist watch list. Too good.*
>
> *The author is anonymous, but worth a try."*

I sent this to exactly 103 journalists.

I tweaked it slightly to appeal to specific targets. For example Jezebel received this:

> *"This was on the front page of Boing Boing over the weekend, but they just did a weak copy/paste job. Would like to see Jezebel cover this properly.*
>
> *He's getting tons of internet love right now, but no one is highlighting what an entitled, pompous douche bag this guy is.*
>
> *A white hipster writing stories about verbally abusing the TSA (including women) because he's on the "terrorist watch list."*

My approach was not scattershot. The majority of emails were sent to journalists who had previously covered the TSA or other civil liberties issues. If done right, you're adding value to the journalist. It is an equitable exchange.

Immediately thereafter, *Forbes* contacted me for an interview.

In a follow up email, the reporter stated she had done a reverse-lookup of my cell number and determined my real identity. The story – outing me as "the jetsetting terrorist" – ran the following week, bringing attention to both the TSA and the bigger issue of classifying a broad segment of the population as "terrorists."

Creating the site and content took three days. And It was methodically crafted to maximize virality. The elements were:

Anonymity: Mystique is powerful.

It's never been done: With so much talk about the TSA, no one had gone quite as public with their experiences on their TSA's terrorist watch list.

Awesome content: There's no shortcut here. I have a background as a writer, and while I wrote with haste, I put care into maximizing the impact of the prose. A collection of generic and poorly written TSA stories would have gone nowhere.

Riding the wave of an ongoing conversation: Controversy over the TSA was a regular part of the public debate. There was a pent up demand for a new angle on an increasingly stale subject.

Solid tagline: "I'm a convicted terrorist. I travel a lot. And the TSA won't leave me alone. This is my diary of traveling as a marked man." I spent a lot of time crafting that.

Going hipster: The original "about me" sidebar read *"How a jetsetting hipster became a jetsetting hipster terrorist."* While subtle, portraying myself as a "hipster" was, in all likelihood the determining factor in making this viral. When you get "terrorist," "jetsetter," and "hipster" in one place, It's too absurd to not spread. You're clicking that link.

(This was, by the way, the only part I changed when my identity was revealed. Calling myself a hipster just isn't accurate. And no one uses that word self-referentially.)

A powerful narrative: There are one thousand ways to tell the same story. I put effort into maximizing chances of this getting picked up by utilizing timeless literary narratives, accentuating the underdog effect, the reluctant hero, and (subtle) revenge themes.

Niching down: The original plan was "The Hipster Terrorist" – Anonymous (and 100% true) stories from a convicted "terrorist" documenting the humorous side-effects of life under the "terrorist" label. From stories about awkward dinner-table conversation when meeting girlfriend's parents, to the baristas at the Starbucks I frequent Googling my name (hilarity ensues).

While this would be a great blog (and a book I'll probably write soon), it lacked any timely discussion to piggyback on. Niching down to the TSA was clearly the right move.

Before this, you manipulated the media with a rather brilliant stunt to drive attention to condition in slaughterhouses and factory farms. Why do you feel justified in essentially tricking or circumventing the news process in order to get your message across? Is this something you think more advocates should do?

The game plan for The Vegan Sellout List was this:

- Launch a site that allowed people to anonymously submit the names and photos of former vegans, and the story behind their rise and fall from veganism.
- Pre-populate the list with 100 former vegans who have a platform (from celebrities to ex-vegans with high-traffic blogs).
- Email all 100 with a link to their entry on the site, and bait them into mentioning it in a blog post or Tweet.

- Concurrently, generate buzz in the vegan blogosphere.
- Parlay all of this to successively bigger blogs, until it hit a huge site that generated serious traffic.
- Pull a bait-and-switch, forcing visitors to watch a video of slaughter-house footage before entering.

"The Vegan Sellout List" was what the internet craved: Offensive, provocative, shameless, and impossible not to have an opinion on.

From launch the goal was Gawker. We would consider it a success if we hit Gawker. (We spent a considerable amount of time trying to identify writers at Gawker who were former vegans to provoke coverage by making it personal, without success. Gawker ran the story in under three weeks anyway).

The Vegan Sellout List Is The Best Worst Thing Ever

 Camille Dodero

Our plan worked a little *too* well. We'd given ourselves a two-month window to build a buzz before getting it mainstream. It hit top-tier outlets like Fox News in under 3 weeks.

When the traffic explosion hit, we weren't prepared. It came so fast and at such volume, it crashed the server. The aborted plan was to utilize a plugin to compel a video view before entering, and with a crashed server the only remaining option was a URL redirect. We sent hundreds of thousands of people to a third-party site that autoplayed a graphic video titled "Meet Your Meat."

In end, the results were massive: At least 200,000 people baited into getting their first glimpse inside a slaughterhouse.

The Vegan Sellout List was vindicated by the results it achieved.

NEWS

Vegan extremists launch Web site to name and shame ex-vegans

By Natalie O'Neill   July 1, 2013 | 4:00am

I have friends working for non-profits who travel in vans to college campuses all year asking people to watch 2 minutes of slaughterhouse footage. On a good day, they reach 200 people. This is important and noble work.

But consider that the Vegan Sellout List may have sent over *one thousand times* as many people to the same footage for three days work. Even if only 10% of visitors watched the video, this is an incredible return on my time investment.

Everyone doing advocacy work owes it to their message to get acquainted with the concept of leverage, and ways to increase the impact of each unit of effort exponentially.

As I asserted in my original statement on this stunt: Before this stunt, most vegans believed the temperature in Hell would have to hit 32 degrees before FoxNews.com would ever send tens (or hundreds) of thousands of their readers directly to graphic slaughterhouse footage.

Regarding why these methods are justified: While the lines are increasingly blurred, I apply two different ethical equations to bloggers versus journalists.

Bloggers: On the internet, being vocally "offended" is the new "look at me I'm cool." It's like being 12 and putting a playing card in your bike spokes.

I've met many of the bigger bloggers in the vegan space. Most of them are awesome people. A few of the more drama-centric ones are clearly acting out their own demons. Like, they couldn't get a date in high school (or now), and it's payback time. (To be fair, this is my take on a large swath of the internet, and is not vegan-specific).

This is exactly the type of person The Vegan Sellout List was designed to agitate for traffic. If you've built a career around creating – or spreading - fake drama, then you're fair game.

Regarding larger online media, it's a more delicate equation. However in this instance it was simple: If they consider a list of former vegans to be "news," they've forfeited all journalistic integrity and have left themselves wide, wide open.

They're for-profit businesses. I have a message. We're both dealing in the traffic economy. In this instance, I just happen to beat them at their own game.

What have you learned about the media and its inner-workings from your campaign?

The unspoken conspiracy that you speak of, that exists between journalists and those seeking publicity is very real. If you have a story that provokes – real or not – they have the time. Give them the promise of traffic and a little plausible denial and you're in.

I've received tremendous insights from *Trust Me I'm Lying* and your Creative Live course. I got to work on The Jetsetting Terrorist the day after finishing the latter. Your point that there is a harmony of interests between journalists and those who wish to hack the media is very powerful, and has proven true.

I've also learned that a big part of your playbook (i.e manufacturing controversy to generate publicity) is given a nitro boost when executed in the activist realm.

I have to be careful here because its clear whose side I'm usually on, but there's a small segment who are attracted to social movements because... let's just say they have an emotional agenda. To use your term, they're "rage profiteers," reveling in the drama economy. And I've been the hidden hand instigating them for a greater good more times than I would admit.

The best case study in this (which I had nothing to do with) was the recent "controversy" around a vegan cookbook titled Thug Kitchen. If you ever do a TMIL update, you have to get this in there.

Thug Kitchen was an anonymous vegan blog, where vegan recipes were written in cartoonish "thug" language. It was funny, the blog became popular, and the (anonymous) authors got a book deal.

Weeks before the book's release, the authors revealed their identity. Surprise: They were two attractive white people from Los Angeles.

Within days, several small anarchist blogs were buzzing in outrage accusing the authors of "cultural appropriation" and "digital blackface" and calling for a boycott. They announced (and eventually delivered) protests at book signings. This went up the chain like wildfire, and hit Vice just before the book's release.

That was four months ago. It's been the bestselling vegan cookbook on Amazon ever since.

I have no knowledge of whether this controversy was real or manufactured. But if the latter, it followed a recipe that couldn't fail:

• Take a target appetizing to leftist & politically radical bloggers (attractive, white, sporty vegans)
• Assign to them some perceived misconduct that fits into one of the top three categories of internet scandal (in this instance: racism).
• Seed excitable elements of the blogosphere with the fake scandal.

If I were the invisible puppet master orchestrating this, I would know that only 0.02% of people will be genuinely offended by the Thug Kitchen authors being white. But another 60% will feign outrage to look cool. And just about everyone else will quietly nod their head's in agreement for fear of being labeled racists themselves.

And what do the authors care? They get six-figures in free publicity. The anarchists get their flavor-of-the-week drama. Win-win.

Why should we believe you? This a question I get a lot myself - to which my answer is: Why should I lie? Lying was keeping it a secret - but I am curious to hear your thoughts. Obviously some people would say you undermine the credibility of the cause with these tactics.

My response is: What's in it for me? I don't have clients (cows in slaughterhouses don't pay), and I don't take credit (I was outed in both instances we're discussing. This would be a longer interview if we got into the stunts I haven't been caught for).

If anyone has a point they think defeats the message that animals are exploited (or that the TSA targets people based on their politics), then by all means lay your evidence on the table.

But attacking a message's delivery device and suggesting it undermines the message itself is the work of someone who lacks an argument.

Credibility is everything, particularly when you're the bearer of a message people don't want to hear. Much different than artists, whose position I envy. When you're an artist, there is virtually nothing that can harm your reputation. Most media tends to be good media.

With advocacy, it's much more delicate. You have to honor the facts at all costs.

The Vegan Sellout List utilized deception of intent, not deception of facts. It was exactly what it purported to be (until the link-redirect): A directory of ex-vegans. The Jetsetting Terrorist was exactly what it claimed: a collection of true stories about a convicted terrorist being harassed by the TSA.

I employ Trojan Horses, not deception.

What's next?

Very little I would admit to.

Despite a compelling interview given by my female co-conspirator, It's looking increasingly unlikely the #2 women's magazine will ever run their "How a one night stand with a radical vegan turned me into an animal rights activist" story. If it does surface, that was all us. While tasteless, a "sex confessional" is just about the only angle to get a message of substance into a publication like that.

On the more frivolous front, an anonymous hip-hop project that will make License To Ill-era Beastie Boys controversy look amateur.

And on the advocacy front, the stakes are too high to reveal my hand. But I will continue to provoke thought into our relationship with animals by any means necessary.

Liberate

Part VI

Prison

This is about what happens after you get caught.

First Post-Prison Statement

Article
Internet
"For the animals, there is no swifter death than a turned back."

After two years in prison, most of it spent muzzled from making public statements due to ongoing legal concerns, this was my homecoming letter.

This is both a homecoming statement, and a thank you letter.

They say the most difficult time one can spent in jail is the time not knowing when you'll get out. For this reason, my two years incarcerated was atypical and arduous. After eight months in county jail, I was sentenced to two years in prison, and for the first time had a fixed term of incarceration. For exactly 5 weeks, I had a date.

Then, in December 2005, South Dakota filed multiple felony counts against me for a nine-year-old mink release. And the remainder of my time was spent serving an open-ended sentence – the most difficult kind. My federal release date was fixed, and then I was to be transferred and begin all over again – same process, different state.

Just days before my federal release date, when I was to be transported to South Dakota, I received word from my attorney the charges had been abruptly dropped. Six days later I walked through the prison gates.

What in large part has been my silence since my release – and for much of the time before – has been deliberate and necessary, for reasons both obvious and not. There is much that has been left unsaid, many stores that will be told in time. After enduring the legal scrutiny to which I have been subjected, in putting pen to pad you accept there may be no such thing as safe ground.

I have had the good fortune of meeting many of those who supported me during my two years on the injured list, and thanking them for their support in person. To the rest, let me thank you now: yours was the gift of freedom – where the lack of a well-funded defense could have seen me imprisoned for 12 years and not two—and the gift of life—in a lifeless world where the absence of letters, books, and funds for food would have meant a slow death.

The true return on your investment does not come in my gratitude; it comes in the ripple effect of your support. The message has been sent: In the event of capture, those who choose to follow their hearts outside the law will be taken care of. The relevant audience of this message is small, but there is none whose work is more valuable.

Sometimes you can't fully process a journey until you've come full circle. After nearly 10 years, I recently returned to Seattle, where this all began. That place where many years ago, belief turned to protest, and protest to something more.

My first stop was the chicken slaughterhouse near downtown Seattle that marked the point of no return for me over a decade ago. A place where, for the first time, I saw the death of those animals I was fighting for with my own eyes. It marked the end of a long, convoluted road. The building that was once Seattle's most prolific killing machine was an abandoned, grown over shell. With its closure easily mistaken as a small victory, I knew they had only moved away; murder in another zip code. Putting their work to an end had at one time consumed me, and staring through the cracked windows I felt only one thing: they had gotten away with it. They had come, killed, and left town. They had gotten away with it.

And they've gotten away with more. An event that night at which I was speaking — marking my Seattle homecoming — brought out not one of those with whom I had fought and stood by all those years ago. The old faces were gone - forsaking what they had once said they would die for, to become every degree of carnivores and apostates.

Looking back, you wonder where all the words went. The chants, promises, and selfless risks. With so many fallen, its hard not to feel alone among the ruins.

Their killing machine won't get every animal – I will never forget reading of the liberation of three chickens from the killing floor of that slaughterhouse before it closed its doors. Somehow I know this culture of soul-crushing-by-convenience won't get every activist. The last decade didn't break them all.

These months since prison have been a homecoming of sorts, a reunion with this movement. The last many years have seen us on very separate but parallel roads. This time since prison has reunited me with what I have for so long been separated from – both the negative and positive.

There remains the destructive impulses to do what feels good over what is effective, to say what is fashionable over what is right, and laying down to die over standing up to fight.

Eclipsing all this is our depth of conscience to feel the pain of a billion animals, and clarity of vision to recognize it as the most urgent of all struggles. We are the last refuge of sanity, and I will always stand by those who know that for the animals, there is no swifter death than a turned back.

Be fearless in your fight,
Peter Young

Federal Prison 101

Article
Earth First Journal
"With prison demystified, we find one less thing between us and animal liberation."

The comically sensitive (and thankfully, now irrelevant) Earth First Journal refused to publish this article after my release from prison. After requesting a guide to federal prison for activists, this draft was rejected for not conforming to some vague, undefined anarchist code. At issue were my undiplomatic words about prison guards, and refusal to portray prison as a daily gladiator fight to the death.

(The editors, who had never been to prison, did not comment on what qualified them to weigh in on the accuracy of this article.)

I settled on two minor, unsubstantial changes (such as omitting the word "thug"), and the article was published.

When prison is the most powerful weapon they have, whose interests do we serve fixating on prison horror stories and selective accounts of a varied experience? Whose interests are served with prison accounts that leave the reader fearing prison as a fate worse than death? To fixate on the negative is to do the opposition's work.

This article is not for the voyeurs. It is not for the thrill-seekers looking for good fight stories. It is not for the anarchists looking to preserve cartoon fantasies of "the struggle." It is not for the former animal liberation prisoners who do a few years and exploit their incarceration to tell embellished prison stories for a little attention.

This is an article for people who are going to prison. No one else.

(Disclaimer: This information was relevant as of 2007. Some facts may have changed.)

In our endless discourse on animal liberation theory and practice, there has remained since the direct action movement began a frightful specter, kept in the closet and rarely spoken of, whose power as a deterrent from the simplest of actions to correct the most horrible of crimes is supreme. The unmentionable is prison.

Inaction cannot with honesty be credited to a lack of knowledge or skill—every address and methodology is for our taking in this information age—and we would more correctly attribute our nights at home to the exaggerated threat of prison.

What follows is intended as a brief summary of the life that awaits an activist convicted of federal charges. My experience extends only to the federal system, however a look at the history of animal liberation prisoners will show it is this system which is of chief relevance to animal liberationists in the United States. Look at our history: all but a few animal liberation prisoners were prosecuted federally. As a final disclaimer, I am unable to comment on life inside maximum (USPs) security facilities—a fate not to be ruled out for those convicted of more serious offenses. However, very few activists have ever seen the inside of a USP, even for arson.

If you, as I, suffered pretrial detention without bail in a county jail, arriving in prison will mark the end of your darkest days. County jail is the worst time you will do—your most comfort-less living, your most difficulties with food, and your most problems with both staff and inmates. You've arrived at prison and it's time to exhale.

Details
The activist convicted of a federal crime will serve 85% of their sentence with 54 days of good time offered per year. The last six months will be spent in a halfway house with work release privileges.

Federal Inmates
The reputation of federal prison playing host to mostly white collar criminals and bank robbers is greatly antiquated. Since the 1980s, federal prosecutions have taken a sharp shift toward drug and gun possession crimes. Currently larger volume drug dealers comprise over 80% of federal inmates. At my facility, I would estimate drug, gun, and immigration cases make up 95% of the inmates. Others include bank robbers and large scale fraud cases.

Custody Levels

Federal prisons are divided into four custody levels: Camps, Lows, Mediums, and Max's (USPs). The basis for the public's image of a federal prison is the minimum security camp. Although the comfort at these prisons have been greatly scaled back since the 1980s due to backlash from "tough on crime" zealots, features such as tennis courts and movie theaters are still very much a reality. These "prisons" lack even a fence. Camps are reserved for low-risk inmates with less than seven years to serve and have the largest percentage of white collar criminals.

Lows are for inmates with 20 years and under. As with camps, they have an open bunk/dorm setup in place of cells.

Mediums are for those with 30 years or less and are much closer to the standard image of a prison.

USPs are for inmates with 30+ years or those deemed a security risk due to trouble at lower security facilities or violent crimes.

It's important to note that any sentence of any length for any crime can result in designation to any security level. Your prison experience and the type of people with whom you live will be most heavily defined by the security level of your prison.

Many factors contribute to one's custody level, including criminal history, severity of crime, history of violence, etc. Small details can have a significant impact. For example, I would have designated to a Camp, but for an 8 year old arrest for "Rioting" at the UC-Davis primate research center. The presence of the word "riot" in my criminal history elevated me two entire levels, from Camp to Medium.

The Bureau of Prisons (B.O.P.) has a fairly efficient system for moving violent and predatory inmates to USPs. Often a single fight can raise one's custody to USP level. This creates a (relatively) relaxed climate even at Medium Security facilities.

For the purpose of animal liberationists, most property crimes are likely to result in a designation of medium security or lower. With crimes involving arson, history has shown it's a coin toss, with USP designation a possibility. Numerous factors weigh in. Josh Demitt and SUV-torcher-turned-snitch

Billy Cottrell were both convicted of arson with no criminal histories. Josh went to a camp, while Billy sits at a USP.

The Prison
As a sample of the physical components which make up a federal prison, a breakdown of the facility where I reside: Dining hall, laundry services, barber shop, commissary, mental health, library, chapel, visiting room, mail room, the hole, rec center (with band, yoga, and arts and crafts rooms, workout machines, ping pong, basketball courts and TVs), rec yard (with soccer field, handball courts, baseball diamond, and track) and housing units.

The Myths
The "survival of the fittest" reputation of prison life is largely obsolete. Most commonly held beliefs on prison life are either echoes of a convict culture long since deceased or applicable only to maximum security facilities. These media-induced horror scenes form the basis for the public's perception of the prison experience simply because knife fights and gang rapes make for good material. The reality of thousands of men playing cards and watching pro-wrestling doesn't sell books. Sexual assault is non-existent. If improvised weaponry exists, it's invisible to my eyes. And in my time in prison, I've neither seen nor been in a fight.

Food
(Note: the B.O.P. overhauled underwent a food service overhaul since my release, and as such some details below may no longer apply.)

Among the most mentioned perks of federal prison is the food. The B.O.P. is surprisingly liberal in this regard, requiring a vegetarian substitute at every meal and extensive commissary options. However, in prison as in jails, veganism as an ethically motivated diet is not recognized and safely navigating the hazardous food landscape requires effort. An overview of veganism behind enemy lines:

Dining Hall: Food in the dining hall can be divided into two parts—the "line" and the self-serve bar. I generally skip the line about half the week. Vegan items served at my facility include french fries, pasta, apples, and potatoes. I find the vegetarian meat substitute is vegan about half the time, and dishes served include vegan chicken patties, soy fajitas, and sweet and sour tofu. The food service manager is usually accessible to answer questions about ingredients. Self serve bar: At my prison this includes an AYCE salad bar, rice, beans, as well as rotating items such as cabbage, corn, and salsa. It is my understanding that all federal prisons have a salad bar.

Commissary: This is the prison store which is visited once a week. Vegans will find it desirable and perhaps essential to supplement their diets through commissary. Selection varies, but common denominator items will include oatmeal, peanut butter and trail mix. My facility also sells organic granola, tortillas and beans, and even soy chorizo.

Common Fare: This is the name for the B.O.P.'s meal plan for people with religious diets. Common Fare is comprised of foods that are common to all religions recognized by the B.O.P. Generally, it is two trays of raw sliced vegetables and whole fruits given at each meal. Other items such as the kosher meats and breads are given but can be refused. Inmates are only placed on common fare if they ascribe to a faith which calls for adherence to certain dietary laws such as Judaism or the 7th Day Adventist faith. It should be noted there exists a curious phenomenon of new arrival inmates being divinely possessed by the power of the Holy Ghost and experiencing sudden spiritual conversion at or around the time of filling out their paperwork in Intake. Many later find this to have been much to their advantage.

Black Market: It is a secret to no inmate or staff member that the prison black market is huge and its largest segment is food. The prison economy works on stamps, which are money. There is simply no food item in the prison which cannot be purchased and the vegan with money will find themselves wanting for little. Well off inmates can quite literally purchase cases of Boca Burgers or have vegan pumpkin pies made and delivered to their cell, should they have the stamps.

Staff
The savage, abusive prison guard is among the staple prison images I was pleased to find mostly false. At my prison, guards are so far in the background, were it not for the daily mail call, I could go for weeks without speaking to or thinking about a guard.

Among the realities of prison I find most frightening is being at the mercy and under the care of profoundly stupid people. From guards to most executive staff, you will live under a group whose ignorance is rivaled only by the inmates themselves. I once had to cut short a conversation with a high-ranking staff member because his speech was so thick with slang I was unable to understand him. My ungrantable request that he speak plain English almost earned me a stay in the hole.

With exceptions, the average administrative staff member is little more than a glorified savage, with military or street criminal background, and all the bad grammar, bullying nature, and lack of education this suggests. My experience strongly affirms a sentiment expressed by George Jackson in *Soledad Brother*, that one of the worst mistakes a prison can make is to assume their jailers have a heart. Too many times I have attempted to appeal to the conscience of a staff member in my dilemmas regarding such things as food, to find my politeness mistaken for weakness and my condition worse off than had I instead beat my chest and barked a demand.

In mentality, nothing separates staff from inmate. The same "code of the street" mindset prevails, with macho posturing rewarded and attempts at cordial dialogue crushed. Any lingering hope for a core of goodness and reason existing deep within all people will find its swift death in prison.

Convict Culture

More than the loss of freedom or friends, I found the shock of a new culture that seemed insane to its very core to be the greatest challenge of prison. Spared a constant physical battle per the common myth, the new prisoner will find instead a psychological battle of life among new customs, manners, language, and priorities. It would be a great disservice to the reader to soften reality with detached sociological language and a tone of cultural relativism so fashionable in discussions of prison. Instead, the facts: On average, prisoners are loud. They are uneducated. They hold women in the lowest regard, tell bad jokes and possess the maturity of 15 year olds. They also have the rest of us very outnumbered, thus it is the primary goal of the prisoner to win their favor without becoming one of them.

Therein lies the most difficult task of prison—tolerance, and a certain level of conformity. What is crucial during the weeks after arrival is to watch. Sit back and take in every detail, from where people sit to how beds are made. Most important is a healthy fear that things can go very wrong at any moment. The smallest transgression can sour one's reputation in a way that can be impossible to reverse. Seemingly tiny infractions such as spending too much time in one's cell can quickly become large problems. Creating one enemy can, in effect, be creating dozens within hours, and should be most crucially avoided. While it takes a certain effort to get beaten up, there is a much less desirable alternative which requires no skill at all, and that is to be shunned.

While it would be my preference to never speak to most everyone in prison, it is inadvisable to keep completely to oneself. There is deep suspicion and a subtle contempt extended to the withdrawn newcomer. Upon arriving, to become friendly with those in your housing unit quickly is wise insurance.

After several weeks of establishing acquaintances and allowing others to be comfortable with me, I then felt comfortable scaling back my socializing and settled into a more isolated routine of reading and letter writing. Even now, I spend 15 minutes or so a day sitting by the TV and talking with other inmates to avoid drifting towards outcast status. This is a smart investment.

Your best asset is something I altogether lacked and was forced to learn: social versatility. In all likelihood no one in prison is anyone you would be friends with or even talk to under other circumstances, but now there is no choice.

To those with whom you share an address, everything that was important to you on the outside is nothing. They do not care about the Hardcore band you roadied for, chocolate almond milk, or your convictions. Prison is a Twilight Zone of NASCAR and Maxim Magazine, and learning to force conversation and connect with diverse groups is of great value. However, at the end of the day, you may find as I do that your only true friend is your radio.

The political prisoner enjoys a significant advantage over the average prisoner. Social standing in prison is based on one vague form of capital called "respect," and keeping with prison's simple-minded ladder of priorities, respect is given for things that defy explanation by a functioning brain.

Among them is mail. There is a powerful effect in receiving the large volume of mail an animal liberation prisoner can expect. Without any frame of reference, inmates assume one to be "something big" on the outside, and extend respect accordingly. Most animal liberation prisoners can expect to have a website set up, and with a majority of inmates having no internet experience, to say you have a website is to say you have your own billboard in Times Square. Additionally, having a case looked at as "exotic" gives one an immediate reputation. Being looked upon as someone into things not fully understood by most inmates places your origins as being in some foreign world, lessening the pressure for conformity—a pressure which can otherwise be stifling.

Overall, the political prisoner enjoys a unique situation which can be exploited to his/her benefit in the convoluted world of prison.

Conclusion

Pulling the curtain away from the specter of federal prison, we find its fiercest threats to be its most hollow. While the hardships of prison should not be downplayed, its realities should not be exaggerated. And with prison demystified, we find one less thing between us and animal liberation.

Vegan Prisoner Playbook

Article
Vice

"There was major irony in the same ethic that I risked prison for being the one that might kill me once I got there"

After extradition to the state of Virginia for charges related to an ID card I obtained with forged documents, I spent six weeks in solitary confinement awaiting resolution of my case. In this bleak existence, I began work on a narrative documenting my journey being vegan while incarcerated.

The handwritten, incomplete story stayed with me for the rest of my incarceration. After my release, I filed it away and forgot about it.

Years later, a food editor for Vice reached out to ask if I had a food-related story I would like to pitch. I remembered my half-finished "vegan in prison" story, completed it, polished it, and submitted it.

In the end, Vice edited out 85% of the story, with only the addendum seeing publication.

This is the full, unedited story; unpublished until now.

No sound short of the slamming of Death's Door signals the end of a plea-sured vegan life than the sound of your Miranda Rights. More than a vaca-tion in a 3rd world country or a tour van breaking down in Casper, Wyo-ming; the greatest test of vegan fortitude of our time is an extended stay in jail. And in 2005, challenge begun.

I am a vegan. 19 years deep into a lifelong commitment to consumer nothing from an animal – flesh, eggs, dairy, skin, or byproducts. This moral code – of reference for all life through my consumer choices and deeds - had brought me to protests-turned-riots, donning cow costumes at meat packer conven-tions, and into slaughterhouses with a video camera at midnight. And in 2005, after a 7-year stretch on the FBI's "wanted" list for charges of freeing thousands of animals from fur farms – it brought me to prison.

For 10 years, I put as much care, craft, and toil into eating as the FBI did into finding me. I ate seitan marinated in sesame ginger sauce and roasted red pepper hummus on sprouted grain pizza crust. I double-fisted dried straw-berries and malted carob balls, drank rice shakes on the beach each morning and Kombucha on my balcony before the sunset each night. Agave nectar was my table sugar, and organic carrot juice my wine. It was decadent, it was pricey and in March 2005 – it was over.

I got arrested.

As I was being booked into Santa Clara County Jail for six federal charges that could have earned me 12+ years, the abrupt end of good food in my life wasn't on the forefront of my mind. But it would be so nearly every moment since.

You know the movie scene where the cell door slams ominously, the new prisoner grips the bars wistfully, and the sound of jingling keys trails off into the distance? It was like that.

Then there are the scenes that find a home on the editing room floor: Mail from homeless palm readers who read about me in the paper, search warrants for my home slid under the cell door, and the part where I ask the guard if he can deliver a message to the kitchen that I cannot eat meat, dairy, or eggs. His response of: "This ain't Burger King kid, you don't get it your way" could be interpreted several ways. I took it to mean that as a vegan, I was in for a very rough ride.

Three times a day, the slot on my cell door opened and shut, through it passing every variety of animal flesh, byproduct, and legal document – everything but an edible meal. The tray's trace shavings of iceberg lettuce brought my caloric intake into the double digits, a brief grim-reaper-placeholder until plunging myself into caloric deficit through the high-impact workout of a nightly letter-writing flurry. Everyone got my pleas for help: The jail captain, kitchen manager, and congressperson Barbara Boxer. My demands were simple: no meat, dairy, or eggs.

In this one-sided negotiation process, leverage was in short supply. My only currency was the arcane legal concept of "making myself a legal liability". The line stretching from starved-to-death-inmate to parents-with-lawyers barrels straight to the nerve center of any big business: their bank account. The business of human warehousing was no exception.

Anyway, my letter campaign didn't work. Silicon Valley newspapers continued their coverage of the "jailed eco-terrorist," sympathetic members of the public kept the incoming mail flow at 15+ a day, and my lawyer solicited my input on trial strategy in the attorney booth while I was shackled to the floor. Yet it all seemed absurdly minor against the rapidly approaching threat of early onset death-by-veganism. There I was, charged with the jailbreak of over 8,000 mink, and not one of them could return the favor.

To keep my mind off the slow death an all-salad diet, I read. I read newspapers. I read mail. I read 800 pages of evidence turned over by the FBI. But as a distraction from food, I would find no escape. It seemed every letter mentioned the vegan restaurant local activists went to after my court date. Glossy Whole Foods ad inserts fell out of the Sunday paper. And the FBI evidence contained everything from health food store receipts for the sandwich I had eaten on the beach the morning of the my arrest, to an inventory list of the pantry in my raided apartment.

I couldn't take it. It had been 10 days. I went to the phone, called a local activist, and sounded the alarm.

The next day I was told the jail had received 200 calls in 16 hours, each one by a concerned vegan demanding I be provided a plant-foods-only diet. It pays to have friends who hate police.

At 7pm, the head nurse was at my cell door.

"Mister Young, what can we do for you?"

I didn't have human contact, my freedom, or any chance of a non-guilty verdict due to the conspiring forces of modern day forensics and a "cooperating" co-defendant, but the next time the door opened in my San Jose jail cell I had a tray of sweet and sour tofu, and that was enough.

It was a victory, but the kind that only lasts the six weeks until Wisconsin extradition paperwork goes through and they throw you on a bus to the military landing strip. Suddenly I became federal property, and watched Silicon Valley fade into the distance while taking in the adverse effects of my change in geography: I was moving from a correctional setting where "vegan" was a word reacted to with hostility, to one where it wasn't even in their vocabulary. I would never regret freeing animals from cages, but there was some major unwanted irony in the same ethic that I risked prison for being the one that might kill me once I got there.

The mythological "con air" is real, and within hours I was on it. Bound, shackled, and airborne with 99 other men holding the criminal prestige of federal charges. The stewardesses were called "US Marshals", and they didn't hand you the in-flight meal, they sort of threw it at you. At this point, I'd given up on ever eating again, but there in that bag were four vegan granola bars and one apple. I had begun the next phase of my imprisonment that morning primed for another food-fight, only to be met with the best airline food I'd ever had.

Oklahoma City: The layover facility for all federal inmates in transit. I was told to expect a stay of between a day and a month. In "Intake," I filled out form after form, each going into my federal file. Medical forms, psychology forms, criminal history, place of residence forms.... My strategy was to leave no form without a plea for vegan food. On the medical form, I was "allergic to meat dairy eggs and byproducts". On Mental Health I was "experiencing depression due to lack of adequate vegan diet". On Religion I was "Seventh Day Adventist vegetarian who does not eat dairy and eggs," They could ignore many things, but not the lawsuit potential of a dead vegan.

Oklahoma was my first experience in a federal facility, and I was seeing the truth of the "club fed" perks I'd been hearing about over the last 8 weeks.

More resources, a higher class of criminal, and better food than county facilities. Everything checked out: A large selection of quality books, purse, snatchers and drunk drivers replaced by computer hackers and money launderers, and food that didn't start out that morning as powder. But still nothing vegan.

When asked, the guards' stock answer, which I grew to know and hate, went, "Your paperwork hasn't been processed yet." I went into scavenger mode, pulling throwaway cereal and potatoes from the trash. No small faux pas in the rigid convict culture, but weighing my options, I opted to trade certain death-by-starvation for possible death-by-inmate.

My paperwork never did get "processed". Two weeks passed, and I was about 12 days past the point of "desperate." After canvassing experienced cons, the advice I found most consistent was that if I was going to eat, I was going to have to find God – i.e. to write the chaplain and claim religious vegetarianism. It was the only thing they'd ever seen get results.

And they were right. On my last day in Oklahoma City, I was handed a meal tray with the most appetizing pasta I'd ever seen. You could say my prayers had been answered.

King for a day, but just one. Next stop, Wisconsin.

Dane County Jail, Madison WI. Hotbed of student activism, liberal thought, and my home for the next many months until trial. The Associated Press courtroom photo in the paper my third day in Madison captured two starved weeks in one ghastly image: sunken eyes, hollow cheeks, vacant stare. It told the story of a body that wanted to die, but with so many to options choose from, hadn't decided on its preferred cause of death.

Now at my 5th facility, I had learned a few things:

First, it was inadvisable to be an incarcerated vegan without money. Supplementing my diet through commissary (prison store) purchases was essential. With this came learning to love my long time enemies, including Fritos, Chili Ramen, and hydrogenated-oil-saturated peanut butter.

Second, in jail as in physics, change only comes through friction, To be heard, noise must be made, guards must be hassled, exaggerated notes of health ailments must be sent to Medical, and no manner of unpleasant behavior spared to force their attention to your dietary weeks. Jail is not a customer service oriented business.

Third, claiming ethical motives for your diet is the quickest shortcut to failure. Opposition to the death of 10 billion animals annually has no box to check on your intake form.

Dane County Jail would be my home for at least six months. I wondered if the influence of Madison's large vegan population - of the town's co-ops, restaurants, and animal rights groups - had seeped through the jail walls. A lot was on the line now. My quality of life over the next six months of court dates came down to my ability to convince the jail of the legitimacy of my vegan diet. In the lobby, waiting to be booked, I went over my lines, considered my angles and prepared for what could literally be the fight of my life. I planned hunger strikes; mass phone assaults from the outside, letters to media contacts....

The nurse called me in.

"Dietary preference?"
"Vegan," I said.
"Vegan it is," she replied.

And that was all it took.

Suspicious, I sensed a trap. For several days I poked at my food awaiting confirmation from a contact on the outside. She'd contacted the kitchen, and everything checked out – the beans: lard-free, Spanish rice: no chicken stock, and the best veggie burgers I'd ever had: totally vegan. Even the buns were vegan. I couldn't have chosen a better town to get federally indicted in.

Some said it couldn't be done, and letters came in expressing that no one would hold it against me if I "cheated a little". But after 13 years as a vegan, above all else in my life my diet was non-negotiable. And now as a caged animal myself, my reasons for it were never stronger.

Six well-fed months later, I plead guilty to two counts of releasing mink from fur farms and was sentenced to 2 years in prison.

So began my return trip. After being designated to a prison back in California, where this all began, I started my reverse course. This time I knew all the tricks, the buttons to push, what worked and what didn't.

Transit between districts in the federal system is grueling. Buses and planes, county jails and federal detention centers. They'll pick you up and drop you off at a half-dozen places on the way, and whether your stay will be a month or a day, you'll never know until you cell door opens at 4am and you hear the words - "Pack up."

Columbia County Jail, Portage WI. My first stop. A jail so deep behind enemy lines, the first day of deer hunting season they shut down the laundry room due to a staff shortage. This was a detail near the top of the list of signs that, as a vegan; you're probably going to die.

Now this would be a fight. By this point, I was in jail #6. I thought I knew all the tricks. But Portage was a level of backwards ignorance the depths of which I had never known. And it was there I added a new tool to the toolbox: the hunger strike.

From the jailer's perspective, a prisoner's wholesale rejection of their food trays was a cause for alarm. The threat of a dead inmate calls not on the jailer's conscience, but their fear of a lawsuit. Any quick cost/benefit analysis on the jail's part would reveal peanut butter to be lighter on their budget than wrongful death litigation, and providing vegan food would soon follow. Or so went my theory.

The moment I was told flatly by a jail doctor:"You will eat what you are given", the battle began. It was loud, it was defiant, it put the custodial staff on overtime, it was a hunger strike. When food came under the cell block door, I paused for a dramatic moment, and flung it back. Other experienced cons backed up the theory behind this power-move, adding that there was something magic about day four of a hunger strike. Universally jails will ignore you through the third day, I was told, and if you clear the 72nd hour, you'll suddenly have their attention.

The guards laughed, made jokes, and told me I would be strapped down and fed by tubes before receiving a vegan meal under their watch. Then, exactly as I 'd been told, I refused my 9th meal and the tone abruptly changed.

My name came over the PA, and I was summoned downstairs. I was brought, handcuffed, into a plush meeting room and seated across the table from the jail captain. The look on his face read defeat. He handed me a pencil and in a surreal moment of acquiescence, said:

"Mister Young, make us a list."

A list of everything food item I wanted, he said, and if their kitchen didn't have it, they would send a sheriff to the store. Oh how the mighty had fallen. As you night imagine, peanut butter tastes a little better when personally chauffeured by a reluctant deer-killing cop. Believe me.

After a well-fed three weeks, I resumed the slow, shackled march on more buses and more planes. I'd spent 10 months in county jails, and had finally graduated to a real prison.

Convict lore held up federal prisons as the Cadillacs of incarceration: movie theaters, residents from exotic criminal trades, and unconfirmed statistics of 48k spent annually per inmate vs. low-20s in the state system.

More than anything, I heard of the food: All you can eat burrito bars, lobster on commissary, and meal trays sized for royalty. The rumors spoke of abundance, but said nothing of any plant-to-animal product ratio. I remained concerned.

12 months in, 12 to go. The year had been one of unabated turbulence, sensory deprivation, media slander, isolation, and malnutrition. I'd launched two hunger strikes, two mob action phone assaults, hundreds of bartering transactions, multiple religious conversions, and countless jail black market exchanges in possible violation of state and federal laws. The days of breaking 800 calories were my glory days of yesteryear. For a year I'd existed in a hazy void of iceberg lettuce and waking hallucinations. To spare animals the suffering of a factory farmed prison, I was suffering in a prison of my own.

As I stepped from the bus in front of the Victorville Federal Prison, vultures circled overhead. A vegan in prison? The birds knew what was coming.

For the muscled and suburban, most first days in prison are characterized by darting eyes scanning for threats of oncoming improvised weaponry. My concern was withheld for the less abrupt but more certain death of flesh-based prison food. By shank or by starvation, I just wanted to get this death thing over with.

As an animal liberator, the first day of prison is like the first day of school, except instead of being made fun of for ill-fitted thrift store clothing they make fun of you for committing what they identify as the world's stupidest crime. I'd heard all the jokes ("Mink? Motherfucka, you look like you got caught stealing your momma a birthday card!"), and put my mouth on autopilot while my mind was on the clock. Six hours until dinner. Survival for the next entire year hung on the alignment of three variables: dining hall menu, ease with which inmate kitchen staff could smuggle out edibles, and the selection of prison commissary. Praying for immediate vegan revolution or presidential pardon, I would settle for dairy-free bread.

A week later my feet were on a table, following up a soy chorizo burrito ($1.69 on commissary) with soy burger (3 stamps on black market) in a sweatshirt lightly stained with pasta sauce (AYCE pasta every Saturday) and herbal tea ($3.49). I wouldn't meet my stolen vegetable connection for another month, but my peanut butter hookup took care of me, and his product went soooo well with the granola.

A year later I walked out of the prison gate with a Hefty bag of mail into the arms of the six friends who met me in the parking lot. The frosting-emblazoned "Happy Freedom" cake was a nice gesture, but I reached right past it for the salad.

"Thanks," I said, "but I'm trying to lose some weight."

Addendum: Advance Prison Strategy For Vegans

After two years and seven jails and prisons, I learned a thing or three about how to get meat-free food in prison. Here's my playbook for imprisoned vegans who refuse to compromise.

Move #1: The Phone Assault
Mob action phone calls work. In prison protests, what is important is not the actual threat, but the perceived threat. A tidal wave of friends and family soliciting the prison with their phone calls in outrage over a legally actionable denial of edible food suddenly recasts you as an inmate with power, influence, and connections. Suddenly, the world is watching. An incentive to comply

is borne through averting a lawsuit, or perhaps even an angry mob storming the prison lobby. After dozens of activists hammered a prison where I was detained in Wisconsin, the captain was quoted as saying, "cooking vegetables is easier than hosing down rioters in the parking lot."

Move #2: Find God

Prisons tend to recognize special diets by way of allergies or religious beliefs. Many faiths advocate fasting as a technique of spiritual enlightenment, bringing one closer to God. Twelve days without a full meal in a prison that only recognized vegan food if it was religiously motivated, and God quickly earned a central role in my life. After 28 years of atheism, I became a born again some-vegetarian-religion-or-another kind of inmate. Claiming an allergy to meat, dairy, and eggs is a tough sell. I've tried, but after many failed attempts, I think the best option is a divine conversion to the Seventh Day Adventist, Buddhist, Krishna, or other verifiably vegetarian faith.

Move #3: Hunger Strike

The rough mathematical basis for this tactic is outlined in the following equation, expressed through the mind of a cop: Hunger striking prisoner = dead prisoner = legal consequences times the concern of public outcry and media attention, squared by the inability to pay an out of court wrongful death settlement.

Move #4: Commissary

The prison store is the abusive partner that you are forced to live with because you have nowhere else to go. The vegan selection in the commissary of the average prison mirrors the vegan selection at an average Nebraska truck stop. Duplex cookies, peanuts, chili ramen, trail mix, and Fritos all make up what I call, "the lowest common denominators of veganism."
Advertisement

Move #5: Trade with Inmates

Because the prison world is the opposite of anything sane or healthy, the most processed non-foods are the ones most coveted by convicts. Even the most accommodating prison will never really get it 100 percent right, and those non-vegan items that will occasionally arrive on your tray give you incredible bargaining power over other inmates. When in possession of non-vegan fare, I would launch the bargaining process by shouting, "I have cake for apples!" and watch the bidding war erupt. When it's over, you'll probably get four apples for that single serving of cake.

Move #6: Black Market

The prison black market is huge, and its largest segment is food. In the prison economy, stamps are money, and for the right price, any food item can be stolen from the kitchen and delivered to your cell. Imagine cases of Boca burgers, or vegan pumpkin pies made-to-order.

Here is a rough price list based on my experiences:

- One five-pound bag of oatmeal (cost: 10 stamps)
- One four-pack of tofu (12 stamps)
- One bag of just-add-water soy meat (12 stamps)

Prison: Support & Survival

Lecture Transcript
Portland State University
Portland, Oregon
"If you don't snitch, you won't get jumped. So, don't snitch."

Shortly after my release from prison, I joined a panel on prison and prisoner support at Portland State University. The panel consisted of myself and two prison support volunteers for other animal liberation prisoners incarcerated at the time.

Anatomy Of Prisoner Support

I was talking to someone last night about how, in going to prison, you see the best in people and you see the worst in people. Worst in people through the people you're with in prison, both guards and prisoners. And the best through the support you receive from activists and supporters. We really take care of our own.

In its stripped-down form, prisoner support is a few basic things. Money in commissary for the prisoner to buy vegan food, buy stamps, and make phone calls. It's books. It's visits. It's calling the jail when the prisoner is having issues with treatment, such as being denied vegan food. And it is fundraising for a competent lawyer.

But as important as those more obvious things, prisoner support is everyone keeping their mouths shut. When someone is facing serious charges, the Feds are looking very closely at people in the defendant's circle. They want to know who's-who, who the defendant knows. They're trying to build a case. It's vitally important that all the associates of that prisoner go on lockdown. That they keep their mouths shut. Stop gossiping. This is a vital component of prisoner support.

What about animals? What is the value of prisoner support for animals? Why is prisoner support good for animals? There's several reasons.

One, we cannot ask people to carry out illegal actions on behalf of animals if we're not going to be there to support them if they're caught. I try to speak out and let people know, if you're out there carrying out ALF actions, you will be taken care of.

Two, stories of prisoners can be galvanizing for other activists and effective outreach tools. I had a fantastic conversation with a woman last night. Are people familiar with the Schumacher Furs campaign here in Portland? She told me the first demo in that campaign was done on the day of my sentencing, as a gesture of solidarity. That's how the campaign started. The campaign snowballed, and the fur store eventually shut down. That's a fantastic example of how prisoner support and the stories of prisoners can serve as a catalyst.

When I was in prison, I received more mail than I could ever answer, more books than I could ever read, more visits than I could ever accept. I'm going to break down specifically the support I received and why it was valuable.

First and foremost was money for an attorney. This literally could have meant the difference between me getting two years in prison or me getting 10 years in prison.

Next, letters. I made friendships I'm sure will be lifelong friendships through the mail. It made every day immensely easier.

Money. Being vegan was made a lot easier by the monetary support I received, allowing me to indulge in some of the extravagances of the vegan options in federal prison commissary.

And then phone calls to people running the various jails. People really came through for me when there were times I was in a bad situation. The best example is a jail were I was held in Portage, Wisconsin. They would not provide even basic vegan food. They were simply not budging. It got to the point where I had exhausted all established remedies. So I had to do two things: Go on a hunger strike, and place a phone call to the outside and request calls to the jail on my behalf.

Word went out on the internet. Calls started coming in. It's hard to know if it was the hunger strike that was the motivator, or the calls. I have no doubt it was both.

But within hours of the phone calls starting, I was called out of my cell. Guards brought me downstairs to the lobby of this jail in small town rural Wisconsin. They brought me in this plush meeting room, and they sat me down at this big oval table in a very nice chair. Across the table from me was the captain of the jail.

The captain of the jail is a guy that you would never see. He's totally inaccessible to prisoners. He had this defeated look on his face. He had a pencil and paper, and slid them across to me. Then he said, "Mr. Young, just make us a grocery list. Tell your friends to stop calling and we'll go to the grocery store every day and buy you whatever you need." So I made the Portage, Wisconsin police department my personal shopping list. And every day, I had the Portage, Wisconsin police working as my personal shoppers.

Sidenote: when I wrote down "hummus," he said, "Don't push your luck."

If you hear anything about a prisoner needing phone calls, call the jail. You're likely to think, "Well, what's a phone call to a jail?" In fact, jailers are terrified of scrutiny from the outside. It makes a difference.

The best form of prisoner support of all, hands down, above all else, are ALF solidarity actions. I would have traded every letter for just one more ALF action carried out in solidarity with my case. There were communiques after ALF actions stating, "We did this in solidarity with animal liberation prisoner Peter Young." There was a mink farm raid in Minnesota. A fox farm raid in Indiana. On my birthday, a fur store in Finland had its windows smashed out. I would have traded every letter for one more of these actions. That is prisoner support in its truest form.

Ultimately what someone who sacrificed their freedom for animals wants to see is activists picking up the slack on the outside. Seeing people continue to take actions for animals makes any jail experience easier.

Myths Of Prison

Consider that most of the literature that exists about prison is written for voyeurs. It's written for people who want a sensationalized account of prison. For people want to hear about the stabbings. Who want to hear about the drama. We don't receive a balanced view of prison. What sells is material written for voyeurs.

I don't care about voyeurs. I care about a person sitting across from me who is going go to prison, and they're telling me, "Look, I'm going to prison for X amount of years." What would I tell them? I certainly would not fill their head with horror stories. I don't want to lie to them either. I want that person to get a *balanced* view of what prison is like.

The fact is, no one person can talk about the prison experience with authority because there are many different prisons. My bottom line here is that when we talk about or focus solely on those horror stories, we do the enemy's work. Fear the most powerful weapon they have.

They can't take our thoughts. They can't take our beliefs. They can't take away our ability to break the law. But they can instill that fear of prison in us so we police ourselves. It is vital we avoid instilling fear in people unnecessarily and instead give a balanced account of prison. We do the animals a disservice by spending our time talking solely about how terrifying prison is.

The reason so many people start talking to police when they get arrested is something that you wouldn't pick up on unless you've been to jail. You see the recent arrests the FBI dubbed "Operation Backfire." The person that held out the longest in this case was Darren Thurston. He broke after three or four months. Some people in that case broke within hours. It seems absurd to me or the average person why they wouldn't hold out just a little bit longer. Why not wait for a plea bargain? Why would you break down in the first day, the first week, the first month?

The reason is that they are in county jail. People don't understand the basic distinction between county jail and prison. How many people here have been arrested and spent even an hour in county jail? I had my first county jail experiences here in Portland. I got arrested at this hotel right over... I don't know where it is. If you hop a freight train out of Portland, you ride right by it. They were having a meat packers convention. I came down from Seattle. I dressed up like a cow. I rushed the stage. It was a PETA sponsored civil disobedience. We got some good media out of it. And I spent a few hours in jail.

Let's say you get arrested for something. You're sitting in county jail. You're locked in your cell 24 hours a day. Your food comes through a slot in the door. It's extreme. The population density is unbearable. It's loud. Everything about it is bad.

People don't understand that's not where you spend your sentence. That's county jail. It's not prison. People get arrested and they're probably thinking, "I can't do this for 20 years. I need to get out." And they start talking to police. You might not be able to do that for 20 years. You don't have to. That's county jail. That's not prison.

When you go to prison it is a different world. The average person is going to have a much better time in prison than in county jail. You get to go outside. The privileges are greater. There is more freedom of movement. There's a library. It's quieter. You rarely see these things in county jail. This is why so many people crack.

Prison Survival

Prison survival is more about communication skills than it ever is about physical might. I was at a fairly relaxed prison. Not terribly rough. There were fights. I didn't ever see them, but they happened. But if you talk to people who have spent a lot of time in prison, they'll generally tell you the same thing. They'll say 90-plus percent of all violence in prison is avoidable.

Once I was sentenced and left county jail, I only saw a single fight. I didn't see any fights in prison. The only fight I saw was at a federal holding facility. I watched a guy get jumped because he was a snitch. If you don't snitch, you won't get jumped. So, don't snitch.

The amount of random violence in prison, in my experience in the federal system, is greatly overstated.

State prison is a different culture. I can't comment on it. It is generally worse than federal. California's state system is a bad prison system. I would not want to go to state prison in California. Good news is that most crimes that are carried out on behalf of the earth or animals generally get prosecuted federally. Generally, the Feds pick up politically charged cases. If you go to a federal system, that's where you want to be. Those are the better prisons. They call it Club Fed for a reason. It's not quite Club Med, but it is certainly a step above state prison. If you have to break the law, I would strongly recommend that you break a federal law.

Having a politically charged case in prison benefited me in a lot of ways. First and foremost, having an exotic case made me a conversation piece. I met people very fast when I got to prison. When I started telling people what I was in for, they couldn't believe it. I told them, "I opened cages and freed some animals," and they'd drag me all around the prison to meet their friends. "Hey, I need to introduce you to this guy. You're not going to believe what this guy's in for." I was shuffled all over prison that way, being introduced as "the guy who freed the animals." People just couldn't believe it because it was so absurd. Being a conversation piece was a tremendous asset.

This is an example of how much of what you'd call "success" in prison is deeply counterintuitive. In my experience being aggressively different than everyone else is something you should try to amplify. I exaggerated my differences because I found it to be an asset in prison. I found that if I drew a line in the sand and said, "You know what, we have mutual respect between us, but I'm not one of you," This resulted in other prisoners not holding me to any kind of convict standard. Whereas a lot of guys come in and try to fit in. Other prisoners hold them to their standard. They're forced to be involved in their prison politics. Which is a bad position to be in.

The secret is to be the person who is a little bit different, who is social, who isn't aloof, but at the same time lets people know, "I don't do my time the way other people do time. I just want to read and do XYZ." In my experience in the federal system, people respect that.

Everything is racially divided in prison. All the white guys would get together to talk about drama between them and other races. I was not invited to those meetings. That was a good thing. Asserting how different you are removes you from the drama.

Prison has been a part of every social justice movement. People go to prison. You can't tuck it away and not talk about it. It can't be an unmentionable. When we accurately converse about prison, we have one less thing between us and what we're fighting for.

Everything There Is To Know About Prison: An Activists Guide

Interview
Unpublished
"Don't fear being the black sheep if the white sheep will lead you to tangled pastures."

After my release from prison, I was contacted by David Hayden, formerly of No Compromise Magazine. While the magazine had ceased publication, David and others were preparing to release a series of printed guides for activists. Among them, a guide to prison.

I answered these questions for inclusion in this guide, which never saw publication.

Sadly David Hayden passed away in 2014.

Where did you serve your time? Was it state, federal, and what security level?

The first half of my sentence was served at seven county jails across the country. The second was served at a medium security federal prison. Its important to note this was not a lower security prison (two levels above minimum, one below max; and the average sentence at my prison was said to be 15 years). Most of what I will be addressing pertains to my experience in federal prison, since this will be of chief relevance to those convicted of animal liberation activity.

What are some of the conceptions you had about prison (both good and bad) that you discovered were wrong?

Myth One: violence was a daily reality. The level of violence in a prison is heavily determined by security level, and being in the state vs. federal system. State prisons are generally more violent than federal, maximum's more violent than mediums, and so on. In speaking with prisoners who have done maximum security state prison time, I never heard it said there was a prison where one couldn't get by with a good attitude and common sense. "Don't bother anyone, no one will bother you" seemed to be a consistent sentiment. There will always be unavoidable problems, but my experience backed this up as a general rule.

My time was served in a medium security federal prison, and seven county jails. In the two years I was incarcerated I was in no fights. I saw only a handful, and only then in county jail or a holding facility (not prison). With the exception of one, both parties were willing participants in the fight, and the violence was easily avoided. With the last, it was several prisoners jumping another prisoner who had informed on others (which in its own way was avoidable through non-cooperation). I was sent to prison halfway through my sentence. From the remaining 12 months I did not see another fight.

Violence may be a daily reality at many prisons, however I do not believe it exists to the extent as has been represented in books and films, particularly in federal prisons. History has shown the most likely designation for those convicted of animal liberation activity — even for arson — is federal prison of medium security or lower. Given this, I would not expect violence to be an ever present threat in prison for anyone convicted of animal liberation activity.

For the reasons of violence (and food) in prison: If you break the law, I strongly advise it be a federal law.

Myth Two: When there is violence, it is often random. Every episode of violence I saw or heard of (with the exception of the above-mentioned example of the police collaborator) was created by a series of bad decisions and easily-avoided mistakes. Most violence in prison can be tied to the following indiscretions: Gambling, debts, snitching, theft, and gang activity. If you don't gamble, don't accumulated debt, don't inform on others, don't steal, and don't align yourself too closely with gangs, you've avoided nearly every example of violence the occurred at the prison where I was housed.

Myth Three: Consequences for breaking prisoner rules resulted in violence. I committed almost every inadvisable prison faux pas one could name, from wearing sandals in the cell block to spending time in the cells of non-whites. With one benign exception, the harshest reprimand I received was a polite explanation that it was best I didn't do that because "some people" might take offense. Prisoners generally give people second chances. It's the repeat offenders who invite drama.

Myth Four: Status and credibility were based on toughness. Instead I found some of the most respected people were respected simply because they were the nicest and most pleasant to talk to. I never found my lack of exaggerated machismo to be a liability. It was much more important that I was seen as being a "stand up guy," generally defined as someone who stands up for himself. People saw that I went to prison for acting on my convictions, didn't inform on others, and held to my convictions in prison (through veganism, etc). This went much further than any amount of muscle-flexing would.

Myth Five: Prison was worse than jail. The only thing worse about prison is that the stakes are higher: you are more accountable because the turnover is less. By every other measure, prison was a much more tolerable and relaxed experience. More privileges, better food, less tension.

Myth Six: Rampant sexual assault. This just didn't happen. I generally gathered this is not part of the culture in federal prison to the extent it might be in state. Those I spoke to who had come from federal max's said that while it may happen at that level, it was not a daily reality. I have also both heard and read that at prisons across the board, this has begun to fade from prison culture since the 70s. I will leave those who have done state time to comment with more authority.

Myth Seven: Toughness and meanness were the norm. Everyone in prison has a line that shouldn't be crossed. Short of overt conflict, I found the day to day demeanor of most prisoners to be non-hostile.

Myth Eight: It seemed that every book I ever read about prison mentioned the same thing: If you let someone do you a favor, they will return later expecting something in return. This was 100% not true.

What was the first day in prison like?

The police brought me to a cell from booking and announced "We've got ourselves a terrorist." I spent many hour languishing in various holding cells before being place in a 6' x 12" box for six weeks.

My first day in general population occurred during my transfer from California to Wisconsin, at the Santa Rita Jail in Dublin, CA. This would be the first of 12 days I did not eat a full meal. Anyone who has been to Santa Rita will tell you: You do not want to get arrested in Alameda County. Calling it a "culture shock" would fall a little short of representing this experience. I had more questions than my mind could process, from where to sit during meals to the meaning of the slang spoken.

My first day in prison was one with a defeated, road-worn feeling of "let's just get this over with." I knew the first two weeks would bring a lot of adjusting, being subtly tested, having to tell my story dozens of times daily, and intense observing (and being observed). The biggest shock at that point was not prison itself, it was the complete lack of direction given to the "new arrival." There is no orientation, no manual, they just send you through the back door of the lobby and lock it behind you. I spent days wondering what was happening. I would see large groups of people moving towards a door and just follow them out, unclear where they were going or why. The first day I had 10 people at my cell, giving me everything from coffee to sweatshirts. I was unsure if these were some of those "we're going to expect something later" gestures I'd read about. But gifts are just customary for new arrivals. People do look out for each other in prison materially, if not emotionally.

Do you have any advice for how people who are going to prison could try to prepare themselves for the experience?

Best to begin with what not to do: Stop reading most literature on prison, including autobiographies of former prisoners. Nothing that gives a representative view of prison would make it to print, because no publisher would accept the manuscript. Erase from your head every prison movie memory and oft-recited prison stereotype. Start with a clean slate.

Put down any books on jujitsu or street fighting, and pick up a book on the principals of communication and influence.

Internalize one golden rule going in: "Try hard, die hard." Any actual or perceived desperation to belong or impress tremendously devalues you in the eyes of other prisoners. I realized early on that a feigned detached indifference is necessary for respect. This is true of life in general, but like all truths, they take on greater weight in prison.

Those things which prepare you for prison are those things which prepare you for life. Making yourself a confident yet pleasant person is all the preparation one needs. The rest is just taking notes.

Is there anything you wish you'd known ahead of time before you were jailed?

Again, the things I wish someone had told me about prison are those things I wish someone had told me about life. There are a lot of lessons I think we learn later in life that we have a hard time believing didn't come to us earlier, and I was forced to learn those things in prison. Those lessons only become more urgent in prison.

Communication skill are of prime importance. As is body language. In prison, people spend a lot of time watching and judging each other from a distance.

In terms of legal advice, one issue I wish had been explained was the significance of the "presentencing report" on prison designation. When the B.O.P assigns you to a prison, the presentencing report carries the most weight (in fact it may be the only thing they look at). The smallest detail can raise your security classification and mean the difference between going to a maximum vs. medium, or lower. It was never explained to me that had I cleared up a 10 year old UC Davis primate center demo warrant (which I later accomplished with one letter), I would have instantly reduced my security classification two levels, from medium to minimum. My prison experience would have been much more pleasant because of it. I would advise anyone in the post-conviction, pre-prison phase to give supreme attention to the facts and wording of the PSR. Defendants have the option of arguing any detail of the PSR in court, and anything that could affect security designation (for example any attempt by the probation office to insert the word "terrorist/terrorism") should be vigorously challenged. This is particularly relevant to those whose security classification sits precariously close to the medium/maximum line.

Lastly, we should be all too cognizant that as activists that prison is not a remote threat for any of us. With this in mind, I would advise anyone to prepare an "In case of prison" folder. It would be wise for every activist to create a list of needs and provide it to trusted friends (insofar as this can be done without raising suspicion of participation in illegal activity). This could include everything from contact information for parents and key people, lawyers numbers, a list of books to send, instructions for caring for animals, and other details on handling affairs on the outside while incarcerated. There is no guarantee of phone access during the early phase of an incarceration. Handling outside business while inside can be difficult to impossible.

How did you "learn the ropes"? (especially as to the unstated inmate to inmate rules?)

I learned about going to prison by going to county jail. This is the only useful training ground for a prison sentence. In this way, I feel for those prisoners who were released on bail prior to sentencing, then forced into the prison environment blind. County jail is where you make all the mistakes and learn all the cultural nuances, without the same level of accountability as prison. I should be clear that my county jail time was very difficult, and I would trade it in a moment for having been out on bail while I was fighting my case. That said, I can't imagine stepping into prison that first day and having nothing to go on but what I'd seen in The Shawshank Redemption.

County jail has a steady flux of prisoners cycling through. The cell block where I spent the bulk of my county jail time in Madison Wisconsin saw a complete turnover (minus myself) about once every three weeks. Thus accountability for faux pas are lessened, because the offended party will not be present for long. This is the chief (and perhaps only) value of county jail time: to ask questions, make mistakes, and study for prison.

In county jail, I was the guy who asked questions. Everyone I crossed who had been to federal prison was treated to my questioning. I wanted to know everything.

Some of the advice I received was quite useful in that it dealt with very ob-scure cultural finer points that transcended common sense. I remember being at the Oklahoma Federal Transfer Center. During lunch one day a man from a medium security prison in North Carolina asked me where I was from. I told him I had spent my time evenly between Seattle and the San Francisco Bay Area. He told me when I got to prison, to tell people I was from Seattle. He said most people form cliques based on geography, and that there is a roughneck element to the Bay Area, whereas the thug culture was much less developed in Seattle. By claiming Seattle, I increased my likelihood of being friends with a gentler crowd. He then asked me about my case, and then later asked my name. He told me when I arrived at prison not to tell people my name was Peter Young. He said to tell them "They call me Peter The Mink Man" (or something). He felt that having an unusual case was an asset, and provided me with an "in" to make acquaintances in prison quickly (which I later found to be true). Giving myself a moniker would invite the question of how I got that name, which provided a non-forced way to advertise why I was in prison, and do so within the first 60 seconds of meeting someone. I found both of those to be excellent pieces of advice.

For those in county jail, ask question and listen.

For the rest, thrust into prison blind, you can only watch and watch closely. It's all in the details, so those are where you should give your attention. The learn-ing curve is steep, but not so steep the plateau is unreachable in short time.

Where not to learn about prison: Anything ever documented on film or in book form. The material is almost without exception outdated, dramatized, exaggerated to sell books/tickets, and the most overlooked defect: they are *selective*. Information may not be fabricated outright, but it is selectively re-vealed, giving the impression of things such as violence occurring with greater frequency than is the case.

What are some common inmate rules?

You have to throw out basic formulas for assessing normalcy in prison. The rules are bizarre and they are numerous. The following is a short list – how things are, not how they should be.

Never reach over another prisoners tray. Don't glance in another person's cell. Don't wear sandals or shower shoes unless en route to the shower (you are expected to wear your boots to be ready to "protect your race" should a fight or riot erupt). Don't "check" (second guess / attempt to influence the behavior of in any way) elder cons. Don't get too close to anyone of another race. Don't do business with someone from another race. Don't enter someone else's cell when they are not there. Don't gloat about having a short amount of time left.

Again, in most federal prisons, I found a transgression of these only very rarely finds violence as its consequence. Instead, the transgressor will more likely find as their punishment a turned back, lost acquaintance, or diminished respect.

What is meant by "prisoner politics"?

Its vague, but to me its a catch-all term for alliances made in prison and the conflicts that arise from them. Race factors into this most heavily. Prisoner politics are who talks to who and the social forces that influence this. Prisoner politics would prevent, say, me letting a non-white person move into my cell. I would be obligated under most circumstances (at the facility I was at) to refuse him entry and then be sent to the hole before it would be allowed.

What is the best way to avoid getting caught up in prison politics?

Most prison truths are counterintuitive. Among these is that being different is an asset. I can imagine others not sharing my experience, but in prison, establishing myself as not "one of them" went a long way towards making my time there much smoother than it otherwise could have been. Those held to a convict standard are those who fit the mold of convicts. By not fitting the mold, I did not find myself held to that standard. I was not made to be involved in prisoner politics because I defied the stereotype of "prisoner."

This is where its essential to ride a very fine line: being close enough with other prisoners that you maintain trust and respect, but not so close you become deeply involved in the culture. I rode this line by spending time with other prisoners (at the table where people watched TV for example), but only long enough to maintain my "in" status. About 15 minutes a day.

There are deliberate efforts one can make to lessen involvement in prison politics.

Simply staying off the prison rec yard was one deliberate step. That is the center of socializing, gossiping, and conspiracies. I gave my time instead to the library, and think my time went smoother because of it.

While there are prisons where there may not be this luxury, in my experience: Don't fear being the black sheep if the white sheep will lead you to tangled pastures.

How did you make friends in prison?

I was friendly and on a first name basis with most prisoners. There was a novelty status that came with the exotic nature of my crimes (and those of most activists). In general I would say having an activist-related case would ease social assimilation.

More than anything else, it was receiving an above-average volume of mail that facilitated my acceptance into the prison social sphere. More than "the guy who released the animals," I was known as "the guy who got a lot of mail," and it went a long way towards making me a conversation piece, which led to contacts and acquaintances.

Very early I decided I wasn't going to get too close to anyone in prison. This is known as "doing your own time" (keeping to yourself / not involving yourself in social circles). I was very cautious about establishing key contacts early on, and maintaining those. This included those known as the "shot callers" (the "leaders" of each race). Once I had established solid base of acquaintances as insurance against any unforeseen drama that may arise in the future, I felt more comfortable "doing my own time". My social circle, if I could say I had one, centered around the library. It was more biased towards different crowd than that on the rec yard, and I enjoyed the conversations I had there more than those had outdoors. My acquaintances were however very diverse, from 17th Street gang members to millionaire hedge fun managers. Just yesterday I received an email from a filmmaker friend I met in prison who was released a month before I got out. He told me he will donating profits from his next film to an animal rights group.

What do you do for fun in prison?

Sneak coffee into the library. I got it down to a fine tuned skill, and Ms. Napoleon almost never caught me.

Once you have been sentenced and are established in prison, there are few lows or highs. Its just one endless day that repeats itself without only very rare peaks of joy or lows of despair. In life I have always found my fun in spontaneity, never structure (like organized sports), and so I found "fun" in the structured environment of prison to be nearly non-existent. The moments that came closest were those in the visiting room with a good friend, talking with the white collar criminals in the typing room, making surprise calls to people I'd never met who included their number in a letter and never thought I'd call, and sneaking coffee into the library. Definitely the last one.

What was a typical day in prison for you?

My schedule was this: Awake at 8am. In federal prison all inmates are required to work, and this work runs the full spectrum from swinging hammers for eight hours to turning on the sprinklers once daily. My work assignment was at the latter end. I am was for emptying exactly 4 trash cans once daily, which I did at 8am. At 8:15am I read whatever newspapers I pulled from the trash cans or read books until lunch at 11:15am. I read 107 books in prison. At 12pm I wrote letters, a never-ending labor of love. The only thing that could pull me from writing letters was receiving them, and at 5:15 I left my cell for "mail call." Soon after, we were called for dinner. At 6pm, I went to the library, to the typing room to work on my less personal more "business-like" correspondence. I also read the LA Times, attended a class on legally forming a non-profit corporation, and made photocopies. At 8pm, I returned to my cell block and handled various affairs such as assembling my outgoing mail and making phone calls. The only variation in my evening schedule came on Saturdays when I watched the Headbanger's Ball program on MTV, which was valuable in providing me a trace of some connection to my previous life in the free world by seeing occasional bands with members I used to see at basement shows a decade ago. At 9:45 we were locked in our cells for the night. I finished reading my mail and listen to various radio programs until midnight.

Where have you done time and how hard was it to get vegan food there?

I've been in eight facilities total, and my experiences have run the spectrum from "you'll eat what you're given" to a jail that had a pre-existing vegan meal plan.

While I understand there are changes being made in the federal system, and deference in this subject should be give to those still inside, I will offer a few words on the state of prison dining in federal prison as of 2007. The BOP required a vegetarian substitute be served at ever meal. I found it to be vegan about half the time. TVP-based dishes were common. Pasta with marinara sauce and sweet and sour tofu were among my favorite regular meals. I can't comment on the extent to which food quality at this prison was better than any other, just that I lived vegan comfortably. Contributing to this greatly was my placement in a facility where the Central American population was over 50% (AYCE rice and pinto beans at every meal), and a very crude but adequate salad bar.

Despite it all, I was lacking some basic nutrients during my two years, and for my first meal in prison parking lot, I went right past the cake for a bowl of spinach and broccoli.

How difficult do you find it to be to get enough exercise while in prison?

I didn't find it difficult because I didn't find it important. I spent my time in prison exercising my mind.

What were some of the "amenities" you didn't expect, but found in prison?

I was designated to the only medium security federal prison in the country (at the time) with email access. It was a pilot program that was being tested at a handful of prisons in the federal system. Very quickly I was barred from email access due to the word "terrorism" in the "Animal Enterprise Terrorism" charges. However the presence of computers with email access was most surprising.

By the time I arrived at prison I had heard it all, and little came as a surprise. For those uninitiated, the presence of craft rooms, typewriters, music equipment, cable TV, and DVD players in the library sometimes come as a surprise. Of everything, I was most pleased to find the visiting room set up to be dramatically better than county jail. At every county jail I was in, the visits were done through glass. In prison, you sit in chairs across from your visitor in a room that resembles an airport gate waiting area.

For whatever reason, people always ask about the showers. I'll say that I was in seven county jails and one prison, and I never saw anything but single person, private showers.

And for all the talk about "life behind bars," I was pleased to find there were in fact no bars in prison. The cells had large hinged doors. Little things like this in prison make a big difference.

What were some of the "amenities" you thought you'd have inside, but you don't really have in prison?

My experience was unique in that I was told by everyone from my lawyer to the judge that I was going straight to a minimum security camp – a prison with no fence. I had heard endless stories about the comforts of camps, from tennis courts to personal DVD players. When the US Marshals picked me up in Wisconsin and told me I was going to a Medium, it was no small surprise. I wasn't preparing for a Medium, and hadn't done my research. So the absence of cell phones, smuggled in food, and movie theaters all came as a surprise.

What was your worst prison experience?

Three months into my prison time I received two books the same day – one I had solicited, one I had not. I was unfortunately not familiar with the content of the book I had requested, and the one I had not was sent rather thoughtlessly. Both had content that would be considered very sensitive in a correctional setting. I never had books rejected based on radical / political content, however these books were something more, and clearly inappropriate in a prison. I was told to pack up my things and moved to another cell block, fired from my job, and told I was being placed on a "high risk status." This would go on to effect my time in prison in countless negative ways, such as the aforementioned denial of email access.

Another side effect was having to explain to the prisoners in my new cell block why I had been moved there. It was assumed the prisoners had run me out of the other cell block, and when I told them I didn't know why I had been moved (I didn't at that point) it only added to the suspicion. One of the guards took the opportunity to plant the rumor among one Hispanic gang that I was a snitch. This created a very precarious situation for me for 24 hours. This was a prime example of how valuable having alliances can be. The "shot caller" for the Caucasian population, who I was friendly with and whose word was law, had seen articles and paperwork from my case that established very clearly that I had not accepted any plea bargain that involved cooperation. He put an end to the rumors in one conversation with the Hispanic shot caller and that was that.

In another incident, I made the mistake of telling a shot caller not to show an interview I had done (with an animal rights publication) to anyone else. With this request I was guilty of "checking" him (trying to influence the behavior of someone higher up on the totem pole), and he threw the magazine on the ground and told me to get out of his sight. Having the shot caller against you is another very precarious situation. I was advised by other prisoners there was only one way to handle that situation: ignore it. To initiate discussion with him would, on some level, be a sign of weakness. A week later he came to my cell and asked if I wanted some coffee, which was an implicit peace-making statement, and that was the end of it.

Other low points: Learning the state of Virginia had indicted me on three felony counts related to an ID I'd obtained there with forged documents. Learning the state of South Dakota had charged me with three felonies for a 10 year old mink release. Cross country transit on planes and buses. The hunger strikes. The holding cells. Every moment under the care of the world's most ignorant and heartless human beings this side of a vivisection lab.

What was your best prison experience?

I don't even need to say it. Passing through that last door into the lobby on February 1st, 2007. It was the best (non-felonious) moment of my life.

What have you learned from your prison experiences?

I've learned I can take the worst they can throw at me.

How has prison changed you?

Taking on a certain fearlessness. After stepping into a room full of tattooed thugs who are looking for a reason to hate you one thousand times, there is no such thing as being intimidated ever again.

What have you found to be the hardest thing about being in prison?

In county jail, its the noise. There's not even a question.

In prison, the volume lowers and the challenges are less direct.

I think most animal liberation prisoners are afraid to speak out on the level of ignorance that exists behind bars. Suffering through a world where finding even the smallest common ground for conversation is a struggle is what I found to be most difficult. A culture of rampant sexism, racism, and willful ignorance takes a toll on your patience and sanity.

How do you deal with the prospect of a long prison term?

I ignored it and hoped it would go away. And it did.

Obviously, prison is not a lighthearted experience, but what has been one of your funniest experiences?

When my lingering South Dakota state charges (for a 1997 mink release) were dropped six days before my federal release date, and I knew for certain for the first time I would be getting out. Right then one thing was established: I would actually be serving a slightly *lesser* sentence than the codefendant who testified against me. I thought that was hilarious.

What do prisoners need from people on the outside?

Simply put: Books. Letters. Visits. A web person. And commissary money for vegan food.

Pre-trial: Money for attorneys, and everyone to keep their mouths shut. The last one can be as or more important than the first.

The Top 7 Things I Learned In Prison

Lecture Transcript
Ignite Talk
Boulder, Colorado
"If you're afraid of breaking unjust laws, be more afraid of not making history."

Ignite Talks are called "Ted Talks with slides." The speaker is given 5-minutes to speak in front of 20 slides which automatically advance every 15 seconds. Timing your words to sync precisely with each slide is everything.

For this unquestionably mainstream liberal audience of just under 1,000, I gave this (short) talk an uncharacteristically irreverent tone.

Can prison be made "funny"? This was my attempt.

I am the most poser terrorist ever. I was literally arrested in Silicon Valley, at a Starbucks, holding a soy macchiato.

In 2005, I was sent to prison on terrorism charges for freeing thousands of animals from farms where they raise them to make coats. So do I regret it? Do I regret it? Fuck no. It was the best thing I ever did. We shut two of those farms down.

But I left one thing out. Before prison I was a fugitive, and I was good at it. The FBI couldn't catch me for eight years. Seriously, the FBI is stupid. You don't need prison advice if they never catch you.

So here are the two rules of being a successful fugitive. Number one, have a real ID under a fake name obtained with forged documents. I got mine at a Virginia DMV, the same place as the 9/11 hijackers.

Number two, don't call your parents. The FBI will stop hiding in bushes outside your girlfriend's house long before they stop watching your parents.

So, if you do get caught, here are the seven rules of surviving prison.

Prison Rule #1

Rule number one, put your crime into one clear sentence. Your crime is your marketing slogan. The way it works in federal prison is this, when somebody asks what you're in for and they don't understand your answer, all they hear is "child porn."

So that's really cool that you're in for "securities fraud" or something, but I could promise you that Big Mike over in cell block six has no idea what that means, and you will be dodging his shank by noon, I promise you.

Prison Rule #2

Rule number two: You will be tested, and you must pass their test. My first day in jail, a guard shoved me into a holding room the size of your bathroom, filled with 50 guys. The whole room went silent. Finally somebody looked at me and broke the silence and said, "What did this motherfucker do, cheat on the SATs?" And for the next two minutes, the whole room made fun of me. But it was a test. It was not a test of toughness, it was a test of confidence.

And there's only one way to pass that test: To make fun of them right back, and that's what I did.

Prison Rule #3

Rule number three: Leverage your weirdness. If you try to act tough and fit in, you are entering into a contract. And the contract is, "Okay, cool guy, you're playing by our rules now." Their rules are stupid. Do not be the cool guy. Exaggerate your differences and do so very publicly.

The first day in a federal cell block, all eyes were on me. A guy challenged me to a game of chess. At the end of it, he said, "Good game," and he put out his fist to fist bump. You guys, I was 27, and I had never fist bumped before. I had no idea what to do. So I'm standing there, putting my fist out thinking, "What the hell does he want me to do?" And the whole room is looking at me. So after 10 seconds of deliberation, thinking, "What am I supposed to do," I went like this:

<displays fist bump done incorrectly>

The whole room exploded in laughter. But you know what? They never messed with me after that, because I was too square to be bothered with.

Prison Rule #4

Number four: You see the guy with the remote? He has power. You must be friends with him. The man has the remote because he has clout. In one jail there was a hillbilly Wisconsin guy who kept calling me a tree-hugger. Word had gotten out in the jail that I had a huge '80s vinyl hip hop collection. And you know who liked '80s hip hop? The guy with the remote. All I'm saying is, I outsourced my self-defense to a guy with a face tattoo who made dynamite in his kitchen for a living, okay? That is next-level gangster, come on.

Prison Rule #5

Rule number five: Manufacture the illusion of rock star status. I got over 3,000 pieces of mail in prison from supporters. Other prisoners thought I was some kind of big deal, and they treated me accordingly. Now, the good news is you can fake this. It does not matter what's in the envelopes, it just matters the other prisoners hear your name everyday at mail call. You know what's better than being known as the toughest guy in prison? Being known as the guy who gets a half dozen letters from girls everyday. And you know what my nickname in prison was? "The Eco-Pimp." True story.

Prison Rule #6

Rule number six: Make your jailers fear you. You can create the illusion there is an army of people who will storm the prison gates if the guards mess with you. And I actually had an army. They were called vegans.

There was this jail that refused to give me vegan food, and they got dozens of angry calls. The jail freaked out, so I got called into the captain's office. He said, "Mr. Young, what do we have to do to make these phone calls stop?" You know what I did? I pulled out a pencil, I made him a vegan grocery shopping list and I slid it across the table.

You guys, I was in jail and I had a cop doing my personal grocery shopping every morning. And I can tell you that food tastes a lot better when it's delivered by your own personal cop concierge.

Prison Rule #7

So when they finally let you out of prison, rule number seven: Have a prison release party in the Hollywood Hills house of one of the child actors in the sitcom "Home Improvement." This has nothing to do with surviving prison, but this is what I did when I got out, and it was awesome.

On a serious note, if we're going to live in a world worth living in, some of us are going to have to go to prison. And if you're afraid of breaking unjust laws, be more afraid of not making history.

Just remember that fear is the feedback you receive when you're about to maximize your potential as a human being. So, the only thing worse than getting caught is doing nothing at all.

Thank you.

Part VII

Government Repression

The more we do to stop them, the more they will do to stop us.

The belief we must respond through inaction will always be more popular.

The belief we must respond through circumvention will always be more effective.

Killing The Cop In Our Heads

Lecture transcript
International Animal Rights Conference
Luxembourg
"Keep your focus on what we are doing to stop them, not what they are doing to stop us."

A journey through my personal experiences with "repression," and why they government is rarely as menacing close up as from a distance.

The Fetishization Of Repression

I'll tell you a short story. I was involved in a legal issue some years ago where I was charged with some crimes and I chose to become a fugitive at the time rather than face a possible life sentence in prison.

I went on the run. I was away from the movement, in a visible sense, for eight years. I got arrested. Then I went to prison for two years. That was a big gap of time. It was as though I was sucked into a space ship for 10 years and then dropped off in 2007. To an extent I maintained activist friendships during this time. I was in touch with the animal rights movement through the internet, but I wasn't so much in touch with the day-to-day conversation of the animal rights movement for a large gap of time. I couldn't go to protests. I was hiding out from the FBI. There were a lot of activities I could not participate in.

When I got out of prison, sometimes I would get invited to give speeches. Now, before I went on the run, I would often attend lectures by animal rights speakers. All I wanted was for them to give me useful information that I could incorporate into my activism and use to help animals. That's all I wanted out of a speaker.

So when I got out of prison and was invited to speak, I found something bizarre. I would always ask, as a courtesy to those who invited me, "What would you like me to speak about?" Almost 100% of the time, they responded, "government repression of the animal rights movement." It was always repression, repression, repression. They always wanted me to talk about "government repression."

To me, being sucked into that spaceship and dropped off 10 years later, this was unsettling and bizarre. I don't remember the climate of 10 years before being such that repression was something we were so obsessed with.

So when I gave these talks, as a courtesy to honor their wishes, I would talk about government repression. I would talk about my experiences, about prison and the various things I've gone through. Yet I was never comfortable with it. I did it as an obligation to the people who asked me to speak because they were my hosts. And so I would say what they wanted me to say.

Then one time I was given a recording of a talk I gave. I listened to this tape, and listened to myself talk mostly about things I thought were useful, tactics that would help activists, and practical advice I hoped could be used to help animals.

Then, during the recording, it was almost like you could hear me turn the page on my notes to the part about government repression. My voice went flat, and I said, <monotone voice> "And now I'm going to talk about government repression." All the passion went out of my voice. As soon as I heard this tape, I realized I was not acting consistently with my core principles. I was acting in conflict with my mission as a speaker which was to help people help animals.

Not only was I not acting consistently with my core principles. I was in direct conflict with them. Through the conversation about repression and my contribution to it, I knew at some level I was responsible for spreading fear. It was not helpful for animals. It was not helpful for activists. It was the opposite.

So I stopped talking about repression. I refused to talk about it. I didn't think it was helpful to animals. When I met Fabienne, one of the conference organizers here, she said, "We really want you to come talk about repression," and I said, "I want to go to Luxembourg but I don't want to talk about that."

So my hidden agenda here is to actually to hijack this talk, that was advertised as being about repression. I'm not going to speak about repression. To the extent that I do, I'm going to speak about it in a way that will be unpopular. I'm going to speak about it in a way that was definitely not what I was invited to speak about.

What I want to speak about is the *conversation* about the repression. The *conversation* that exists currently. I would much rather stand up here and offer something actionable you can use to help animals than tell you what hole you should hide in to protect yourself from the government boogie man.

I'm not going to speak about repression, I'm speak about how we respond to repression.

The Defeat Is In The Response

In the United States, the conversation about repression has become very fashionable. Fashionable to the extent it has overshadowed the actual conversation about what we can do to help animals, which is the most important conversation we can have.

To this end, I will offer a short account of my experiences with government repression. Whether it's prison or getting my house raided or finding out a friend was working for the FBI. The people dominating the conversation about government repression have rarely experienced it themselves. As I'll share with you, I've experienced it from all sides.

The current narrative about government repression goes like this: Someday, in the near future, we're all going to go to prison as terrorists for the rest of our lives for passing out vegan literature. This is an obvious slight exaggeration, but this is generally how the conversation has been twisted.

Because of this conversation, today many people are afraid to do even the most minimal level of activism because they're afraid of going to prison. This is what it's come to. That is why the conversation is so dangerous.

There are certain people among us who want to preserve this narrative. They want to take the worst examples of government repression, give a disproportionate amount of attention to those examples, and then embrace crippling fear as the only appropriate response.

You are not going to hear that from me. I reject that conversation entirely. It's toxic. And that's actually why I wanted to give this talk.

De-Hipsterfying Victimhood

The conversation about repression has become trendy. I would like to make activism for animals that involves risks trendy. Perhaps in trying to challenge this conversation, we can make that happen together.

I don't think the people who dominate this conversation are ill-intentioned. It doesn't make them any less dangerous. I'm not talking about anybody who addresses the conversation about government repression in a sober way, in an analytical way. I'm talking about a certain segment of the movement, most of whom are not even activists, who focus entirely on spreading fear through talking about repression. Yet curiously, when it's time to actually put work in for animals, they're nowhere to be found.

Doing The Enemy's Work

Before we contribute to this conversation, we have to ask ourselves: Who's interest does this serve? You always have to know your outcome. So what is the outcome when we talk about government repression? Are we just trying to make ourselves feel like we're part of a cool action movie, or is this actually useful? Is this repression we're so afraid of actually an obstacle in helping animals? Or do we just like to pretend we're living inside of a spy novel?

When I got involved in activism, people would get arrested for crimes to benefit animals. When that would happen, we supported those people. And that's important. I was the recipient of a large amount of prisoner support and I'm very grateful for that.

Yet when we did that, we never lost our focus. We would help people who needed help in prison but our focus was always on the animals. Some of us have lost that.

We see people in prison now whose cases are exploited to drum up fear, oftentimes without the support of those prisoners. I know for a fact there are people in prison at this moment who do not like the way their cases are being used to drum up fear and to say "look at what can happen if you go out and break the law for animals."

When I was in prison, my case was portrayed in this way: "Peter Young is facing 82 years in prison." On paper this was true. Practically speaking, I would not have gotten 82 years. But people like to take the worst case scenario and highlight that. Even after I was sentenced to two years in prison, people still said, "Well, he *could* have gotten 82 years in prison." What's the point in focusing on that? Whose interest does this serve?

Cowardice From The Safety Zone

I was at a conference several years ago. It was a unique situation. There were three people in the room who had all been charged with the crime of "Animal Enterprise Terrorism," including me. This is also a law, the Animal Enterprise Terrorism Act. This law is the focus of most of the conversation about repression. "The Animal Enterprise Terrorism Act criminalizes vegan leafleting and we're all going to prison as terrorists." People genuinely believe this.

The speaker had also been charged with Animal Enterprise Terrorism. This is a room of maybe a couple hundred activists, and the speaker said, "How many people in this room are afraid of Animal Enterprise Terrorism Act?" And nearly every single hand in the room went up. Then the person said, "Okay. Now, how many people in this room who have been charged with Animal Enterprise Terrorism are afraid of the Animal Enterprise Terrorism Act?" Again, there happened to be three people in the room who had been charged with Animal Enterprise Terrorism, myself included. None of us raised our hands.

Now, that does not mean the three of us are brave or courageous. It means that we have seen the threat close-up. We have demystified it. We understand it. We understand how the law works. We don't look at it's reputation, we look at the actual threat. We have a more sober analysis because we've seen it close-up.

The people who fear government repression the most tend to be those who have experienced it least. They are the people on the sidelines, not the people actually putting in work. Because if you're putting in work, you're more focused on your goal and helping animals than you are with some distant threat.

We can look at this by looking at the numbers. The raw data. In my estimation in the United States, there's probably, and I'm being very generous here, fewer than 15 organizers who are so effective they actually have reason to fear prosecution under the Animal Enterprise Terrorism act. That number is actually probably less than 10, maybe even less than five.

The conversation you hear about the Animal Enterprise Terrorism Act is not scaled to the actual number of people who have a legitimate reason to fear being prosecuted by it. This is not to say it's not a real thing. It's not to say the AETA does not give out larger sentences to people than they otherwise would have received. I am not diminishing the actual threat. Yet we should look at the true threat, not the exaggerated threat.

In the US, there are probably fewer than 20 people who have carried out ALF actions who have not been arrested, and who could still be charged due to statute of limitations issues. Fewer than 20 underground activists who have something to fear from the Animal Enterprise Terrorism Act.

By these numbers, on the maximum end, there are fewer than 40 people who legitimately have something to fear from the Animal Enterprise Terrorism Act. Yet the AETA is discussed by activists almost constantly. We must scale the conversation to the true threat and not the perceived threat.

Deficienecy Of Perspective

Did everyone see George from Brazil speak yesterday? He said something I thought was amazing, and really highlights how much privilege goes into this conversation about repression. He spoke about how Brazil had a daylight raid of a lab, and there were 200 beagles taken from this lab. It was an awesome story. He was saying in Brazil, people who break into buildings to rescue animals do not fear going to prison. They fear getting shot and killed while they're carrying out raids. In Brazil, although we have a lot of guns in the United States, getting shot while committing a crime is a greater and more realistic threat in Brazil than it is in my country.

This should put things in perspective. There are people committing actions who legitimately have reason to fear being shot and killed. Yet they still carry out these raids. In my country where there is not a realistic threat of being killed, we remain paralyzed by fear over the Animal Enterprise Terrorism Act.

Not to mention the fact in Brazil, 90% of the people in prison have HIV and assault is rampant and going to prison is possibly a literal death sentence. Whereas, in my country, the prisons are basically a joke.

The last point I want to make before talking about my personal experiences is a concept I would like everyone to hopefully think about. It is the cop that exists in your head.

The Cop Inside Your Head

I have dealt with a lot of police in my life. I think a lot of us in this room have, certainly people who have experienced it much more than myself. Yet the cop I'm afraid of most is that cop that exists in my head. These are the voices that tell you you should scale back your activism to be 100% sure you never go to prison.

The cop in your head is that little voice that tells you to keep a low profile so you don't get put on a terrorist watch list. The cop in your head is that one that tells you anytime you break a law, whether it's minor or major, that you're going to get caught and go to prison. The cop in your head is the one who makes you feel like there's a grand conspiracy to put you in prison for the rest of your life. Although that might be an exaggeration for most all of us, on some level, I think we all have that cop in our head. The one that tells us to pull it back, don't be so extreme, don't do as much, restrain yourself.

Identify that voice, identify that cop in your head, and kill it. Don't let it speak, because it wants you to fail.

We let that cop speak to us in ways we would never let anyone else speak to us. Can you imagine if somebody came up to you and said, "Oh, don't do that thing, you're too weak to handle a weekend in jail"? Can you imagine if somebody came up to you and said, "You don't have the courage to deal with interacting with police so don't do anything that might invite a police interaction"? You'd want to fight that person. I wouldn't let anyone speak that way to me.

Adventurist Activism Aversion: The Two-Question Test

The psychology of repression-obsession is often that people like to feel there is an enemy they're fighting who sees them as so much of a threat, that they actually have something to fear.

It's like playing a video game. It's not fun if nobody's shooting back at you. We get psychological satisfaction about feeling like we are being repressed when there is no government repression. When we have no evidence repression is actually happening to us.

If we must talk about repression, I'm proposing we put it to a test. The one thing we must do if we ever talk about repression is ask ourselves, "What is my intention?" If you write an article, if you do a workshop, if you give a speech, you must ask, "What is my intention behind talking about repression? What is the outcome I seek? Whose interests am I serving?"

As an example, the subject of prison. There are many things I could say about prison that I won't say publicly. I ask myself, whose interest will it serve if I talk about this bad thing that happened in prison? That would serve the interest of the animal abusers. It would serve to instill fear. It doesn't pass the test, so I won't talk about it.

The second test we must put it to is this question: "Is the repression we're talking a legitimate road block to our activism, or just a perceived one?"

With many things, there's a gap between the perceived threat and the actual threat. Especially in the conversation we have about government repression.

An Anthology Of Repression

Let me go into the repression I've experienced. The intent here is to show that the conversation can go two ways. When people talk about, for example, getting their house raided by the FBI , it's very easy for the takeaway to be fear. You could leave this room with some fear. My intention instead is to show these things we fear are almost never as bad close-up as they are from a distance. That's true in all things in life. People say speaking in public is the most scary thing there is and usually, if you get out on a stage, it's nothing.

The repression I've experienced falls in this category. Much scarier from a distance than it is when experienced close-up. This is the takeaway message I wish to leave.

Repression Anecdote I: So when I first got involved in activism, there was a large conversation happening about surveillance of activists from the government. And I thought, this is weird because I've never seen any evidence of this surveillance. I was suspicious this was propagated by people who were, say, a little self-important. They want to feel like they're being watched. But I wanted to know: is surveillance a legitimate concern?

One day I received an unexpected summons to appear in court. I showed up in court and was told I was being charged with vandalizing a street sign. The specific accusation was that I had taken out a pen and drew a skateboard under the person on the crosswalk sign. I was guilty. I had done this for no reason except that it was midnight and I thought it would be funny. My only thought was: "How did they know?"

As it turns out, my friend and I were under surveillance. The sign was outside of his house, and his house was being staked out by the police. They were investigating some small-scale ALF vandalism that had happened around the Seattle area. Butcher shops getting their windows broken, actions like that.

They believed we were involved, so they were surveilling us.

The Lesson: Being under surveillance could be intimidating. You may think, wow, the police are following me. I had a different perspective.

The fact that I was *only* charged with vandalizing a street sign told me that they're really, really bad at their job. I was out vandalizing things every god damn night. I was 100% guilty of everything they were investigating, and the only thing they caught me for was drawing on a street sign?

I took this as incredibly empowering because my thought was: If all they know about is the street sign, that means the police are very bad at doing surveillance. They aren't following us very often at all.

That was my first lesson that the government is not good at what they do. You'll see that pattern emerge as I go through these examples. They're keystone cops, and that's been my experience time and time again.

Repression Anecdote II: A month or so after I got charged with the sign vandalism, I had my house raided by the police. I was living in an abandoned house in a wealthy neighborhood outside Seattle. Several activist friends and myself lived in this house. So the police raided it.

Two days later, there were a couple of newspaper articles about this. The headlines read, "Police raid animal rights radicals safe house." Something like that. A very sensational headline. When you read the article, you got the impression the police relied on their investigative techniques, savvy, and genius to determine we were living in this house and staged this big raid at the house. The fact is a cop in our town was doing a routine check of the house and noticed there was a light on in what was supposed to be an abandoned house. That's all it was.

The Lesson: Here was a case of "government repression": Police stakeout house, raid house, arrest activists, make a splash in the media. Yet being on the inside, then seeing how it's portrayed in the media, you see the police will always exaggerate their skill in solving a "crime." That whatever happens is the product of their investigative ability. That's rarely the case. Most arrests are made because of snitches or dumb luck.

Years later I was arrested at a Starbucks on suspicion of trying to shoplift

CD's. If you read police statements afterwards, they made it sound like they had me under surveillance. This is the kind of thing we see time and time again. They try to spin dumb luck as investigative savvy.

These are yet more examples of repression that is not as scary when you see it close-up. You realize most of what the government accomplishes, they accomplish through dumb luck and informants.

Repression Anecdote III: Two years later I became a fugitive and I went on the run for eight years. It was a choice I felt I had to make because at the time, I believed it was possible I would serve a life sentence. It was a choice, yet the prosecution and the exorbitant maximum sentence was a clear form of repression. I was pulled out of my activist work and forced underground.

The Lesson: There is a very clear image that is elicited when you speak of being "on the run." It elicits images of fleeing through the woods in face paint. In fact, being a fugitive was kind of fun. You get to live under a fake name that you get to make up. You have an excuse to not talk to relatives you probably don't like that much. It did cause me hardship.

But being a fugitive is not as devastating when experienced close up. Once you get an ID under a different name, you're no longer looking over your shoulder. You just continue living.

Again, the severity of the threat was not within a light year of the reality.

Repression Anecdote IV: The next significant form of government repression I suffered was my co-defendant being arrested. He was not as good as being a fugitive as I was. He was arrested quickly and ultimately ended up testifying against me.

At the time, my illusion was that if we're activists, then we are rock solid, we are never going to break, we're willing to die before we would talk to the government. I was certain this was how everyone was.

My co-defendant broke under a very light amount of pressure. Before his second court date. This was a massive wake-up call. I learned the trust that functions best is that which is tested least.

The Lesson: Had I known this, I would have learned how to carry out ALF actions myself. Working alone was a model I had never considered. During the years I had been an activist, I would read ALF literature. It would always say, okay, here's what you do: you go out, you find between one and four other people, you form a cell, and then you go out and break the law for animals. The one thing they never said was that it was possible to work alone.

I wish somebody had introduced working alone as an option. Because I just took what I'd read about the "two to five people" model as an immutable rule. That you had to work with somebody else. When I look back on my personal history, I could have done perhaps just as much ALF work by myself, with a greatly reduced risk.

The lesson is that in every instance you can, if it's a situation that is legally compromising, always work alone.

Repression Anecdote V: Ultimately I was sent to prison. This is the ultimate form of repression, short of death. Having your freedom taken away. There's a lot I could say about prison. There are many stories I could tell. One thing I feel obligated to say is that I had in my head an image of what prison was. When I finally got there, the day-to-day reality at the prison I was at was it's a lot of guys with neck tattoos and slippers sitting around watching wrestling. That was pretty much how I spent my two years.

The Lesson: I found that what I considered to be the ultimate form of repression was not even 10% as bad as I thought it would be. What they don't really tell you is that when you read a book about prison, or see a TV show about prison, they splice together clips or stories of people getting stabbed. Those things happen, but they're taking possibly years of footage or material and distilling it down to 30 minutes. Or you read a book and it's a collage of the craziest stories from their seven-year prison sentence condensed into 30 pages.

What I least expected was that, although there is violence in prison, in my experience, at least the prison I was at, I found almost all of it to be avoidable. If you didn't get into debt through gambling, you didn't get involved in gangs, and you didn't get involved in drugs, you could safely avoid 95% of the violence.

Repression Anecdote VI: Meanwhile, while I'm in jail, the FBI is going scorched-earth across the country to interrogate people they believed were linked to me.

What at times was worse than jail itself was sitting in a cell not knowing who's door they were breaking down. Not knowing what those friends might say.

The Lesson: This taught me an important lesson, which is to educate your friends. If you're dating somebody who is not steeped in activist culture or security culture, have a conversation with them about how to deal with police.

When I was on the run, nobody knew I was a fugitive. Not my girlfriend, no one. But I always had a talk with them that perhaps at the time seemed suspicious. I would just say, "Hey, listen if the cops ever come here's something you should read." And I would just leave literature around about dealing with police. There were several people who had no activist history who knew not to talk to the police, and refused to when the FBI came knocking.

Often times that my non-activist friends were better at dealing with cops than my activist friends. There's something weird about human psychology where the more you talk about something, the worse you are at it. The activists who were so outspoken about "security culture" were often the worst at it. Some people did talk to the police. They violated that code that you don't talk to the police about your friends. That did happen to me on a couple of occasions.

You should never talk to those people again. I shut them out. I'll never talk to them again. That's the ultimate crime in my world. You should never talk to somebody who talks to the police about you, ever again. That's unforgivable.

Repression Anecdote VII: When I was arrested, there was a woman doing jail support for me who the FBI thought was a friend of mine, pre-arrest. The FBI was following her from jail after her visits. They were very obvious about it. So she ran a red light to evade them. The FBI decided to run that red light too. She looks in the rear view mirror and sees the FBI car smashed into by another car. Full-on collision.

The Lesson: I hope you see the pattern emerging here: They're keystone cops. Police are rarely as scary close-up as they are from a distance.

Another example came in getting a close-up view of an FBI investigation. I was of course privy to all the FBI documents related to my case. It's reasonable to assume the most powerful domestic investigative agency in the country would be thorough in their investigation into a crime of "domestic terrorism."

My legal paperwork told a different story. After driving onto the property of multiple mink farms, and leaving tire tracks that would have linked us to every single one, one thing was glaringly missing from the FBI's investigation: The never looked for tire tracks. What would I would expect to be the simplest and most basic "first step" in investigating crimes carried out in series of muddy fields was totally overlooked.

The lesson here: Investigations themselves are not as menacing close up as they are from a distance.

Repression Anecdote VIII: In jail, while awaiting trial, I learned the FBI had placed an informant on me. Another prisoner who had turned informant was tasked with extracting information from me. He was really bad at his job, by the way. Very obvious.

The Lesson: The subject of informants, particularly outside of jail, features very heavily in the conversation on government repression. After dealing with them both in an out of jail, I can tell you two things about informants.

One, they are very bad at their jobs. Comically so.

Two, they are effectively neutralized in one very simple way: Compartmentalize your life. There are the very small number of people who know of your illegal activities because they are directly involved in them, and there is everyone else. There is a firewall between both. And in that way, informants are 100% neutralized. They are not to be feared, because there is nothing they can say. Your life is compartmentalized.

Repression Anecdote IX: I spent four months of my prison experience in solitary confinement. This is the most severe form of repression within the prison framework. Locked in a cell 23 hours a day.

The Lesson: There is no positive angle I could give on solitary confinement.

It is as bad as it sounds. But the one takeaway from that experience is the power that comes from knowing you can take the worst they can throw at you. I experienced the worst form of imprisonment and came out unbroken. For the rest of my life, I can walk with a sense of invincibility, knowing I can take the worst they throw at me.

An unintended side effect of the government attempting to intimidate us is that when they do, they demystify their own tactics. Many of us will break. But some of us will emerge with a new level of fearlessness, because we've experienced the threat close up. Their attempts at intimidation backfire. Because we emerge no longer afraid.

Repression Anecdote X: When I got out of prison things got very interesting as far as repression. There are very few people in terms of ALF activity the government can put a name and face to. The government was almost obligated to follow me around.

We caught them following us on multiple occasions in the months after prison. One example, some Los Angeles friends put together a "get out of prison" party for me a week after I was released. Three people flew out from Philadelphia for the party. Two of whom were known activists, and one I'd never met. When they were returning to Philadelphia, the person behind the counter at the airport referred to this third woman as a name that was foreign to the two people she was with. They had known each other for two years.

She was confronted about this inconsistency and admitted she worked for a private intelligence firm. She'd flown out to my party to spy. I feel like there should be a Geneva Convention for spying. You don't go to parties. That should be off limits, right?

At the house I moved into after prison, we had garbage men show up at our door one day. They said, "Why do you take the trash cans out to the curb every Thursday but they're always empty?" We were momentarily confused, and then realized: Oh, wait a minute, because the FBI comes at 4:00 a.m. and steals our trash.

The Lesson: They don't need a warrant to take your trash. If you have anything of any evidentiary value, flush it or burn it.

Repression Anecdote XI: A year later, I had a storage unit searched secretly.

They call these "sneak and peak" searches. I know this because the laptop I stored in the unit was only placed there after the battery had died. When I came back a year later, the battery was fully-charged.

Over the next couple of years I would have my house raided by the FBI twice. People think of an FBI house raid as a SWAT-style, kick-down-the-door, storm-in-with-guns-drawn cinematic display. In the particular house I lived in, most mornings I awoke to a Paramore song from roommates loudly playing Rock Band upstairs. The FBI raid was far less thunderous and dramatic. About five agents strolling through the house half-yelling, half-talking, "Search warrant."

Both times, their primary target was computers. They wanted our computers. The first time they took over a dozen computers from our house. Computers hidden under beds. Computers under boxes hidden in closets. Every computer but one: My laptop, sitting literally on the couch, as FBI agents walked by for over 3 hours. They totally missed it. These are the "professionals."

During the second raid, we had a house guest. They perceived her as a weak link and took her outside in an attempt to turn her into an informant. But they didn't do their homework. She was an ivy league law school grad and practicing attorney. Bad move.

When the FBI was leaving after the second raid, they were talking super tough, "We got all your stuff." Then they backed out of our driveway and ran into a pole. Destroyed the back of their car right in front my house. It was awesome.

The Lesson: Even an FBI SWAT team isn't as intimidating close up.

Repression Anecdote XII: Soon after this, I got into a dispute with my ex-girlfriend over text message. The FBI was at her house literally the next morning, trying to capitalize on the dispute. Clear tip off they were monitoring my phone communications in real time.

Soon after this, I was at a conference like this one, and a woman approached me in a very friendly fashion. We talked a little, had dinner and so on. Soon after she took me on a vacation to Southern Utah, which she paid for. As I later learned, she was working for the FBI.

It's mildly flattering when a woman you barely know offers to take you on an all-expenses paid trip. It's even more flattering when you learn the FBI paid her to do it.

There are many more stories I could share. In all of them, the government failed to extract any legally compromising information.

The Lesson: When you compartmentalize your life and limit all information to a "need to know" basis, the governments best attempts to infiltrate your life and social circle will most often fail.

Three-Part Repression Mitigation Framework

My intention with this talk was to leave you with three takeaways:

One, kill cop in your head.

Two, keep your focus on what we are doing to stop them, not what they are doing to stop us.

Three, nothing is ever as scary close-up as it is from a distance.

And remember, if you're among the rare people who experiences true government repression, who knows, you could get a free vacation to Utah out of it.

The Outlaw's Guide To Security Culture, Activism, & The Law

Lecture Transcript
Animal Rights National Conference
"I'm not a lawyer. But I am a criminal."

A criminal on a panel of lawyers, I give a short talk on the fundamentals of the best protection against repression — "security culture," and not getting caught.

I'm not a lawyer. But I am a criminal.

As such, I have experience with both security culture and prison. I'm going talk about both.

In preparing for this talk, I was flailing around to come up with a definition of security culture. The definition I came up with was:

"Managing the flow of information to minimize legal threats to both yourself and the movement."

More simply put, if everybody keeps their mouth shut about things they shouldn't talk about, nobody gets in trouble. Or as someone said to me years ago, "Nobody talks, everybody walks." That's a good mantra we should all tune into here.

I had the misfortune of having a co-defendant who breached the most fundamental rule of security culture, which is to never talk to law enforcement. And I shouldn't even say a fundamental rule of security culture. It's really a fundamental rule of being a human being. When I was in kindergarten I remember being taught that you don't tattle tale on the next kid. That's fundamental.

Anyone who is an activist on any level should be prepared to be asked to speak to law enforcement one day. We must be prepared to adopt security culture into our lifestyle to protect both our movement and protect ourselves.

Time and time again, we see the number one legal threat that people face that gets them in trouble is the threat of loose talk. Whether that is gossiping about things they shouldn't gossip about, whether that's bragging, whether that's saying anything during an interrogation, whether that's talking on the witness stand, or whether it's just talking to old friends about crimes they may have carried out years ago, and it turns out later that person was wearing a wire and was planted back in their life by the FBI. That happens.

Security culture means not discussing illegal or legally sensitive information with anyone but your attorney. Not speculating about legally sensitive activities of others ever.

And the latter happens so much. "Oh, you know, this raid happened, and so and so, I noticed they weren't home that night." That speculation is dangerous. It's vital that people don't speculate about things. Keep your mouth shut.

I've been at this conference only 36 hours and have had people ask me if I could list off the things that I wasn't caught for, and confirm my role in crimes they suspected I carried out. This happened to me just last night. I had people tell me they would like to carry out an illegal action, asking me how they can do that, and asking for my personal experiences with that type of illegal action. Again, asking me to incriminate myself in actions I've never plead guilty to in any court.

About half of us are laughing right now. I hope the other half understands why the first half is laughing. Because it is absurd. But too many of us don't understand why it is absurd.

When the FBI raided my house and took my computers a few months ago, I had an activist ask me in a crowded room if there was anything on my computer that was going to get me in trouble. Again, you see the pattern of people either incriminating themselves, or trying to fish for someone to incriminate themselves.

When I was arrested on felony charges five years ago, I had already thought through how I was going handle it. I refused to talk to the arresting officers. I refused to even give them my name. The cops call it "lawyering up," where you just say, "I want to talk to a lawyer. I'm not answering any of your questions."

And I was in a very sensitive place where I knew that anything I said could hurt me. In fact, my lawyer finally came in and took my first meeting after I had been incarcerated for about 48 hours. I remember being so security conscious that I didn't even trust whether he was actually a lawyer. I thought he may be FBI. And I said, "Give me your wallet." And he was just like, "Give you my wallet?" And I said, "Give me your wallet." And he gave me his wallet, and I flipped through it and I eventually decided if he was an FBI agent, this was a very elaborate ruse. And so I thought it was too elaborate to carry out so I decided to trust that he was in fact a lawyer.

But I knew that it was a difficult case I had when I got arrested. We're talking about a high-stakes case, and not being aware of security culture when you're in jail can be very devastating. I knew when I went to jail not to talk to other prisoners at all about anything related to my case, even seemingly benign information.

And this later came out to have served me very well. One, I was guilty as hell of what they were charging me with. But I didn't want them to know that. And two, because if I had talked about my case to other prisoners, I would have probably earned myself more prison time. It turned out later the FBI actually put an informant on me in jail. He was an actual prisoner, and he was getting a reduced sentence to inform on other prisoners. I had alarms go off in my head with some of the questions this person asked me, so I cut him out of my life in jail and it later turned out that he was working for the FBI in some capacity. So that saved me.

I would later have a police officer from South Dakota pose as a reporter to get information out of me. A total set up.

I can wrap everything up and just say, words can literally be deadly weapons.

No one talks, everyone walks.

Questions

Audience question: Give us any tips to spot an informant or FBI agent?

I want to stress that there is no formula. People need to discard this notion that there is a checklist of things that, if it matches up, someone is an informant. Or if it doesn't match up, you can cross them off your list. Because that checklist doesn't exist.

The informant they planted in my life, who took me to Moab, was the opposite of somebody you would ever think would attempt to fit into the movement. So opposite, it was actually disarming, because I thought, "No FBI agent would be this bad at their job." This was literally my thought process because she was so over the top in defying activist stereotypes. She had openly conservative politics. She admitted openly that most of her friends were cops. My thought was: "No FBI agent would be this bad."

There's no formula. Obviously if someone is told that their line of questioning or their behavior is inappropriate and they don't correct it, that should be a major red flag. And whether or not that person is an agent, the ex-communication process should probably be initiated. So people need to be told once, maybe twice that what they're doing is inappropriate and dangerous. But if they don't get it, those people need to be cast out.

Audience question: What's the best advice on writing a prisoner a letter?

I can only speak for myself. I really appreciated anything that tried to build a personal connection. Because I think when you're in prison, what's most valuable is an ongoing dialogue with somebody. So try to ground yourself in their reality in some way, even if you know very little about them. Or talk about yourself and maybe you might find that you have a lot in common so you can have an ongoing conversation.

If you have no intention of writing a second letter I would make that clear up front so they don't invest a lot of time in their response. Every prisoner is different. Just take your first letter and ask, "What would you like to hear about? Is there anything you don't want to hear about?" Some people don't want to hear about others having fun outside because prison is so boring. And I actually loved hearing about people having fun. But that's really hard for some people. So just ask.

Audience question: Can you talk about security culture in relation to social networking sites like Facebook?

Non-existent. There's no such thing.

Why The Best Defense Is A Good Offense

Lecture Transcript
California State University
Long Beach, California
"The government rules by fear much more than they rule by bullet."

As one of only a few former animal liberation prisoners, I would frequently be invited as a speaker on the subject of "repression," always to reinforce fashionable fear-based narratives. Were I to comply, this subject would almost certainly generate cheap applause, but ultimately serve only to spread fear when fear was already in no short supply.

To the frequent dismay of event organizers, I hijacked these talks every time to offer a different message.

It was not long before I was no longer asked to speak on repression.

Let me say upfront, I despise this subject of "government repression."

Of all the talks I could possibly give, of all the subjects I could possibly talk to you about, this is one where I'm the least likely to tell you what you want to hear. So I'm going to hijack this talk, and tell you what you don't want to hear.

The subtext to most conversations on "government repression" is: "Tell people how they can hide from the government."

I don't want to get up here and spend precious time at a podium telling a room of activists what kind of defensive stance they can take to protect themselves from this looming specter of government repression. I would much rather get up here and give you something actionable. I would much rather give you something you can take from this room to actually help animals, rather than describe what rock you can best hide under to protect yourself from the FBI.

In talking to people, I always get the sense that in asking, "how do we resist government repression?" what people are really asking is, "How do I make myself safe? How do I protect myself? What rock do I hide under?"

I want to remind people that what we're working for is something that is much bigger than our safety and convenience. But if we want to talk about being safe, I can talk about that.

How To Stay Out Of Prison

Let's talk about the most effective response to threats like the Animal Enterprise Terrorism Act. This response is going to give you a 100% success rate in avoiding prosecution. Something the success of which is unmatched in reducing your risk exposure.

That thing I'm talking about, of course, is staying home and watching TV. It's having no original thoughts. It's doing absolutely nothing to help animals. That's something that guarantees you can protect yourself from prosecution.

What else can I say? Is there some magic pill that's going to allow all of us to be effective yet still guarantee the government will not come after us? Of course not. I would assert that's not even a question we should be asking.

When I got into this movement, things were very different. Today it seems like the highest goal, the top of our pyramid of priorities, is staying out of prison. I can tell you, when I got involved in this movement, I accepted it as a fact that I was going to prison one day. That was just a given. That was the culture at the time.

I feel like I speak for a lot of my friends at the time that we accepted a few things as facts: We were in this for life. We were in this for something that's much bigger than ourselves. A few of us are going to go to prison. And that just comes with being an activist. It's a package deal.

I don't mean that in a chest-thumping bravado way. It was a part of the culture when I got involved. And today I feel like people have adopted a defensive stance. This is a big step backwards.

By design, laws like the Animal Enterprise Terrorism Act are weapons that are being used when people become effective activists. So the magic pill to avoid prosecution, by this formula, is to stop being effective. To stop causing friction. Because it's gotten to the point now we accept it as fact that if we cause any sort of discomfort to the opposition, that somehow we're exposing ourself to the risk of prison. That's what it's come to.

How To Effectively Resist Repression

If the question on the table is how we resist the government and the FBI, I'm going to give some case studies. These are many people who have effectively resisted the intended effects of the Animal Enterprise Terrorism Act since it's inception, which is to both imprison us and spread fear.

Last May, right outside of Reno, there is a company called SRI that imports primates from China to be used in laboratories. Their headquarters was burned to the ground and effectively caused that company to temporarily cease its operations. And I would argue, by the description I gave of the AETA with its intention to instill fear in people, that the people who burned down that building very effectively resisted the AETA.

Eighteen months ago, outside of Salt Lake City, the ALF released 7,000 mink from a fur farm. That's a fantastic way to resist the AETA.

And about two months ago, some anonymous individuals pried open a pen outside of Minneapolis and released three wolves, rendering the AETA effectively void by ignoring it and acting with their hearts.

So the way you resist government intimidation is not to succumb to the neutralizing effect that is it's intention. To not lay down and die. And resistance of what they're trying to do to us right now is something that's done as much on the psychological front as it is on the streets. And that's the main message I'm trying to impart here.

This is a war we have to win inside of our heads. And fear is something I've been talking to a lot of people about lately, and how fear is the only weapon they have against us. That's all they have to hold over our heads: fear. The fear of prison, the fear of consequences.

And as an example of the psychic hold that government intimidation has on us, this summer I was invited to be a part of a project. It was called the Fur Farm Intelligence Project. And it was a very simple concept. The intention was to map out the entire fur industry. Basically to come up with a complete list of all the fur farms that are active at the time, and all other infrastructure sites like auction houses and so forth. No one had mapped out the fur industry in many, many, years. So I was asked to get involved and do my part in compiling this list. And the mission, to put it even more simply, was to create the largest list of fur farm addresses to date. Part of this was that I drove around the country taking pictures of fur farms, while other people did internet research. And so the animal rights movement would have a very large database of addresses to be used in our campaigns.

The response I got to this was incredible. Both before I got involved in this project and after, almost invariably the response I got from activists was, "Aren't you concerned about the legal consequences?" It was incredible because by no measure was this illegal. By no measure was anything we were doing even coming close to anything that stepped outside the bounds of legal activity. Yet there was this understanding that because we were going to publicize addresses in the fur industry that had previously been kept secret, that it was going to make the opposition uncomfortable. So therefore, in some roundabout way, it must expose me to a potential prison sentence.

That's the psychic hold that the FBI has on us. That anytime anybody embarks on a project that's going to make the opposition in any way uncomfortable, we say, "That's got to be illegal one way or another." Even if you don't know how, it *must* be illegal. And that's what it's come to. It's incredibly tragic.

It's gotten to the point where anything that involves you turning off your computer and going outside the house is somehow understood to expose us to legal prosecution. Exactly the intended effect of government repression. As Camille Hankins said earlier, the intended effect is not to go after the Animal Liberation Front. Those people know what they do is illegal, and they know they're almost never going to get caught. The intended targets are all the people in this room, people like myself, people who work above ground to help animals.

And anytime you do anything that involves going outside and making people uncomfortable, the default response is, "Oh my God. Are you worried about getting arrested?" And I think that highlights our failure to be resilient against mild government intimidation.

Federal Bureau Of Internalization

We walk around today with that cop inside our heads. That cop that says, "Ah-ah-ah. Think twice. Don't do that. You know, that's going to make somebody uncomfortable. You might get arrested."

When I got involved in this movement we distributed literature that these days would be almost unheard of. Not necessarily legally speaking, but unheard of because people would never consider to distribute the literature we distributed. We distributed pamphlets on raiding farms and making incendiary devices. This is something everybody did when I got involved in this movement, but these days it is almost unheard of. It was something we did without a second thought.

Today, the government has had its victory by planting a cop in the heads of all of us. The cop that has you ask, "Can I say that? Should I do this? Should I not do that?" We've internalized the threat of laws like the Animal Enterprise Terrorism Act. And the threat is an *implied* threat. And it's not even a threat they've actually followed through on.

What does it take for us to just lay down and die? Do they have to merely make an implied threat? Do they have to make an explicit threat? Do they have to make an explicit threat they follow through on to some minimal degree? Or do they have to actually follow through on the full weight of their threat until we start to alter our behavior? What is the line? I would argue for the last of that list.

They don't need to police us all individually if we're all policing ourselves. Think about how much easier it is to put a cop in the head of everyone in this room than it is to put a cop outside the house of everyone in this room. They don't have to plant an informant in the life of everyone in this room. They just have to put that cop inside your head so you're policing yourself. So you're effectively doing their work. That is their very deliberate intent.

Repression Role Playing

Certain elements within the movement increasingly fetishize being perceived as victims of "repression." There then becomes a social and psychological incentive to exaggerate the extent of the repression. The subject of government repression was once confined to discussing activists who have been arrested and needed help. It was confined to real problems. It has now turned into outright hysteria over laws that haven't even been applied yet, people who haven't even been arrested yet, and tactics no one has ever been arrested for.

Talking about repression and police surveillance and informants is fun. It makes us feel like we are a part of something exciting. But it is the worst form of adventurist-leftism when we exaggerate the threat and omit facts which challenge doomsday mass-arrest scenarios, and continue to drum up fear over legal threats the government has barely followed through on.

Again, their intent is to spread fear. Their intent is not to target underground activists, but the rest of us. I've never met a cop who I thought was smart, but I think the higher-up architects of government repression are smart.

The Privilege Of Fear

With this in mind, what we call "repression" simply doesn't rise to the standard of repression to any movement that isn't comprised of first-world people with first-world problems. Our standards of repression are scaled to our privilege, and this brings us to our present circumstance – a 30-year-old movement that has seen only a few people sentenced to unusually long prison terms. Every person in prison is a tragedy; however, the statistics do not justify the dominant sentiment that we are an exceptionally "repressed" movement.

Introducing: Status-Seeking Repression Vendors

The conversation currently is dominated by people who have never been targeted by the government, telling each other how scary it is to be targeted by the government. The conversation is dominated by people who have never been to prison, telling each other how scary it is to go to prison.

I'm saying this as someone who has been and continues to be targeted: the threat to our movement is not government repression. It is our response to it.

It's interesting because I feel like some days, the opposition couldn't be dumber, and some days I feel like they are very, very shrewd. The truth is probably somewhere in the middle. But I think it is very shrewd on their part to draft the laws like the Animal Enterprise Terrorism Act and neutralize all of us. This is what I've seen the last few years, with the perspective of having gotten involved in activism pre-AETA ,and then seeing how things are now. The effect is noticeable. And the world needs more people acting on their conscience and less people looking to their left and then looking to their right before deciding what to do.

It's important to keep in mind the privilege that we have and how people in other less privileged countries are willing to risk their lives for what we won't give six months in jail for. Think about that.

Warrior's Pledge

In the year 2000, while I was a fugitive, someone gave me a cassette tape. It was a fuzzy audio tape of a former ALF prisoner named Rod Coronado speaking. He gave a talk at the Environmental Law Conference in Eugene. And I used to listen to this tape often while I was fleeing the FBI. He said something on that tape that I'll never forget, where he gave a fantastic quote:

"Going to prison is like going to the DMV - it's just something you have to do."

This mindset echoes that of the culture when I got involved. We just accepted it as fact that a prison sentence was going to happen one day. That's what I signed up for. It doesn't mean I'm going to court a prison sentence. Yet when I got involved, it was something I did accept as being part of an involvement in this movement. Because if we truly felt the sense of urgency that we all claim we have towards what happens to non-human animals, it's very likely that a lot of us would end up in prison. That's part of the animal rights movement that has tragically been lost.

Fear is a very emotional subject. People talk about fear, but nobody talks about numbers. And I feel obligated to speak statistically. Who does get arrested? How many people get arrested? How many things happen for animals, that would definitely subject somebody to prosecution, but yet the activists are never caught?

I compiled what I think was the first complete list of US ALF actions. I went back to 1979 and compiled every report of an ALF action I could find going back 30 years. And when I sat back and looked at this list as a whole, some of the statistics that I came up with were quite interesting. There were approximately 1,300 ALF actions since 1979. Of those 1,300 actions, fewer than 40 resulted in arrest. And only a small handful of those arrested actually resulted in any substantial prison time.

These numbers I'm giving you clearly reduce the legal consequences for staying active for animals, in any illegal capacity, to what I would argue is a statistically insignificant threat. What else can we glean from the stats I just gave you? Thirteen hundred actions, 40 people arrested, maybe 10 or 15 that actually did any kind of real prison time. Those are just the numbers. So again, the only kind of response to government repression I personally will ever endorse is something that translates into doing more for animals, not less.

Unfortunately, we have the latter right now. People's response is almost invariably translating to actions that will do less for animals, and people actually doing less for animals.

Best Defense Is A Good Offense

So I will never advocate a defensive stance. The best defense is a good offense. And by that, I mean, maybe the best defense against this is everybody in this room going out there and doing more for animals, If you just double your efforts. Consider how they'd have their hands full. I'm sure they want us all in prison, but they're not going to get us all. And the more we do, the more other people get involved. It creates a snowball effect.

I said before, the purpose of intimidation is not to deter the ALF. The ALF knows what they do is illegal and they know based on those numbers, there's little chance they're going to get caught. And we see now, because they can't catch the ALF, they're going after people who are above ground.

Take myself for example. My house was raided by the FBI a month ago. I haven't done anything illegal in years. But because I do talks like this, they target me. That seems to be what has happened. When they raided my house, they were ostensibly investigating a raid of a laboratory going back over five years in Iowa. And that was the pretext under which they were able to raid my house and take almost everything I own.

That was a direct effect of the fact that they can't catch the people that carried out that raid in Iowa. So they go after people like myself. People like us. It's not the people that are working underground, it's for people like us. That's what they want. They want us to be afraid. That's the intention of government intimidation.

They want a cop inside our heads, one that has us questioning our every move. Can I pick this piece of literature from the table? Is it even legal for me to have this piece of literature? Am I going to be put on "the list" by showing up at a talk like this?

This mythical "list"... I'm so sick of hearing about this ridiculous list. I want see this "list." I don't think it exists. But there's this specter of "the list," like it's a big black binder somewhere with the words "The List" on it that has the names of everyone... Who cares? If everything gets you on the list, that means everyone's on the list, so who cares about the list? But it's those cops that have us questioning our every move, and their voice is always telling us, "Always err on the side of safety," instead of increasing your efficacy as an activist.

The Real Prison

When we look for signs we've lost our freedom, we look at: Are there prison bars in front of us? Are we in prison? That's how we gauge whether or not we've lost our freedom.

We're not considering a more insidious loss of freedom. That voice inside our heads that jails us as much as prison bars. The psychological freedom that is lost from having to question ourselves all the time, from having to ask ourselves if we can go to a conference or a protest. That's the kind of freedom that you don't know you've lost, and may be the most tragic of all.

When I was in prison, I knew I wasn't free. But at least I knew it. I'd much rather be that person than somebody who sits inside their house and is afraid to look at an ALF website, and doesn't realize they've just become duped by the biggest fraud in activist movements right now.

Because the government rules by fear much more than they rule by bullet. I've only had a gun put in my face by a cop once. But I've had them try to make me afraid on a daily basis. Think about that.

So the way you resist government intimidation is to locate that cop that's inside your head, and kill it. Kill it.

Then act in a way that, no matter what happens, you can live with dignity knowing that at least you did something. That at least you didn't lay down and die.

Questions

Audience question: I feel like a lot of people in other countries have an attitude that's a lot more carefree about some of these laws. They just do things for animals anyways. It seems like they're under more oppression, but they're doing a lot more compared to the United States.

Right. It's an inverse correlation. It's absolutely true. Laws in the US are nothing compared to some laws that exist in other countries. Without the benefit of being versed in all those laws, I do know that other countries have faced much more severe repression than we do, yet are doing a lot more for animals.

What's the message? How do we duplicate that here? I would argue that obviously a country like England has a much richer culture of animal liberation activity than we do. You definitely get a movement over there accepting it as fact that prison is a very strong possibility. The first question that is asked is never, "How do I stay out of prison?" Look at other cultures and take strength from what they've done. It's not the top of their priorital scale to stay out of prison.

Like I said, I don't think anyone does anything that they believe has a 100% chance of getting them into prison. Or even a better than 50% chance. And again, most of what we're talking about here are not things that are illegal by the letter of the law. These are things that they make illegal because we're being effective. Nothing that I've said during this talk applies strictly to underground action.

We look stupid. I think they laugh at us over there. I really do. I think that we get people in the UK who look at us and say, "That's all you have to deal with?" There's ALF actions that were carried out in the UK where they literally knew they were being followed en route to the lab they were going to raid, and by the time they arrived felt only moderately confident they'd shaken their tail. And they still went ahead and raided the lab. These days you get one knock at the door from the FBI in this country and people drop out forever. That's what it's come to.

When I got indicted, the FBI made the rounds around Seattle, knocking at the doors of my friends. Pretty routine, happens all the time. And I would say over half those people, the first time they got a knock at their door, they just vanished from activism forever.

Audience question: Have you regained some of the possessions that were taken away from you from the FBI? The computers, the shoes?

No. I don't expect that will happen. Their only burden is to claim, and not prove, that whatever they took is being used in some ongoing investigation. So in theory the statute of limitations, as long as that's running on whatever crime they're investigating, they are allowed to hold on to those things. And they took 15 computers, and 10 phones, and just about everything I own and botched the paperwork and so forth. So no, I don't expect to see those things back.

Audience question: The two gentlemen who were caught for the fur farm raid in Utah. How were they caught?

The BJ and Alex case in particular is interesting because it covers all the bases. And it's a good case study in how people are indicted and the anatomy of an FBI case against activists. BJ Viehl and Alex Hall are the two people who released hundreds of mink from a fur farm in Utah. They were implicated in several ways. The most damning evidence was cell phone records. Their cell phones, so the FBI alleges, were on them or in their car at the time of the liberation.

How many people realize that when you have your cell phone on, even when it's not on, it leaves a permanent record of everywhere you go because it's constantly broadcasting a signal to the nearest tower? That's a permanent record. Clearly they didn't think of this at the time. So the FBI has cell phone records. They could see their cell phone just bleeping across the map, down to the fur farm, staying there for the time of the action, and bleeping its way back home after the action. So that was the most damning evidence.

Also, one of them allegedly dropped a car key at the fur farm. Like a cell phone, it didn't exactly place him at the scene of the crime, it simply just placed his key at the scene of the crime, or his cell phone at the scene of the crime. But it is very difficult to work around something like that in front of a jury.

They also had informants in the case who in the end didn't really give them much to work with, but they did plant one woman in the Salt Lake City

Animal Rights Movement group. She attended meetings. She actually targeted me at a conference just like this. She approached me after the conference. And she's this attractive blonde woman, and she's saying, "Hey, I have some questions for you," and proceeded to sort of orbit my friends and I all weekend. She was working for the FBI.

There were things like bank records. One person had dropped a car key, so he used his credit card to hire a locksmith. So they see, okay, we found a car key at the fur farm - which activist hired a locksmith recently? That was another way they caught him. They could see through his bank records he had hired a locksmith.

The mistakes that were made were not paying for things in cash, carrying a cell phone to a crime, things like that. There's other things you can't shield yourself from. There's always going to be informants. They're in this room right now.

The number one way people get caught is through loose talk. More than anything else it's people not knowing how to keep their mouth shut.

Audience question: Peter, thank you so much for your talk today. Last weekend I attended the Animal Law Conference in Boston and they spoke about the iPhone in particular. I guess some cell phone records purge themselves after so long, but the iPhone in particular can be your best friend or your worst enemy. And just in general, cell phones, many people might not know this, even if your cell phone is off, it can still track you. So anytime you're even having a conversation that's sensitive, the battery should be out or it should be away. And even cars, like Chevrolet has OnStar. Those microphones can be activated without your knowledge, so even talking in a car without your cell phone in the car, your conversations can be monitored.

Totally true. Laptops have built in cameras they can activate remotely. Built in microphones they can activate remotely. What you said is 100% true. Your cell phone is a roving microphone, they can activate it remotely, this is totally verified. They can turn on your cell phone, even when it's turned off. They can hear every conversation within ear shot.

And I'll tell you this, you said taking the battery out. I don't have any reason to think that is not effective, you obviously need power to power a microphone. But, I'm going to tell you this: A year ago I saw a clip from Fox

News. And there was a story about how law enforcement can now listen to you through your cell phone even when it's turned off. And you had the news caster holding up the cell phone saying, "The only way to protect yourself is to take out the battery." And she takes out the battery, on the air. Now, if we can all accept that Fox News is an apparatus of the state, why is the news caster on Fox News telling me to take the cell phone out of my battery?

Now I don't know how it would be possible for them to use a cell phone when the battery's out, but immediately I'm thinking, "Is there some sort of 10 minute power reserve on most cell phones? Why is she telling me that this is going to protect myself?" I'm immediately suspicious.

Just consider cell phones a liability all the time. The iPhone in particular — and I would not be surprised if this is deliberate, back-door dealing on the part of the government and Apple — you can't take the battery out of the iPhone. You need screwdrivers or a hammer to get the battery out. And everybody has one of these things. Pay attention to what they're selling you.

Audience question: I would actually advise people to keep the cop in their head. Most importantly the leaders, the ones who are organizing events, they need to keep the cop in their head so that they can make sure they can keep doing demonstrations year after year. Response?

I would argue that most of the cops in our heads are overly disempowering. If somebody says to themselves, I'm not going to do XYZ because I'm afraid, it's very, very rarely based on some sort of objectively proven cause and effect relationship. Almost never. It's more a vague fear that "Maybe, in some roundabout way that I can't really put my finger on, this might expose me to some legal risk. So therefore I'm not going to do it." And that's the kind of cop I'm arguing against.

I don't think anybody should do anything where the relationship is a very direct cause and effect relationship. Where if I do this, this is going to happen to me. None of us want to be martyrs, none of us are courting imprisonment. So it's two different things. But most of these cops I speak of that exist in our heads do the enemy's work much more than they do the animal's work.

Audience question: What do you think is the best way to recruit and retain members? Is it just rallies and the conferences? Or should we try to build community?

336

I accept the role of community in movements, but community is always a by-product of a movement. It comes naturally. I'm not sure that's something that we should direct our efforts towards. You have people now who call themselves "culinary activists." They do cooking blogs. They do potlucks. It's gotten to the point now where we can put a revolutionary spin on the most inane thing imaginable.

The community aspect is going to come naturally. I'm much more interested in what people are doing, not what's going to get them together to hang out. That's not something we should emphasize.

What's important in our activism is that we not delude ourselves. If you go to a protest, don't lie to yourself about what you're doing. Be very honest with yourself about your impact. Same thing with having a potluck. Don't say you're a "culinary activist." That's criminally pretentious. You're just eating.

This is not a food movement. Everybody talks about food. And we didn't talk about food in 1996. There was no vegan food to eat. We were just fighting for animals.

Seduction Is The New Waterboarding:
I Was Seduced By An FBI Informant

Article
Unpublished
"If I had one flaw the FBI could always count on to exploit, it was that I'd do anything for a story."

Solicited by Vice as a follow up to my vegan-in-prison article, this story was passed on by editors for reasons unknown (after requesting legal documents to corroborate this story, their legal department vetoed the story).

This is a story about the time the FBI paid a woman to seduce me.

I am America's "#1 domestic terrorist threat."

All I did was release a few thousand mink from fur farms. For this crime of "Animal Enterprise Terrorism," I received two years of prison and a lifetime of FBI attention as a convicted "eco-terrorist."

I have had my curbside trash stolen by police, my ex-girlfriends questioned, my luggage ransacked by the TSA, my travels communicated by the FBI to fur industry executives, and my houses raided - twice.

And then there was the time the FBI sent a blonde woman named Taylor to seduce me.

It started at an animal rights conference...

At first impression, she was exactly what you'd expect an FBI agent to be. Like spending an hour making exaggerated nodding motions every time I opened my mouth while on a panel for a contentious debate: "*The Animal Liberation Front: Terrorists or Heroes?*" It was the conclusion of an animal rights conference in Salt Lake City, and there was nothing notable about a woman approaching me at the podium post-talk with a smile and a question.

Her name was Taylor. She wanted advice on starting a dog adoption program or something. I was better qualified to instruct her on picking locks to get inside labs that researched on dogs, but I did my best with her question. Undeterred by my failure to offer even basic guidance, she asked what I was doing after the conference, and could she join my friends and I for dinner? I didn't object.

Clue #1 the girl flirting with you is an FBI agent: Everyone who knows her thinks she's FBI

We agreed to meet later. When she stepped away from the podium, I was immediately mobbed by local activists who gave me a warning: Beware. That bouncy blonde, they admonished, had been lurking around the local animal rights scene, and was seriously suspected of working for the FBI.

It wasn't the part about the FBI infiltrating animal rights groups that seemed implausible. When there is a flank of your movement that burns down slaughterhouses and breaks into labs, a little federal infiltration is obligatory.

It was the flimsy basis for their suspicion that I wasn't sold on, which amounted to three pieces of "evidence": One, Taylor wasn't vegan. Two, she dressed a little too conservatively. And three, she sat quietly and took notes during local animal rights group meetings.

I just rolled my eyes. Many people get involved before giving up dairy and eggs, considered an ethical baseline for animal rights activists. Two, if being a conservative dresser was grounds for suspicion, well, I did most of my shopping at Banana Republic so they'd have to blacklist me too. And three, this was the 21st century, where covert digital recorders meant FBI agents didn't have to take handwritten notes. It wasn't just weak evidence, it was no evidence at all.

I did some follow-up inquiries with locals, and the most substantive "evidence" that came back to me was from one friend who said:

"Always be suspicious of anyone so easy on the eyes."

I should have listened.

Clue #2: She employs desperate, amateur courtship moves

We reconvened after the conference at a vegan restaurant in downtown Salt Lake City. Seated at opposite ends of the group, she texted me under the table, flirting in a way anyone post-high school would classify as either amateurish, aggressive, or desperate. When the conversation turned to how badly she didn't want to spend the night at her place due to a roommate conflict, I could see where this was going.

We shared a bed in a spare bedroom of the conference organizer, the warnings of local activists hanging in the air. At 1 a.m. we stared at the ceiling while she peppered me with questions: How did I meet my friends in Salt Lake City? Did I still break into farms? Why did everyone think she was an FBI agent?

There is something disarming about someone so bad, they couldn't possibly be doing what it seems like they're doing.

And it got worse. Only an FBI agent would turn to someone in bed, and in the most hollow, emotionally vacant way possible, say:

"There's something about you I find really... attractive."

Was she being paid to seduce me? If I had one flaw the FBI could always count on to exploit, it was that I'd do anything for a story.

Clue #3: She asks permission to photograph activists at protests

I left town, and soon after Taylor was in touch to request a favor: As an ostensible "journalism major at the University of Utah," she wanted me to call on my contacts in the local animal rights group and secure her permission to photograph their protests for the student paper. I made some calls and cleared it with local activists.

Later that week she attended a circus protest in Salt Lake City and photographed everyone. The photos never ran in the paper.

Clue #4: She contacts you days after a major act of "eco-terrorism"

Three months later I was back in Salt Lake City visiting a friend, but I didn't contact Taylor. We'd spent two days together after the conference, but she was fun in an "empty calories" way, and the undue interest in the details of my activist life left an aftertaste that didn't exactly incentivize future contact.

A week after my return, the Animal Liberation Front cut fences and released 7,000 mink from a fur farm just north of Salt Lake City. The FBI seemed to make me a suspect every time a cow got loose from a dairy farm, and I told the friend I was staying with:

"Prepare for an FBI visit."

The FBI never came, but an email did: 48 hours after the ALF raid, I received an email from Taylor. How have you been? When are you coming back to Utah? The timing, occurring after the largest fur farm raid in five years, should have been immediately obvious. *Should* have been, but wasn't.

She asked another question: Would I like to accompany her on an all-expenses-paid trip to Moab?

She had a two-day-a-week hostess job at a high-end resort, she said, and I was invited for the three-day trip. We firmed up the details on the phone: Stay at the resort, live like the rock starts who often stayed there (the Beastie Boys had just left), and make Moab our playground. She'd pick me up Friday morning.

Clue #5: She asks you to implicate yourself in a major felony

When I got into her car on Friday, she didn't launch into interrogation mode right away. She let me put my seatbelt on first.

"Do you know who freed those mink in Kaysville last week?"

This is another point where an FBI informant gets so obvious, its actually counterintuitive, and you think: No actual FBI informant would be this bad.

As an interrogative move, this whole thing was pretty shrewd. Bait a suspect into a free trip from Salt Lake City to Moab, and enjoy a captive interrogation subject in the passenger's seat for five solid hours.

I stonewalled her questions. She was undeterred.

How did I know so-and-so? Who did I live with when I was on the run from the FBI? Am I *sure* I didn't know who released those mink last week?

At my breaking point, I laid down the law: These questions are intrusive and egregiously inappropriate, I told her. I know you're a new activist, so this is your warning.

She didn't relent.

We drove most of the five hours in silence.

Clue #6: Her godmother is a district attorney

"Don't break any laws here." She said, entering Moab. "My godmother is the county prosecutor, and she's mean."

Clue #7: All her friends are cops

After her waitressing shift, she picked me up downtown and announced two things. One, her Moab friends had invited her to hang out. Two, I wasn't allowed to meet them.

"Don't take this the wrong way," she said, "But most of my friends are cops. And I know how you feel about cops."

I'm not an anarchist. I'm not even a "radical." I just care about animals and dislike cops. In my world, cops were foot soldiers of the animal abusers.

But there was also zero chance I would pass on a story like this: The convicted eco-terrorist partying with police. I pressed her to reconsider, and she conceded to strict terms: I can attend the cop gathering, she said, if I promised not to talk to them.

The gathering, I learned, was to convene at midnight inside a closed movie theater managed by her high school friend. After hours, and unbeknown to the owner, he invited friends to enter through the alley for secret, illegal screenings of unreleased films. As we pulled in, I counted five police cars in the theater's back lot. This was going to be good.

She whisked me in the back door and through the lobby like Lindsay Lohan's lawyers shielding their client up the courthouse steps. I caught a quick glance of several cops ransacking the concessions counter, double-fisting Jujubes and Milk Duds, in a building they weren't allowed to be in. I'm no lawyer, but two minutes in and I was pretty sure I had implicated half of the Moab PD in felonies ranging from abuse of power to burglary.

She hid us out in the back row, and I spent the next 100 minutes moving my eyes between the screen and the backlit silhouettes of at least 10 Moab police.

If you thought it couldn't get any weirder, you're way off: The movie was the Big-Brother-is-watching-themed Spielberg film *Eagle Eye*.

> *"The Federal Bureau of Investigation can now hear everything you're saying."* – *Eagle Eye*

The next day, the cumulative evidence for her FBI-status had stacked so high, she had almost brought me full-circle: She was so obvious, she wasn't obvious. Overt inquires into criminal activity. Photographing activists. Family in the

DA's office. All friends are cops. A brilliant cover, in the way that the best way to shoplift a lawnmower from Target is probably just to push it out the front door.

The next day I orchestrated my own rescue, placing an SOS call to a friend in Salt Lake City who drove down immediately. Before my escape from Moab, I met Taylor to retrieve my un-password-protected computer, which had been in her possession for a full eight hours. It was the last time I ever saw her.

Clue #8: The FBI admits she is FBI

Five months later two Utah animal rights activists were arrested as suspects in the mink farm raid. Defense lawyers provided me with court documents revealing the un-shocking truth: "Taylor" was an FBI informant.

Endnote: Seduction is the new waterboarding

One attorney told me she's reviewed documents stating the FBI's new favored intelligence operatives are "females, aged 19 to 24, recruited from college campuses." One FBI asset exploited feelings of amour to ensnare activist Eric McDavid in an unactualized bomb plot that got him over 20 years in prison. In my personal sphere I have seen the FBI exploit fractured relationships to turn former partners into informants, even increasing compliance by planting false rumors to stir up ill feelings. One friend learned his girlfriend was a paid spy working for private intelligence. This spy was employed by the same firm that recently posted fake online commentary about me (hide those IP addresses, Big Brother).

For anyone marked as a "domestic terrorist," separating friend from fed is delicate game. So if we meet at a conference, it doesn't mean we can't have coffee. I'll just need three forms of ID and time for the background check to clear.

Outtakes

Excerpts from radio, print, & online interviews

Straight from the editing room floor, a collection of interview outtakes from over a dozen sources. The only criteria for inclusion here was if I felt these excerpts offered value either as actionable insights or voyeuristic curiosities.

What is the most important part of forming an ALF cell?

Find people you trust, find people who aren't easily scared. People who understand how important it is to keep your mouth shut, to not talk, to not gossip. People who are empowering, and not disempowering. The hardest part is finding people to work with. There's no formula for it. I wish there was. I've met very, very few people in my life I felt were worth working with. Very few. If you find people like that, hold on to them. Those people only come around a few times in a lifetime.

How did you get involved in the Animal Liberation movement?

I became vegan in 1994 though my involvement in the punk rock and straight edge hardcore music scenes. Bands such as Raid and Vegan Reich were part of a unique subcultural phenomenon in the early-to-mid-90s which combined a staunch anti-drug and alcohol message with militant animal liberation politics. These bands brought many people into the fold during that period and inspired a surge of animal liberation activity. The era saw a new and zealous breed of activist, many arrests, and even more broken windows. Music is a powerful outreach tool, and very often a stepping-stone to activism. Two weeks after seeing Earth Crisis play Seattle in late 1995, I attended my first animal rights meeting at the University of Washington.

Can you tell us one of your first ALF raids?

It is over-dignifying to label this an "ALF raid," but I will describe the first small action that I claimed as an ALF action.

One other person and myself chose to target a restaurant in the Seattle-area that sold primarily animal flesh, both because of its logo (a happy-looking pig) and its very large plate-glass windows. We found multiple rocks, parked a block away, broke out every window, and spray-painted "Meat is Murder" and "ALF"

This kicked off a prolific small-scale sabotage campaign across the Seattle area. Our targets were primarily restaurants, retail outlets, and distribution companies. This campaign lasted nearly one year.

I soon began to question the strategic value of this form of small-scale sabotage. I also began to question targeting anything on the retail level. Our justification at the time were that the actions generated media, which introduced the idea of the suffering behind "meat" to an unknowing public. Secondly, that some level of direct, street-level response to those who profited off of animal suffering was better than none at all. I think this was flawed on several levels.

First, most ALF actions will generate some media. Therefore actions should be chosen based what their immediate effects are going to be for animals. The type of action that will generate the best media coverage should be a secondary concern, but still a concern. Every effort should be made in an ALF action to maximize its impact in the media (for example, supplying footage of the action). Yet even when we broke windows at butcher shops we found the Seattle media covered these actions heavily.

Second, saying "something is better than nothing" presupposed that downstream, retail targets were our only options. At the time, we were unaware that everything from a large laboratory rabbit breeder to a meat research facility were nearby. There is no excuse for wasting risk-exposure on a small, symbolic target when a large, high-impact target is in close proximity.

A third folly was in assuming that smaller actions were lower risk. It was a flawed equation. It takes less risk to empty a well-chosen mink farm than it does to break windows at a fur store. Most fur stores are on highly trafficked roads, with the risk of detection high. Fur farms are most often in a rural setting, with no one but a sleeping farmer anywhere nearby.

Tell us how it was for you on the run knowing the most "intelligent" police of the world could not locate you.

After my arrest, the FBI denied in court that they made any effort to find me: denied the use of wiretaps, informants, surveillance, or any attempt to locate me at all. I know this to be false from the many reports I have received since, from people who have been questioned and placed under surveillance by the FBI during the years I was wanted. It would seem the FBI does not like to be embarrassed by their failure to capture "ecoterrorists," and to save face would rather deny they tried at all. All of their skill and investigative powers failed to locate Rod Coronado for several years, failed to locate me, and still fails to locate Daniel Andreas San Diego.

You were indicted on two charges of Animal Enterprise Terrorism (AETA). Were you ever targeted by law enforcement before you were arrested on AET charges?

In 1996 and 1997, I carried out a well-intentioned (albeit nonstrategic) sabotage campaign at Seattle-area meat distributors and butcher shops, among other targets. Suburban Seattle police quickly honed in on me and a friend as primary suspects, and was later revealed we were under significant surveillance.

In one instance, the police pulled a friend and myself over at 2 a.m. near past ALF targets. Seeing dark gloves in the back seat, they impounded the car and applied for a search warrant. The warrant was denied; however, the stop strengthened their suspicions that we were behind the wave of ALF sabotage. Soon after, they raided the house I was living in.

All of the above police attention was inspired only by broken windows, spray-paint, and slashed tires of delivery trucks.

You were the first to be convicted under the Animal Enterprise Protection Act. What do you think your conviction and sentencing means to activists in this country?

In terms of sentencing there is nothing precedent-setting about my conviction. They took a gamble with the Disruption of Interstate Commerce charge — which could have seen me in prison for 12 years or more — and in stretching the definition of "extortion," lost.

This prosecution might have a small historical significance in that these are the first federal charges filed for a live liberation. Historically, non-arson cases have been the prosecutorial domain of individual states.

Although there are no significant implications of my conviction, there are many lessons that can be taken from my overall case that are worth mentioning. The first being that you can be offered a plea bargain involving giving up names of friends and associates, throw it back in their face, and at the end of the day receive the same sentence offered in the plea. I invite all future collaborators to take note. Prison is a lonely place without any mail, friends, or integrity.

On this subject, another lesson can be taken: A willingness to put oneself on the line to save lives should not be the sole qualifying factor for inclusion in a liberation. Some people will fold before they've even been read their rights. My co-defendant Justin Samuel was not a man who belonged within a thousand light years of anything requiring resolve or fortitude, and before his second court date had offered his full cooperation with the federal government in their prosecution of me. All those whose hearts lead them outside the law should be mindful that some people will fold before the fingerprint ink has dried. Some belong back at the outreach table.

Another lesson we can take from my case, although not new, is a reminder on the investigative zeal of the FBI in breaking down our movement. This applies even to those who remain within legal bounds. In the months following my arrest, the FBI combed through thousands of pages of paperwork and address books confiscated in search warrants of an address believed link to me. Subsequently they proceeded to question, by my estimates, between 50 to 100 or more people believed to be friends or associates of mine around the country. Search warrants of several homes were executed, cars impounded, and phone records subpoenaed. Clearly they were not seeking information on 8-year-old mink releases. They wanted more names for their list.

You worked with someone named Justin Samuel who snitched. What would you tell him and to all those who informed and will inform in the future?

You're only hurting yourself. Your crimes transcend activist politics. Someone who sacrifices a "friend" to save themselves is someone who is universally reviled, inside activist circles and out. Even your parents will never look at you the same again. While you may save yourself prison time, you condemn yourself to a lifetime of scorn and self-hatred. You can't hide from your apostasy, and you can't hide from yourself.

Is it worse to have been caught and arrested or worse to have your friend Justin Samuel enter into a plea agreement with the US Attorney Office?

It is a special kind of degenerate who throws another activist into the flames to save himself 2 ½ years in prison (this is the gap between Samuels maximum sentence given his clean record and the time he received for collaborating).

And it's an even rarer breed that invents facts and events to appease his captors. A gentleman with whom I shared a friendship during my stay at a facility in Chicago had spent time with Justin. They had both been in the same jail during a previous sentence. He remembered a young man who spent much of his time sobbing over his sentence and consequently being taunted by other inmates. The image of a person who breaks down when he's four months to the prison door accurately captures the kind of person Justin is.

How does it feel to be one of the few activists not rolling over and helping the authorities?

Soon after my arrest the prosecution approached my attorney and offered a plea bargain. I was facing four felony "disruption of interstate commerce" charges which, if convicted on, would have realistically brought 10 to 20 years, and no less than eight. I was offered a deal of three years in exchange for full disclosure of my friends and affiliates in the 8-½ years since my indictment. They wanted to know where I had been and the names of those I had been with.

Two months later we were successful at having my felony charges dismissed by highlighting the flawed legal theory behind them. I was then facing a maximum of two years. We were re-approached with the same request, this time in exchange for a one year sentence which would have seen me out of prison in several months. I requested of my lawyer that he bring me no further offers that involved giving names to any law enforcement agency.

These plea offers powerfully illustrate the federal government's agenda: I was not even asked to implicate anyone in any crime, merely to prove names (the type of person with whom I associated being deemed somehow significant). At no point have I had anything to do with the FBI. Anyone reading this with whom I may have crossed paths for one minute or called a best friend for years can live confident that my silence is non-negotiable. Every day I served after March 10 2006 (the release date offered in the plea offer) I served for them.

How does it feel to remain unbroken? It feels like an extra year to finish every book on my list. I don't know what else to say.

How is an animal liberationists treated by fellow inmates and the authorities in prison?

In prison, having an exotic case is helpful with inmates and a liability with staff.

Early in my sentence a man I had only spoken with on one or two occasions approached me and said "Mr Young! The mink man. You may not see it but a lot of people here respect you and what you did." I recall being told by an inmate whose family owns a slaughterhouse and who considers himself very much "right wing" that although he didn't share my views in the slightest, he considered me a better person than most of the people there because "at least I stand for something." Such comments were common.

As for staff, I give them something to talk about. Offering a little spice to their otherwise empty lives is charitable work I am happy to perform. I should be receiving community service credit.

Talk about the difference between regular protest and direct action.

Protesting is the formula we all know. Generally you will pick a target. You will go stand outside. You'll have signs. You may have a bullhorn. You maybe will chant and pass out literature. The idea will be to educate passersby, to put pressure on a business to stop certain practices, or to generate media attention.

Direct action, on the other hand, is bridging that gap between out wants and our actions, As it applies to the animal rights movement, direct action historically has meant working outside of the law to achieve change for animals. That could be anywhere from burning down a slaughterhouse to going to a fur farm and releasing animals.

What's an example of good direct action and one of negative direct action?

I would be the first to say the Animal Liberation Front has had its share of actions that aren't effective. There are rules and principles the ALF should apply to its actions that are often disregarded. The most important thing is to make sure that what you do has a high likelihood of having an impact. The ALF is most effective when it gets away from symbolic property destruction, and leaves that to the above-ground facet of the movement. The ALF works best when it focuses on getting direct results.

By results, I mean directly saving animals. Getting animals out of labs, getting animals factory farms, or carrying out some economic sabotage or destruction of property that will directly translate into the lives of saved animals. For example, as I just mentioned, burning down a slaughterhouse. Despite not affecting the demand for meat, putting that slaughterhouse out of commission, even just for a couple days, could translate into saved animals.

Ineffective direct action would be actions I started out doing. We would go out, break the windows at McDonald's or a butcher shop, and we would spray paint "meat is murder" on the building.

I risked a lot of prison time for actions that weren't effective. I should have been putting my efforts towards actions that saved animals.

What would you like to see more of in the animal liberation movement?

Number one, creativity. I mean this on the whole spectrum of actions, from outreach to those things more clandestine. We live in an age of information and amusement overload, and getting the attention of the public is more difficult now than ever. Thinking outside the box is not just wise strategy, its life or death for our movement and the animals. Look outside the movement for innovative tactics that can be applied to the struggle for animal liberation. Read books like *Catch Me If You Can* for examples of people who gave themselves to a mission and accomplished it in unprecedented levels through tactical innovation. Its sad that those working towards much less noble ends dedicate themselves so much more fully to their mission than we do to helping animals.

On creativity, lets talk about aboveground, civil disobedience oriented groups which could be formed for maximum impact. Lets talk about a group that once a week picked up corpses from the dead pile of nearby slaughterhouses or factory farms and dropped them overnight in front of fast food restaurants, while following up minutes later with a press release. The media attention would be huge, and many would be awoken to the suffering behind the meat consumption. Or what of a group that forcefully entered labs week after week with cameras in the daytime to document what lay within. Either they would be arrested for presumably minor trespassing charges which would force attention to vivisection through the ensuing media coverage, or video documentation would be obtained which could then be released to the media. It would be win-win.

Making our actions count/going for the throat. Remembering that direct action is best applied to the weak links in the chain - to industries on their last leg or easily defeated targets. Going for maximum impact.

One thing often ignored is that while you may know you are committed for life, everyone around you is going to sell out in two years. You'll be standing alone. We're reminded of the turnover rate of activists time and time again. Rather than focus on gaining experience or floundering about experimenting with various tactics; rather than going about your activism with the belief that one day you will reach the plateau where everything has come together: where you have a rock solid circle to work with, enough experience to do something grand and effective, and enough data to make the best possible decision on where to direct your energies; we must act as though our time is short. Everything can change in a minute. Your friends will disappear, you will be caught for something small and find yourself on probation, constantly monitored, and with a large suspended sentence over your head, and you will wish you hadn't indulged yourself in the small things. You'll wish you had skipped ahead to something more strategic. In my vision of a perfect world, everyone would push themselves early and start big.

If animal rescues are so simple, why don't they happen more frequently?

Live liberations of animals happen infrequently because of the difficulty in finding homes for domesticated animals. These actions would happen more if there were broader awareness about the scale of wildlife farming in the U.S., and the prevalence of animals that can be released directly into the wild. There are many thousands of pheasant farms, deer farms, bobcat farms, and many others to be found if you do your research. Wild animals have no greater right to freedom than a chicken in a factory farm, yet targeting confined wildlife operations allows the ALF to liberate thousands of animals without the burden of homing them. Addresses of fur farms are widely available, and other wildlife farms in one's area can be found via the internet, or a local state Department of Agriculture or Department of Fish & Wildlife office.

Is there anything about the animal liberation movement you feel is counterproductive?

Overemphasis on internet activism. The folly of belief that action follows information. We have seen an astronomical skyrocketing of information available to us with the internet, and have not see an proportional rise in actions. There is such as thing as too much information. We are at the point of sensory overload, an information glut that distracts us from our mission. In this information age, there is no information unavailable to us. No tactic, skill, or other how-to knowledge not at our fingertips. There is information on who is using animals and what kind of animals they have. Every slaughterhouse and lab address in on your screen in a moment through Google. Every skill, from using grappling hooks to social engineering, is available on the internet. So why then have we not see a corresponding rise in actions? It is because information does not always function as a catalyst, it just as often functions as a distraction. This is counterintuitive, but consider just how much more information we have access to now over even 10 years ago. And then consider why we have not achieved total vegan revolution. We are not informed, we over informed. We are not educated, we are distracted. Remember: Animals don't die in cyberspace.

What would you like to say to animal rights activists?

Lets re-frame what it means to be a compassionate person in this society, to be an "activist." Ask yourselves if we are a force for change; or a community, scene, or lifestyle. Is being vegan an "identity" or a defiant statement complimenting even more defiant actions? And what are those things we allow into our movement that are pacifiers disguised as weapons? These are all questions we must ask ourselves as we continue to fight for space in the landscape of ideas, and move our way towards cultural progress and movement relevancy. A time will come when in a moment events are swung into motion that will bring our message to the minds of the public in one profound and lasting way. We might do well to ask ourselves what this shift of culture and consciousness will require, and bring it to pass.

What separates the Animal Liberation Front activist from the average activist?

A difference between those with a warrior mindset and those more passive is what I call "line of sight compassion". That is, a warrior just as motivated by the suffering they don't see but know is happening, as the suffering they do see. Why are circuses and rodeos the biggest protest targets? You can see the animals. Yet in Seattle where I lived, I found many well-disguised labs and slaughterhouses that went "out of sight, out of mind." The people I know who have been serious about getting things done have compassion that can see through walls. They know these horrors are not limited to the lobster tank at Wal-Mart. It's everywhere.

There's a tremendous peace that comes from an acceptance of prison as a possibility. The how's, why's, and where's of direct action are all at our fingertips. It's the fear that is the biggest obstacle we face. Only when fear is conquered do we become a true threat.

In 2003 one animal liberation activists was accused of placing bombs in Chiron and another company related with HLS. He is still on the run. It seems that her is forgotten in the movement. Do you think it is possible that he is never captured?

Daniel Andreas San Diego has been a fugitive for over ten years. If he is using the internet, he will likely experience some sadness at his name being mentioned less often in recent years. While living with the many sacrifices of being on the run, he will also face the added burden of feeling he is doing it alone. I would say a couple of things to Andreas, were he reading this.

It would be an error to use the internet as a gauge of the hearts and minds of the movement. I know there are many people who think about him and his sacrifice every day, and cheer him on silently.

I was told after my release from prison by someone from an activist publication they had deliberately not mentioned me in its pages while I was a fugitive because they felt that to give my case attention would be to encourage the FBI to hunt for me more fiercely. I think there is a sense that to talk openly about Daniel Andreas San Diego is to somehow stimulate more interest in the government's search. With Andreas having been placed on the FBI's "Most Wanted Terrorists" list, and having three appearances on America's Most Wanted, anything the movement can do is probably of no consequence. But this fear may explain why the movement doesn't focus more attention on the case of Daniel Andreas San Diego.

Do you still think that inactivity is worse than jail?

Everyone has a line they decide will not be crossed — an acceptable risk level, and consequences they will and will not bear. When that line falls this side of intervening in any animal abuse that might in any way intrude on the comfort or convenience of their life, it makes claims of being committed to animal liberation disingenuous. A relatively short (and unlikely) prison sentence to save one, or hundreds, or thousands of animals should be an acceptable trade for anyone.

I have put my freedom on the line for non-human animals because, were I in a cage, I would hope others would make the same sacrifice for me.

What would you say to all those punks and vegan straight edge kids that are just interested in shows instead of fighting for animal liberation?

Doing nothing but going to Hardcore shows, yet adorning yourself in vegan tattoos and militant t-shirt slogans is like putting on blackface and going into East Saint Louis. Its insulting, clownish, and makes a mockery of people who are really dedicating themselves to animal liberation.

How could the ALF become more effective?

When I sat back and reviewed the timeline of ALF actions, I looked at the patterns. I began to ask what were some of the mistakes that ALF has made. What are some of the things they could do better.

One of the things I noticed is that there was a very sort of scattershot, opportunistic approach to ALF Actions. You'd have people breaking out windows one night at a McDonald's, and people smashing a fur store the next night. I wondered, "What if these 1,300 ALF Actions had all been focused on one industry?" We would have seen the collapse of several smaller, vulnerable industries.

I began to ask, what if the ALF had a greater strategic basis for what they were doing? How powerful could the ALF could be? If every action that happened in the last 30 years had gone after a vulnerable target that functioned as a linchpin in a small industry, the ALF could have achieved massive victories.

If you read inside literature such as trade publications for these industries, they talk in candid terms about just how vulnerable they are. I have a memo from someone inside a fur feed supplier near Seattle. I don't think he ever intended it to be public. He talks about how if the cost of fur feed increased just 10 or 15 percent, the entire mink industry in this country would collapse. That's the razor-thin margins we're talking about. I saw another fur trade publication talking about how one pelt processor south of Madison, Wisconsin is absolutely crucial to the survival of the entire mink industry in the US. How if that business didn't exist, there's literally nothing that could replace it. The fur industry would be at a standstill.

A focused ALF campaign against as few as one or two small buildings could be devastating. You have a processing window in the fur industry of only a few months. Let's say a crucial building was decommissioned for a few months. You literally would destroy the entire year's crop of mink.

Any niche industry is vulnerable. Foie gras is extremely small. To give an example of what I'm talking about, at one time about 15 years ago, there were only four slaughterhouses in the country that killed horses. The horse slaughtering industry was very small. You had one man named Jonathan Paul, with others, who went and burned down one of the four horse slaughterhouses. That horse slaughterhouse had to permanently close as a result. For other reasons, in the next few years, the remaining three shut down. Effectively, you have no horse slaughtering industry in this country right now, in part because of ALF activities.

You mentioned the history of the ALF is being told by those who did not participate in it. How do we ensure the history of the ALF is accurately told? What are you doing to preserve that history?

I will keep this short and direct: There are people currently who are attempting to maneuver into positions of ALF "historians" who not only had no involvement in ALF activity, they were actively shut out of it because they were deemed to be security liabilities. They were deemed to be untrustworthy, braggartly, dishonest, and egotistic.

It is unfortunately not difficult to carry out these deceptions, twist history, and posture as speaking for those who do not support you. The nature of the ALF makes this simple, because outside of communiques, the ALF cannot speak for themselves.

To preserve the true history, I have a small press called Warcry. I've put out five books now. I have a book by Keith Mann, who's a former ALF prisoner, titled *From Dusk 'Til Dawn*. I just put out a collection of ALF newsletters from the 1990s, titled *Underground*. I have a book by Rod Coronado titled *Flaming Arrows*. These are titles I've released to capture the history of the ALF, with more coming.

How did animal rights activists get ranked up with Al Qaeda on the "most wanted" list?

Put yourself in the post 9/11 law enforcement world. You have your boss in D.C. or at the local precinct, or up and down the whole ladder of law enforcement. That boss is saying, "We're fighting a war against terrorism." At this point, your obligation as a foot soldier is to be a part of this war on terrorism. Let's say you're in an FBI satellite office in Des Moines, Iowa. You have to look around your town and say, "Okay, I have to come up with some terrorists because that's my job now, to fight the war on terrorism."

Now, if there are no domestic terrorist to speak of, which there almost never are, you don't have the option of saying, "Hey boss, no terrorists here. Give me something else to do." You have to create a terrorist at that point. The fact is the animal rights movement are really the only people out there putting their money where their mouth is in the way that the ALF does. So it just makes us the most likely people to assign that label to.

We've heard you say two incredibly badass things that we wanted you to expand on. First, you said there's always a way into a building. What did you mean?

In the mid-90s, I would go to labs, both private and university labs around town. I would go there at 1 a.m., with my skateboard, and just look around and see what would happen.

Almost every single time I put myself outside of a building I would always see ways in. And if it wasn't apparent how to accomplish this at night, it was apparent how to accomplish this in the daytime so I could come back at night. Everyone says "I could never do that," but I had no formal training. Yet nearly every time I put myself in front of a building I was able to get inside.

Why is the animal liberation movement so misunderstood by law enforcement?

It is the simplest of concepts that much of the public and all of our opposition will never understand: Our only motive is to deliver animals from confinement. Our only drive is the curse of empathy. There is nothing "in it for us," no hidden agenda. Our movement exists to alleviate suffering. The animal liberation movement is analogous to all human based liberation movements, as should be clear. Yet too frequently, this point is not grasped.

At my sentencing, Judge Crocker said, "I don't believe your crime had anything to do with animals." In this instance, an inability to see the lifting of a latch on a cage to save an animal as an act of conscience is the dysfunction of a confused person. Yet when lives are saved in less direct ways, the connection between our actions and their compassionate motives are even more easily lost. This is the unfortunate side effect of a movement and its tactics which are ahead of its time. I never fail to remind those who question our motives that no one does these things for fun. No one stands outside a research lab to call attention to the horrors within for pleasure. No one works undercover in a slaughterhouse for the thrill of it. No one risks their freedom to remove rabbits from a vivisection breeder at 3 a.m. for leisure. And no one goes to prison because they enjoy it.

Recently your house was raided again by the FBI. What happened?

At 11:30 a.m., March 15th, eight to twelve FBI agents from both Utah and Iowa entered our house shouting "search warrant." They corralled all of us into the living room, and spent the next 7.5 hours searching our home.

The search warrant named me (and three other non-house-residents) specifically, and called for the confiscation of anything related to "animal enterprise terrorism." They took 15 computers, eight phones, and many boxes of paperwork. Ostensibly, they were seeking evidence in the 2004 raid of the University of Iowa, in which 401 mice and rats were rescued and research equipment destroyed. This action was claimed by the Animal Liberation Front.

Since the raid, agents have been tailing residents of the house on foot and in cars, and sitting outside our home. It feels like a prolonged siege, continuing with the prosecutor's allusions in court that the raid has provided evidence in the Iowa case, with which they seem to be drum-rolling further legal action. The raid of course yielded no such evidence, and this is a psywarfare operation on their part as much as an investigative one.

The raid comes after a succession of suspicious events and people in my life over the past six months. It is clear they had been planning this for some time.

Why are you being targeted for a search?

The first theory is the FBI's claim a diary seized at the home of Scott DeMuth (a non-vegetarian, 17 at the time of the raid, who has been charged for an unspecified role in the University of Iowa action) contained a reference to someone referred to as "P." The context of this mention has never been stated. It is important to note DeMuth and

I have never met. Yet this shared first initial of someone mentioned in a diary is touted as somehow tying me to the Iowa liberation.

This along with similarly weak "clues" they claimed to have cobbled together, including flight records putting me in Minnesota a month before the Iowa raid, a Radio Shack receipt from Illinois around the time of the raid, and other circumstantial trivia.

The second is that the Iowa prosecutor is making the absurd claim that the entire ALF is a single conspiracy. This is how he is attempting to extend the statute of limitations, saying that as long as there is not a five-year gap between any ALF action, it is all one vast conspiracy, and the statute of limitations resets every time the ALF carries out a new action. This is absurd in a dozen ways, the most serious of which is that it presupposes everyone who carries out an ALF action knows one another and conspires together. The entire Iowa investigation is marked by these sorts of legally unsound acts of desperation.

The third theory is simply that I am public in my support for the Animal Liberation Front. I speak to the media, publish articles, and give talks in defense of the ALF These thought-crimes and speech-crimes are enough for the FBI to make anyone a target. These raids provide them an opportunity to seize computers and paperwork, and build their intelligence on the animal rights movement.

I expect they have wanted to get their hands on my computers and files for years. The Iowa investigation merely provided the pretext.

What were the reasons you focused your attacks (or rather, the ones you were caught for) on the fur industry?

Fur industry targets were chosen as part of a wider underground campaign in the mid-to-late-90s, where approximately 60 fur farms were raided in a three-year period. There was a time where we felt that a small group of autonomous ALF cells across the country were going to bring down the entire fur industry. Before the momentum was lost in 1999, we were on course to do exactly that.

Why did you focus on fur farms?

We began to sit back and weigh the risk/benefit ratio for various actions. We asked ourselves where our efforts would be most effective. We considered options from trashing the office of a local slaughterhouse, to cutting offshore fish farm nets, to disabling delivery trucks for a vivisection breeder, and beyond.

Data circulating on the survivability of ranch raised mink in the wild brought us to print a list of fur farms off the internet and visit mink ranches in the area. Nothing we'd seen seemed quite so feasible and with so great a life saving potential as what we saw at those mink farms outside Seattle. Thusly, we chose mink. Two to five per cage, 5,000 cages per farm.... The idea sold itself.

The short answer to "why mink" is: When you're staring at a list of fur farms four weeks before pelting season, and there is a car with a full tank of gas in the driveway, there is little room for negotiation with your conscience. You get in the car and drive.

With so many fur farms and others raided, why animal farmers take the hint and get out of the business?

The fur farmers and the meat packers of this world don't take the hint and get out of the business because clearly we are not using the right kind or quantity of hints. Some hints require a photocopier and others require a flashlight and a thick pair of gloves. What's important is that we all offer the hints that our hearts tell us are best. But remember: not all hints are created equal.

What are the exact circumstances of the release of the mink from fur farms, and what were the consequential effects for the animals themselves?

Fencing was stripped away and the cages opened. This is the short formula for a fur farm liberation.

The fur industry has a short checklist of soundbites they feed the media on the fate of liberated fur farm prisoners. The animals are hit by cars, die of heat exhaustion, were all recaptured, do not leave the farm at all, and/or die from exposure/starvation. Each of these is easy to refute. Mink are a native species which have been showing to survive in the wild. Mink populations in areas such as northern Utah are almost entirely descendants of fur farm escapees. We are talking about something entirely different than releasing a dog or cat into the wild. These are genetically wild animals held captive. Any arguments against releasing mink also ignore the brutally obvious point that mink and fox on fur farms are bred to die. Death is already a certainty. Fortunately, that is not the case for those animals freed into their native habitat by activists.

People say that a rescued animal can be replaced. What do you think about that criticism?

When is a live liberation a net gain for animals, and when does that animal just get replaced? It is a question worth looking at. There have been older activists once active in the ALF who came to the conclusion that sabotage at a lab was more likely to translate into saved animals than removing the animals themselves. I think the question isn't so simple, and we have to look at it on a target-by-target basis.

With labs, I don't think there is a clear answer. Research projects have been massively delayed, or stopped altogether, by ALF raids, and in those instances liberating the animals likely resulted in a net gain of saved lives.

There may also be actions where you are simply freeing space in cages that will be filled within days by an order to Charles River. This critique has merit, and should be looked at. But the bottom line is activists will never know how a liberation will convert to saved lives, and it never means you don't try. It places an unfair burden on the ALF to always know the exact impact of their actions. You do everything you can and live more nobly knowing at least you did something.

With fur farms, the equation is more clear. At a fur farm, breeding is done on-site. Farmers don't often sell their breeders to other farms (although some do) to preserve the proprietary value of their particular genetic stock. When animals on fur farms are released, the animals are simply gone, and the farmer must start from scratch.

The effect of a liberation is likely to be much more direct when the target either breeds animals on-site, or there is no commercial breeder to replace the animals liberated (such as a wildlife research facility or pigeon breeder). However fuzzy arguments for which there are no clear answers should never deter the ALF from liberating animals when it is within their ability.

We also have to consider those things that are less measurable. Things such as the educational impact of showing the public images of abused lab animals, the public relations impact on the vivisection industry when the public gets a glimpse of these animals, and the galvanizing effect on other activists when they see the ALF spiriting animals from labs. All of these factors make the value of liberating animals above debate.

What do you say if you shut down a business, and people criticize by saying, "There are people who are now out of jobs. You care about people more than you care about animals"? What's your response to that?

Take an example of a pig on a factory farm. It spends its whole life in a metal crate, never sees the light of day, is crammed into a truck after X number of months, is shipped off to a slaughterhouse, gets strung up, has its throat slit while it's fully conscious. I don't quite see the rights of the slaughterhouse worker being terribly important. I'm more concerned about the greater injustice, which is what's happening to the animal.

You do not have the right to kill without provocation. I'm talking about animal researchers, I'm talking about anyone who kills for a living. If you take the dissenter's same logic and apply it to a situation where humans are victimized, it falls apart. It's an inherently speciesist argument. What about the guards at a concentration camp? The analogy is very direct. It's unfortunate we have not evolved as a culture to view animals the same way we see humans.

These people live their hipster life or their academic life. Bu they never really feel it. This transcends an abstract ethical calculation. It's life and death for these animals.

What evidence did they use to connect you to specific fur farm raids?

The FBI primarily used wire cutters that they found in our vehicle. These were sent to the FBI crime lab, where they performed what's called "forensic tool mark analysis." They did a microscopic zoom view of the bolt cutters. Then they matched the specific grooves on the bolt cutters to wire samples that were taken from the fences of these fur farms. They found that, I think on one or two of these fur farms, there was a perfect match. That was used as the basis to indict us for the whole multi-state campaign.

I understand you also faced under-reported charges in the state of South Dakota. Can you talk about this?

While serving my federal prison sentence, I was charged on the state level with three felony counts of third degree burglary, first degree vandalism, and "Animal Facility Trespass". The cumulative maximum sentence was 22 years. This indictment pertained to a then 9 year old release of 2,400 mink from the Turbak Mink Ranch in Watertown, South Dakota. This farm subsequently shut down.

As you can imagine, bringing charges for a 9-year-old property crime is almost unheard of. These charges were filed soon after my federal sentencing, and unquestionably were brought by a combination of the media attention around my case, my somewhat defiant statement to the court, and the political vendetta of one small town prosecutor.

The charges were dropped one year later after I agreed to never return to the South Dakota ever again.

What was the prison experience like? What have you learned about yourself?

To read a line on a page about me having served 22 months incarcerated doesn't capture my experience. I was in seven jails, one prison, spent weeks in transit, 20% of my sentence in solitary, and after my federal case endured two additional multi-count state indictments (South Dakota [mink release] and Virginia [ID card charge]). It was 22 months of unabated turbulence. There is a lot more to "going to prison" than just going to prison.

With so much time spent without stimulus, you are forced to retreat into your mind and hope you find your way back out when the experience is over. Prison is a psychological journey, and psychological assault. The theft of identity, endless noise, and limiting of one's exposure to the world all take a toll. And then there are the valuable lessons: patience, appreciation of the small things, social flexibility, and all those things learned from a life spent looking backwards. In more concrete terms: how to maintain sanity for 5 days with only the business section of an old newspaper, skills for communicating with Chula Vista drug runners, and acknowledging all those things you should have done and said before stepping out of the world for a minute.

Above all, I've learned I can take the worst they can throw at me.

Let's say you shut down a fur farm. How long would it actually be shut down?

We shut down two farms quickly with little effort. They're still closed.

When was the last time that you actually did something illegal?

If had done anything since what I went to prison for, I certainly wouldn't tell you on this radio interview.

Do you have any regrets?

I will let the burden of guilt and regret fall on the bloodthirsty killers of the world.

Fugitive 3.0: Accelerating Your Own Collapse

Lecture transcript
Farmhouse Conference
Hollywood, California
"Start with breaking the dominant culture's rules. Then break the rules of your tribe."

This book opens with the talk that preceded this one. This final transcript is from the same conference, one year later.

In this follow up, I give a warning to my generation of activists, now finding a paradigm that was once an energizing asset to them is now a tragic liability.

What happens when you develop a world view at 18, decide to take it to the grave, surround yourself with a half-dozen others with the same paradigm, and militantly keep out any diversity of thought?

The unsettling answer is told across the dozens of activists from my era working subsistence-level jobs, lost in an increasingly irrelevant echo chamber, talking about endlessly about their "glory days," and finding their high school paradigm isn't aging well.

This is both a final warning to those for whom it's not too late, and an epitaph for those who will never recover.

I opened my talk last year with an anecdote of meeting Bill Nye when I was 13 years old. I spoke of how he was friends with my dad and we were hanging out, and he said, "Peter, I want you to remember something for as long as you live," and he looked at me and said, "Don't ever, ever, ever get a job." He said, "It's not worth it." And I talked about how I've worked less than 18 months in my adult life since then.

As a follow-up, our conference organizer Shane recently ran into Bill Nye and reminded him that in a very roundabout way, he was responsible for an eco-terrorist going to prison. Shane, can share this story?

Shane: So a friend and I went to a filming of "The Soup," and it was like their end of the year, "Let's invite all our friends over" party. And Bill Nye was one of the random guests, and I was like, "Oh my God. You know, what are the odds? I've gotta tell him Peter's story." As we were leaving, we got stuck in the elevator with him and his wife, and I was like, "Oh my gosh, 30 seconds. There is this guy who you knew his dad in Seattle, and you told him never get a job, and then he later turned into this like eco-terrorist/FBI fugitive, and then went to jail all because of you." And he was like, "That doesn't sound like advice I gave. I probably told him to maintain ownership of his distribution." I was like, "No, no, no. You told him not to have a job."

Peter: Listen, my memory's very clear on this. Bill Nye told me to never work for another man again.

I'm not going to give last year's talk again, but that anecdote was central to my story, that turning point where Bill Nye cornered me and told me to never work again.

My last talk was largely about being a fugitive, which is kind of a metaphor for the theme of this conference, which is "collapse." It is a metaphor in that when you become a fugitive, when you flee from the FBI, you're forced to start from scratch. You take on a new name, you leave all your friends behind, you can't call your parents. You're starting from nothing, and that's what I had to do. I was looking at a maximum of 82 years in federal prison. So I soberly assessed the situation and said, "I have a lot of life left, and I'm going to fight for the life the government is trying to take from me." So I went on the run. I was on the run for eight years.

What was significant about last year's talk for me personally was that I was told by lawyers, very firmly, to never, ever talk about those years as a fugitive because there could be serious legal repercussions. But I eventually decided, "I'm going to talk about it anyway." So the last talk was my "coming out" talk. It was very satisfying to unburden myself of that story. Those were stories I had never been able tell before. I was never legally allowed to admit that I had knowingly evaded the law. That in and of itself is a crime. So that's what the last talk meant for me.

What I didn't talk about last time is how I've actually been a fugitive three times in my life. I told you the first time, being a fugitive from the law. The second time was when I got out of prison, I was told that I can never talk about my years as a fugitive. After prison I was around nothing but people who would ask things like, "Where were you in 1998?" But I couldn't talk about those 8 years for legal reasons. So it was like being on the run all over again, with an entirely different period of my life I had to deny, lie about, or shut the door on.

What I'm going talk about now is the part I couldn't talk about in my last talk, which is how I felt like I've become a fugitive for the third time in the years since prison. I got out of prison in 2007. And there's another kind of fugitive status I've endured. Another kind of clean break and starting new. I'm talking about fleeing the subcultural confines that I had been trapped in for so many years. I was publicly typecast, in certain circles, or at times by the media, as an almost cliche political "radical." This is something I never identified with.

In many ways, I was forced to conform. It's interesting how, if you receive social incentive for something like being in a band, you can find reasons to be in bands for your entire life. Even into your 40s and 50s. Or if you get known for something as trivial as being a dumpster diver, that you can find reasons to continue being a dumpster diver, even long after those tactics have stopped serving you.

The best way to capture this is an anecdote from prison. I was in jail in downtown Chicago. It was a very bad jail. And I was there for about two months. The first day I got there, this guy sat down and wanted to play chess with me. So we played chess. The whole room was watching. 50 people staring us down. At the end of the chess game, every prisoner is looking at me, trying to feel me out, see what kind of person I am. He goes to fist-bump me.

Actually, I need a volunteer. Would you come up here real quick? *<points to audience member>*

So the guy says, "Good game, man," and he puts his fist out. So put your fist out. *<motions to audience member>*

And I'm sitting there, and the whole room is looking at me, and they're going to judge me based on what I do next because I'm the new guy who is under scrutiny.

Here was the thing: I was 27, and I'd never fist-bumped before. He had his fist out, and I didn't know what he was trying to do. I'm staring at this fist, thinking, "What is this weird prison ritual?"

So finally, after a long pause, I go like this: *<drops fist downward>*

And the whole room busted out laughing. Here was a 20-something square white guy who didn't know how to fist-bump.

The message here is that I had gotten 27 years into my life and never fist-bumped anybody. Now, I'm not saying that your life goal should be to be around a lot of people that fist-bump in a non-ironic way, or that fist-bump-ing makes you "cultured." But what was telling to me when I look back at this story, is that I was so deep in my subcultural niche that I had never fist-bumped in my life. I was 27 years old. I was so deep in the punk rock sub-culture that I didn't even know what that was. It's staggering to me to think about this now. So in the years since, I feel like I've been trying to break from that and diversify my life.

So I get out of prison, and the urgency of this crystallizes. This need for me to diversify my influences. The need for me to get out of my punk rock subcul-ture and diversify.

Does anyone in here know who Anthony Robbins is? A lot of us do. Tony Robbins, the archetype of the cliche motivational speaker? I had read some of his material in prison. I found it very practical. And when I got out of prison, he was speaking at the Long Beach Convention Center. It was a two day seminar for $2,000. So me and a friend went down there, found a hatch in the service hallway, and found ourselves on the scaffolding that went above the entire seminar. This seminar was $2,200, okay? We got up into the scaffolding, wound our way around, and eventually we're four stories above this small crowd of people, each paying $2,000 to be there. We positioned ourselves right above the stage. I spent two days watching his seminar from the scaffolding.

I received more out of those two days watching this so-called "cliche motivational speaker" than every punk rock song I'd ever listened to combined. More practical, useful, actionable advice than I'd ever gotten from any punk record. Now, no offense to any of lyric writers whose records I may or may not have listened to in high school, but what was interesting is that the punk rock scene that I came out of told me to not look outside of itself. It told me that people like Anthony Robbins, the "rich white guy" telling you how to live your life, were the enemy. That scene militantly enforced not looking outside of itself.

That weekend was an experience I identify as me making a break from my past, a wake up call that I needed to start looking outside of the activism scene and expose myself to new knowledge. If I'd been fed these lines that all "rich white guys" were the "enemy," what else was the that scene lying about?

So I accepted the limitations of the subculture that I came out of. This came to a head recently. I've been thinking about punk, or activism, or, radical-whatever, and how most people I know who come from these worlds are doing the exact same thing they were doing 15 years ago. They consider themselves "consistent." I consider them tragic.

There's a few people who actually took the best parts of subculture and did something great with it. But they're few in numbers.

By and large, most of the people I know from that era are in lifestyle-cryogenics. They're taking it to the grave. They're taking proud mediocrity to the grave. But mediocrity is nothing to be proud of.

For a long time, I was very proud that I was staying within these very rigid boundaries. I was sure I had a lock on the truth. And I look on that Anthony Robbins seminar as a moment where I realized there's more out there.

I was recently in a Barnes & Noble. I look over at a magazine. *Inc. Magazine*, the business magazine. I see a friend of mine on the cover. A woman who was an anarchist friend from Olympia, who I knew 10 years before. She was a rabid shoplifter. She was a classic anarchist. She's on the cover of this magazine. The cover says she's worth $200 million. I don't want to say her name. I don't think she wants any public association with an eco-terrorist, so I will leave her name out of this. But we go back.

We met up recently. And I asked her, "Do you ever talk to any of those people from Olympia?" And she said, "You know, I try," she said, "but every single one of them is doing the exact same thing they were doing 15 years ago. And we don't have anything to talk about."

Smash cut to 24 hours later I was talking to another friend of mine, who was a fixture in our local punk rock scene. I asked him what he was up to. He told me he was building a house out of stolen pallets on squatted property, playing in a punk rock band, going on tour, and playing to 30 people every night. I'm principally supportive of this, but that was exactly what he was doing 15 years ago. And I juxtaposed those two phone calls, and I realized how I've become a fugitive from the confines of that era.

I will close by saying let's all figure out how we can accelerate our own collapse. Let none of us be doing the same thing we did 10 years ago. Let none of us be doing the same thing we did three years ago. Let's all figure out how we can reinvent ourselves and become reborn. Take the best parts of what we learned and parlay them into things much bigger.

I ended my talk last time like I'll end it now, which is to say that the best lives go to those that break the most rules. In my last talk, I was referring to society's rules. Today I'm referring to the rules of your contemporaries, the rules of the people around you. So start with breaking the dominant culture's rules. Then break the rules of your tribe.

Whatever you do, if you've done it before, then it's worth tearing down and doing bigger.

The best way to honor your mission is to accelerate your own collapse.

Seeds Of Conspiracy

Animal Liberation

Free The Animals (Newkirk)

From Dusk 'Til Dawn (Mann)

Flaming Arrows (Coronado)

Underground: The Animal Liberation Front in the 1990s (various)

Recon. Raid. Repeat.

Interdisciplinary

Final Confession: The Unsolved Crimes Of Phil Cresta (Wallace)

Confessions Of A Master Jewel Thief (Mason)

Burglar's Guide To The City (Manaugh)

Catch Me If You Can (Abagnale)

Flawless (Selby & Campbell)

Security is always more a psychological barrier than a physical one.

Psychology

Art Of Deception (Mitnick)

Influence (Cialdini)

Self-Liberation

Never trade time for money.

At various times, Peter Young has been a fugitive, protester, author, prisoner, felon, spokesperson, entrepreneur, hobo, saboteur, publisher, speaker, and criminal of conscience.

By various federal agencies and trade groups, he has been called a terrorist, eco-terrorist, domestic terrorist, "special interest" terrorist, burglar, accessory after the fact, danger to the community, armed and dangerous, flight risk, escape risk, and unindicted co-conspirator.

Today he runs internet businesses and continues his lifelong, unbroken succession of conspiracies.

He can be contacted at:
peter@peteryoung.me

Also by Peter Young

Jetsetting Terrorist

...and at least a dozen other books under fake names.

Photo credit: Melissa Schwartz @ Schwartz Studios

Recon.
Raid.
Repeat.

Lightning Source UK Ltd.
Milton Keynes UK
UKHW021456090921
390292UK00014B/1149